Masculinities in
American Western Films

Masculinities in American Western Films

A Hyper-Linear History

Emma Hamilton

PETER LANG

Oxford • Bern • Berlin • Bruxelles • Frankfurt am Main • New York • Wien

Bibliographic information published by Die Deutsche Nationalbibliothek.
Die Deutsche Nationalbibliothek lists this publication in the Deutsche National-
bibliografie; detailed bibliographic data is available on the Internet at
http://dnb.d-nb.de.

A catalogue record for this book is available from the British Library.

Library of Congress Control Number: 2016947536

Cover image: Paul Newman and Robert Redford in *Butch Cassidy and the Sundance Kid*
(1969). Directed by George Roy Hill. Reproduced with permission from 20th Century
Fox/The Kobal Collection.

ISBN 978-1-906165-60-4 (print) • ISBN 978-1-78707-043-1 (ePDF)
ISBN 978-3-78707-044-8 (ePub) • ISBN 978-3-78707-045-5 (mobi)

© Peter Lang AG 2016

Published by Peter Lang Ltd, International Academic Publishers,
52 St Giles, Oxford, OX1 3LU, United Kingdom
oxford@peterlang.com, www.peterlang.com

Emma Hamilton has asserted her right under the Copyright, Designs and Patents Act,
1988, to be identified as Author of this Work.

This publication has been peer reviewed.

Printed in Germany

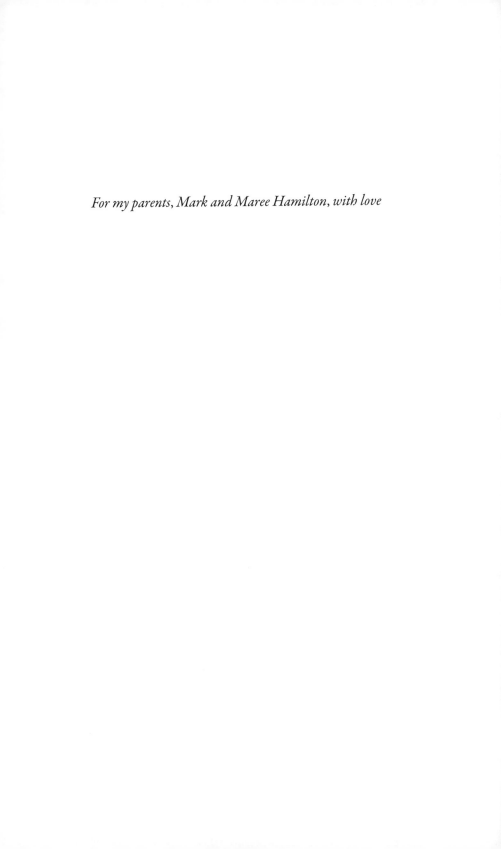

For my parents, Mark and Maree Hamilton, with love

Contents

List of Figures   ix

Acknowledgements   xi

Introduction   1

CHAPTER 1
Gender, History and the West   13

CHAPTER 2
'He's not a man! He's a sack of money!': Corporatism and the
Male Breadwinner   43

CHAPTER 3
'Back home they think I'm very strange. I'm a feminist':
Re-Evaluating the Feminine Other   71

CHAPTER 4
'You're the party done all the suffering': Representing
Stereotypes of Native Americans in the 'Pro-Indian'
Western Cycle   101

CHAPTER 5
'A pistol don't make a man': Technology and Masculine
Gender Performances   139

CHAPTER 6
'Who are those guys?': Understanding American Intervention
in the 'South of the Border' Western   175

CHAPTER 7

'As unmarked as their place in history': Black Westerns,
an Alternative History of Masculinities?   207

Conclusion   245

Filmography   257

Bibliography   263

Index   277

Figures

Figure 1   Howard Kemp (Jimmy Stewart) awakening in
            hysteria in *The Naked Spur*.   51
Figure 2   Amy Kane (Grace Kelly) and Helen Ramirez
            (Katy Jurado), planning to leave town together in
            High Noon.   91
Figure 3   Jessica Drummond (Barbara Stanwyck) is a woman
            with a whip in *Forty Guns*.   95
Figure 4   Rachel Zachary (Audrey Hepburn) struggling
            with the discovery of her Native American
            heritage in *The Unforgiven*.   115
Figure 5   Randolph Scott as Steve Farrell, the travelling
            gun salesman, in *Colt .45*. The iconography of the
            crossed Colt .45s is consistent throughout the film.   151
Figure 6   The death of Mapache (Emilio Fernandez) in the
            final apocalyptic massacre in *The Wild Bunch*.
            The vivid demonstration of violence through film
            techniques such as slow motion and inter-cutting,
            and the use of new technology such as squibs,
            were revolutionary.   172
Figure 7   The iconic finale of *Butch Cassidy and the
            Sundance Kid*, with the title characters played
            by Paul Newman and Robert Redford, captured
            freeze-framed, guns drawn against certain death.   178
Figure 8   Harry Belafonte plays against his sex symbol
            typecasting as the hustling 'Preacher' in *Buck and
            the Preacher*.   236

Acknowledgements

The writing of this book has been facilitated by the support of staff at the University of Newcastle, Australia. Colleagues within the School of Humanities and Social Science and the English Language and Foundation Studies Centre were (and are) generous in their mentorship and support of me as an educator and emerging scholar and were endlessly patient in their discussions of this and other projects, which was very much appreciated! I would especially like to thank Associate Professor Josephine May whose contributions to this volume have improved it immeasurably. I am grateful to bask in her presence. I would also like to thank my family and friends for their love and support. I would especially like to acknowledge my parents, to whom this book is dedicated: my father, Mark, a lover of cowboy flicks (especially *The Magnificent Seven*), whom I hope to meet again on the trail; and my beautiful mother, Maree, who is still riding alongside and thankfully shared her love of *Butch Cassidy and the Sundance Kid* with me many, many years ago.

Introduction

No historian can fail to acknowledge the enormous and transformative potential modern audiovisual media may have on the conceptualization and communication of historical ideas. Nor can historians ignore that film raises important, perhaps discipline re-defining, questions regarding what history is and how it is validly transmitted. Indeed, the way in which the filmic medium is approached by historians today will directly impact the histories we write tomorrow and the continued relevance of the discipline beyond the academic sphere. Certainly, central in the debate over the uses of film in telling history are pedagogical concerns regarding the increasing use of film as an educational tool. This debate critiques the capacity of cinema to carry an adequate information load, to prioritize historical content, and to engage skills of critical analysis in classrooms where time, expertise and individualized attention may be lacking. For some, it can be disturbing that not only do historical films feature as popular adult entertainment that doubles as historical education but, more importantly, that the future guardians of the past, children, are increasingly educated about history through the use of film.[1] The historical film clearly cuts very close to the bone for historians: practically, theoretically and emotionally.

I began to grapple with the implications of historical film on our ideas of history while conducting a study of the iconic Western, *Butch Cassidy and the Sundance Kid* (George Roy Hill, 1969), a film which won four Oscars and enjoyed enormous box-office success. The film, based on actual characters and events, follows the two bandits of the title, Butch (Paul Newman), the brains, and the Sundance Kid (Robert Redford), the gunslinger, through their bumbling criminal career, which culminates with their exile in Bolivia. The film finishes with the pair captured freeze-framed, guns drawn against

---

1   Scott Alan Metzger, 'Pedagogy and the Historical Feature Film: Toward Historical Literacy', *Film & History* 37 (2007): 67–68.

the certain death of the surrounding police force. Although the focus of my research is the ways in which gender is historicized in Western films, concepts of historical time became critical to the analysis. How is history constructed in the Western? Can a film only be historical if based on 'real' events and 'real' events? How is the past connected to the present? What role does the gendered representation of the iconic cowboy have in communicating historical ideas? What happens when the lights go down and we are left alone with these images on the screen?

To make sense of these questions I noted the perspective of foremost film historian Robert A. Rosenstone, who has attempted to apply postmodern theory to film. Unlike previous scholars who examined the possibility for historical films to actually convey the historical past, or who examine historical films in terms of what we can learn about the production context, Rosenstone suggests that a 'good' historical film inevitably and anachronistically intermingles elements of past and present, in the process complicating, indeed *de*lineating, the traditional linear narrative structures of history: 'they render the world as multiple, complex and indeterminate, rather than as a series of self-enclosed, neat, linear stories.'[2] But *Butch Cassidy* may be seen to construct a more complex exemplary relationship between the represented historical past and the present of the viewer. In this film important historical cues are given that make the past immediately connected with, and relevant to, the contemporary issues surrounding the viewer context. In doing so, rather than *de*lineate time into separate and disjointed historical moments, *Butch Cassidy* actually provides a sense of time as being *hyper-linear*.[3] That is, film acts to facilitate a temporal 'jump' from the audience's own time (the time of filmic release), back

---

2   Robert A. Rosenstone, 'History in images/history in words: Reflections on the possibility of really putting history onto film', *American Historical Review* 5 (1988): 1182. Rosenstone would later expand on this, suggesting film is the medium to provide a truly postmodern history in *Visions of the Past: The Challenge of Film to Our Ideas of History* (Cambridge: Harvard University Press, 1995), 206–207.

3   A conceptual parallel may be found in the notion of hyperspace, the ability to shift objects from one geographical location to another without the loss of time. I am arguing that film, in essence, enacts a similar concept on notions of time.

to an earlier temporal period for the purpose of establishing an *exemplary* link between the past and the present. In so doing, film makes explicit, obvious and immediate the links between past action and present reality, for the purpose of illustrating historical continuity and/or discontinuity between both temporalities. Westerns may be seen as a prime vehicle to facilitate this process as they are inherently historical and deeply rooted in ideological conceptualizations of both the self and nation. Moreover, because the symbols and motifs of the Western are instantly recognizable, they provide a constant and unchanging territory that easily facilitates the leap from one temporal location to another.

This book undertakes a two-fold analysis inspired by the questions and concerns about history and film first prompted by this analysis of *Butch Cassidy*. Firstly, it explores, at the theoretical level, the way in which history functions on film. Specifically, a paradigm for understanding the historical film, termed 'hyper-linearity', is offered. This paradigm suggests that, rather than the historical film acting to reflect the issues surrounding its production context or as an opportunity to represent the past 'as it was', the historical film creates deliberate temporal links between the represented historical past and the present reality of the audience. In so doing the past assumes particular and explicit relevance to the present, and a specific relationship between the two time periods is created.[4] This relationship is one that is 'hyper-linear' in nature, where the actions of the past are accentuated and seen as immediate, obvious and directly relevant to making sense of the present, to the point where this relationship can at times be causal in nature. Further, this relationship is maintained through

---

4   For reasons of clarity and methodological validity the temporal relationship maintained here is twofold: between the past represented on film, and the time of the film's release. However, it is possible to conceive of a third and more complex temporal relationship that exists when watching a film in a contemporary context. Here it could be argued that the audience autonomously uses the historical cues constructed in such films to make the historical past relevant to their own context, in so doing demonstrating an intuitive awareness of themselves as historical subjects and a desire to create meaning through historical connection. Such an assertion, whilst theoretically interesting, taps into a rich field of audience studies and as such is not demonstrable within the confines of this work.

the discarding of events that, although historically relevant, disrupt the viability of this hyper-linear relationship and this goes towards accounting for the filmic 'gaps' in historical representation; that is, events or perspectives that, although historically relevant, are ignored by the filmmaker. The viability of 'hyper-linearity' as an approach to the historical film, including how it functions within a film, and the implications this approach has in relation to audience understandings of history, will be the primary focus of this volume. In exploring the theoretical nature of history on film, a greater insight should be provided both into how film functions in an historical manner, and also into how historians can effectively use film in a way that encourages positive pedagogical outcomes.

In Westerns, the hyper-linear function can illustrate three main relationships between the filmic past and the production context, which can create a new historical understanding for the audience. The first relationship that may be constructed is *positive continuity*, in which the past is represented in such a way as to illustrate a positive, socially reaffirming connection with the present, which encourages the audience to feel comfortable in their heritage and to use this as inspiration to construct a meaningful future. This positive continuity is seen in *The Magnificent Seven* (John Sturges, 1960) for example, where a group of men with specialized skills undertake foreign interventionism and, in this setting, rediscover and assert their dominant hegemonic masculinities. This film connects past American interventionism in South America with then contemporary interventionism in South America and South East Asia in a positive light, reaffirming American ideology and identity and the patriarchal hierarchy that underpins it.

The second relationship is discontinuity, whereby we are shown that, although the past and present may have certain parallels, these will not and should not continue, and the audience is therefore encouraged to shape the future in a different way. Usually such films show the beginnings of this divergent transformation in them and the audience is provided with the illusion that through watching they have effected change. An example of this is the 1972 Sidney Poitier film *Buck and the Preacher*, which provided a representation of the African American voice in the West and connected this to Civil Rights issues and the emerging 'Blaxploitation' genre.

The third relationship is the more ambiguous notion of *negative continuity*. Here, there are parallels between the past and the present, which is undesirable, yet it is also seemingly unavoidable, as any avenue to effect real change is unclear. These films are underlined by the embedded nature of structures and protagonists who are unable to change or effectively combat them. This can be demonstrated obviously in films that explicitly address racial discrimination or class inequality. In *Butch Cassidy*, this negative continuity is not *shown* but *embodied* in the characters through their gender representation. This film uses, at the most fundamental level, the manifestation of undesirable and destructive masculinities as a symbol for structural mechanisms that allow for the perpetuation (and repetition) of negative historical experiences. Thus negative and destructive gender forms come to embody the ideological and structural continuity in American society that has allowed the continuation of negative and destructive actions, from frontier settlement to the Vietnam War. This film illustrates both the place of gender as a distinct organizing category and, more than this, the role of gendered behaviour and patriarchal institutions as, cyclically, a symptom and driver of detrimental continuities of national policy and character. In this way personal gender construction, broader concepts of national identity, and historical continuity are inescapably linked and mutually (negatively) reinforcing concepts.

The other and inter-connected intention of this volume is to link gender representation and historical analysis using as evidence Western films produced in the period of the 1950s and 1960s. This connection between the representations of gender, the functioning of history, and the Western, are linked and mutually beneficial areas of analysis for a number of reasons. Westerns broadly may be seen as the most significant American film style and even as far more than a film style but as the expression and re-evaluation of American national values and identity founded in the frontier experience.[5] As such, and due to its longevity, the Western provides an integral link between changing perceptions of the past and the way in which these perceptions intimately relate to the contemporary construction

5   Harry Schein, 'The Olympian Cowboy', *The American Scholar* 24 (1955): 309.

of national and personal identities in the United States. Central to building this connection, however, is not the props, or even the setting, it is the man. The gender representation of the central male protagonist, instantly recognizable, subsequently commodified and often imitated, is the central expression of history in the Western films, where his conduct comes to represent an historical past, a national type and value structure, and works as the open gateway by which the American audience connects the past with their present. Using an interdisciplinary approach and highlighting the relationship between gender construction and historical representation in the Western genre shows not only the way in which gender norms are historically contingent, a point both illustrated by and insulated within Hollywood structures; but, more than this, it also shows the way in which the construction of gender at the private level relates intimately with the maintenance of broader social institutions and national forms of identity at the public level.

This study focuses on the 1950s and 1960s for a number of reasons. It derives from the hypothesis that these interdisciplinary links can most distinctly be made at a time when the Western film, gender and history were potently interlinked. Moreover, the Westerns of this period are under-analysed in the manner conceptualized here. Specifically, while scholarly interest has increasingly been piqued by the so-called 'remasculinization' of America following the Vietnam War, especially during the 1980s, this study aims to examine the prior decades as the period of American '*de*masculinization'. Evidence for this demasculinization is reflected in Western films of the 1950s and 1960s and this, in turn, affects concepts of history and the relationship between history and then-contemporary national identity and institutional structures. It is important to acknowledge here that the decade of the 1970s is sidelined in both this work and other works on remasculinization. The reason that this period has not received extensive attention here is that, whilst the 1950s and 1960s are seen as a period of demasculinization, and the 1980s a time of concerted remasculinization, the 1970s are perceived as a period of transition between these two states, where films such as *Taxi Driver* (Martin Scorsese, 1976) and *The Deer Hunter* (Michael Cimino, 1978) began to reintroduce the Vietnam veteran into the American domestic context and grapple with the implications this reintegration would have on American identity and gender. This reintegration would ultimately be resolved in the remasculinized images of the veteran (and broader American masculinity) most commonly associated with the *Rambo* franchise (Ted Kotcheff, 1982; George Cosmatos, 1985; Peter MacDonald, 1988).

The concept of 'remasculinization' is particularly associated with Susan Jeffords' *The Remasculinization of America: Gender and the Vietnam War* in which the author argued that cultural artefacts of the 1980s, including television, film, and other representations associated with the Vietnam War, put forward a 'masculine point of view.' As distinct from 'masculinity' and 'men', this 'masculine point of view' was seen by Jeffords to be an ideal, hegemonic masculine standard that, although unattainable, allowed for male identification with individual characteristics and the overarching system of dominance it portrays. This acted to reinvigorate traditional forms of American national identity founded in patriarchal power structures and the maintenance of strict gender difference.[6] Thus, in Jeffords' analysis, representation, individual gender identity and broader national identity and policy are inherently linked and mutually constructive factors. Jeffords' work acts here as a reference point: if such a remasculinization occurred in film representations inter alia as she claims, then there must have been a prior process of demasculinization. This volume seeks to explore if and how demasculinization occurs, and what its implications are for historical understandings of identity.

This volume will examine the fracturing elements in men's gendered identities, faced as they were with a multitude of challenges on the economic, gendered, technological and racial frontiers. Particular factors that contributed towards this notion of demasculinization, and case studies of films that particularly highlight these factors, will form the foundation of each chapter and will be examined in light of their hyper-linear relationships between the represented past and present. These demasculinizing factors include, for example: men's changing economic power bases in *The Naked*

---

6   Susan Jeffords, *The Remasculinization of America: Gender and the Vietnam War* (Bloomington: Indiana University Press, 1989), xiii.

Spur (Robert Mann, 1953); the increasingly public role of women, using
High Noon (Fred Zinnemann, 1952); the re-evaluation of the treatment of
First Nation Peoples following the Vietnam War, including a reflection on
the capacity for film to represent 'Indigenous' stories, using *The Unforgiven*
(John Huston, 1959) and *Soldier Blue* (Ralph Nelson, 1970); the impact
of technology as related both to notions of 'progress' and violence, in
Colt .45 (Edwin L. Marin, 1950) and *The Wild Bunch* (Sam Peckinpah,
1969); finally, the re-evaluation of foreign interventionism in the wake of
Vietnam, using *Butch Cassidy and the Sundance Kid* (George Roy Hill,
1969), and a reflection on inter-racial discourses following the Civil Rights
Movement, using *Buck and the Preacher* (Sidney Poitier, 1972).

It should be noted that in seeking out films to form the research for
this book I have focused primarily on theatrically released films with wide
distribution, with the inclusion of a small number of straight to television/
video titles. All the films selected here could be considered 'popular' in
the sense that a majority were theatrical releases, have a leading actor who
was or would become a well-known performer, and, in most cases, were
either well received at the time of their release and/or would go on to be
recognized as genre staples. Popular films were chosen because they were
the films most viewed at the time by the movie-going public and therefore
raised the most questions about the ways in which history was constructed
in films for many people. This study does not grapple with the rich field
of audience studies, although certainly there is potential to apply these
understandings to this field. The sheer popularity and studio output of
the western genre in the 1950s and 1960s would make it difficult to choose
westerns that did not fall within a 'popular' category. The films studied in
composing this volume covered a wide span of history – from the 1930s to
the 1990s – however, the focus of the research was on films released during
the 1950s and 1960s. Whilst concern for having a reasonable selection of
films within the period of consideration is evident, films were not sought
out on the basis of theme, relationship with historical subjects, star or other
purpose. My aim in selecting films for a research base was to engage with a
truly popular discourse and to seek to explore the validity of hyper-linearity
as a model that, in these Westerns, allows for a greater understanding of
history and changing gender norms over time.

The 1950s and 1960s are well known not only for the immense popularity of the Western genre in both film and television, but also for the production of sub-genres of subversive or revisionist works. Westerns such as *Run of the Arrow* (Sam Fuller, 1957), *Hud* (Martin Ritt, 1963), *Cheyenne Autumn* (John Ford, 1964), *Hombre* (Martin Ritt, 1967), *Will Penny* (Tom Gries, 1968) and *Little Big Man* (Arthur Penn, 1970) offered revised visions of the Old West to draw attention to then contemporary American policies at home and abroad. This would also translate into so-called Acid Westerns, those expressive of countercultural values beginning with Monte Hellman's *The Shooting* (1966) and *Ride in the Whirlwind* (1966), and also into Italian Zapata Westerns, films situated in a Revolutionary Mexican setting that were, typically, overtly political in tone such as Damiano Damiani's *A Bullet for the General* (1966).[7] The films selected for analysis in these chapters include revisionist films but not exclusively so and, indeed, which films can be classed as revisionist is itself up for debate. On the one hand this volume illustrates that revisionist Westerns cannot be ignored as major innovators of the genre that reflect upon the capacity to utilize Western conventions to illuminate contemporary politics and these were sometimes incredibly popular films in their own right. However, this volume also seeks to question to what extent 'traditional' Westerns and supposedly hegemonic masculine performances also pose sometimes subversive questions about the narrative of American history.

I argue that in the portrayal of men, and the embodied masculine gender performance they each present, some Westerns of this period draw a hyper-linear connection between the events of the represented past and the context of the film's release. In particular the represented past reflects upon men's reintegration into society after the Civil War or 'Indian Wars', social and economic change prompted by events such as the Gold Rush, adjustment to the closing of the frontier and shifts in economic structuring. This reflection creates links to the events of filmic production: post-World

---

7   See, for example, the work of Jonathan Rosenbaum, whose work is especially associated with the Acid Western, especially *Dead Man* (London: BFI Publishing, 2000) and Carlo Gaberscek, 'Zapata Westerns: The Short Life of a Sub-Genre (1966–72)', *Bilingual Review* 29 (2008): 45–58.

War II reintegration, changing women's roles, and changing economic structures. In examining these films a clear shift in historical attitudes is evident throughout the period. In 1950s Westerns this hyper-linear connection is ultimately more likely to be of a positive nature, arguing that hegemonic masculinity and the patriarchal structures that support it can adapt to change; however, this does not detract from the slow erosion of the masculinity that takes place. Here men are often forced into competition with each other and, what Eve Sedgewick refers to as the 'homosocial bond' is tested by the pressures of greed, racial minorities and women.[8] In the Westerns of the 1960s, however, it is more common for this homosocial bond to break down and the notion of a stable and positive hegemonic masculinity is portrayed as illusionary. By the end of the decade, although some elements of these films may be read as illustrating a breakdown or devaluation of traditional hegemonic values, I also question whether a subtle repositioning of masculinity takes place that presages the shift towards remasculinization in the 1980s using in particular the 'black Western' *Buck and the Preacher*.[9]

In Western films gender becomes a potent vehicle through which a hyper-linear understanding is communicated. Firstly it is significant to acknowledge the centrality of film in charting changing gendered ideas. Unlike traditional written scholarship where gender can either be ignored or neutralized the visual nature of the medium and its nature as a collaborative exercise means that gender performance moves to centre stage. Beyond this the gender performance of the central male protagonist presents the embodiment of historical ideas. At a structural and national level the central place of the hero in embodying and exploring national values, actions and structures is a significant connection between past and present. At

8   Eve Sedgewick as cited in Cynthia Fuchs, 'The Buddy Politic', in *Screening the Male: Exploring Masculinities in Hollywood Cinema*, eds Steven Cohan & Ina Rae Hark (London & New York: Routledge, 1993), 194–195.

9   It is important to note here that, with a mind to the flaws of strict and arbitrary periodization and to the nature of filmic production, where a film may be produced well before the final release date, some films of a later date will be used in this discussion, with a rationale for inclusion at the commencement of each chapter.

an individual level the manifestation of gender representations on-screen allows for a critical examination of the ways in which men's gender individually relates to broader national ideas and patriarchal standards, is impacted by contextual factors and adapts over time. I frequently use the word 'patriarchy' in this volume and do so with the intention to convey that patriarchy is, as Allan Johnson stated, '*not* simply another way of saying "men." Patriarchy is a kind of society [...] in which men *and* women participate [...] a society is patriarchal to the degree that it promotes male privilege by being *male dominated, male identified*, and *male centred*.'[10] In this way it is acknowledged that patriarchy, masculine gender performances, hegemonic ideas of gender and the lived experiences of men (and women) are distinct, changeable concepts that may align or fracture for different men dependent on a variety of other facets of identity as well as across time and place.

Generally, then, the validity of this hyper-linear approach to historical film, which sees the construction of a 'hyper-linear' relationship between the represented past and the present of the filmic release, is explored here. This relationship is constructed to illustrate a positive or negative continuity, or a discontinuity, between the events of the past and the contemporary reality of the audience when the film is released and encourages the perception that the historical past has direct and meaningful relevance in informing that present. Following this, the potential impacts this paradigm for history and film will have on conceptualizations of history will be explored: on the one hand, the effect of this may be to enrich audience understandings of the relationship between the past and present. Certainly, a view of the past that is informed by the concerns of the present in other historiography has not received the same level of criticism as has been levelled against film for, potentially, performing a similar function. Indeed, as Frederick Jackson Turner, the foundational Western historian himself suggested in 1910: 'a comprehension of the United States of to-day, an

---

10   As cited in Judith M. Bennett, *History Matters: Patriarchy and the Challenge of Feminism* (Manchester: Manchester University Press, 2006), 55. Indeed, it is important to recognise the ways in which men and women can be individually disadvantaged or privileged in a patriarchal society depending upon other facets of their identities including race and class.

understanding of the rise and progress of the forces which have made it what it is, demands that we should rework our history from the new points of view afforded by the present.'[11] On the other hand, and perhaps more pertinent to current educational concerns, is the underlying sense that a hyper-linear relationship positions the past as relevant only for the use of the present, and it is this that is responsible for emptying the historical meaning from film and relinquishing audiences from a responsibility to maintain historical memory.

11   Frederick Jackson Turner, 'Social Forces in American History [annual address as the president of the American Historical Association at Indianapolis, December 28, 1910]', in *The Frontier in American History*, ed. Frederick Jackson Turner (Malabar, FL: Robert E. Krieger Publishing, [1920] 1985), 330.

Gender, History and the West

Within the proliferation of 'screen' cultures of all types, film continues its rise as an important method by which students, and the broader public, engage with the historical past, yet it is a site of contestation amongst professional historians who remain concerned about the methodological foundations of using such a medium to inform our understandings of the past. The foundational proposal of this book is that film profoundly informs social understandings of the past in ways that are incredibly complex. Films do not simply reflect our present but construct a hyper-linear relationship that equally informs our understandings of both the past and the present. Specifically, the Western film and, potentially, historical films more broadly, construct a hyper-linear relationship with the past that does not simply reflect the concerns of the present nor attempts to accurately represent the past but, rather, constructs a fluid relationship between the two that privileges both temporal localities and sees each as mutually informing and constitutive. This is a distinct theoretical model in the field of history on film. Hyper-linear connections are illustrated throughout this volume via a consideration of the represented post-Civil War period given life in the Western film genre, circa 1870 to 1900, and the release period of the 1950s and 1960s. They are examined with a particular view to exploring the elements seen as fracturing and ultimately demasculinizing men's personal and patriarchal national identities in both periods.

These two periods are considered for several reasons: most obviously, the post-Civil War period is the most commonly presented historical period in Western films and the 1950s and 1960s was the period during which the Western across multiple media formats enjoyed the height of its popularity. Logically, this correlation suggests that there is some synergy between the themes and issues represented in the post-Civil War context that spoke to the concerns of the Civil Rights Movement and Vietnam era. This volume locates such concerns around a locus of gender: both periods were times during which white hegemonic masculinity underwent renegotiation, even breakdown, in the face of mass cultural, social, economic, and technological change. In particular, post-Civil War shifts in economic and technological structures, women's rights movements, and race relations and racial movements relates, hyper-linearly, to post-World War II shifts in these same arenas. In Western films these shifts are illustrated specifically in men's employment and economic status, the interactions between white male characters and female, Native American and African American counterparts as well as in America's relationship with its neighbours. These historical shifts fundamentally called into question the traditional values and foundation of hegemonic gender identities and the patriarchal institutions that privileged such identities. At a national level these shifts called into question the patriarchal, white ideals that formed the cornerstone of American ideology: a country founded upon available land, fulfilling its Manifest Destiny, providing equality, democracy and opportunity to all people willing to seize upon it. The exposure of the gaps between this American myth and reality is characteristic of both periods. Certainly theorists of masculinities such as Michael Kimmel, E. Anthony Rotundo and Raewyn Connell have reflected on the crisis tendencies associated with modern masculine gender performances, and have highlighted these periods as particularly transitional for definitions of American manhood.[1] Susan Jefford's reflections on the 'remasculinization' of the male image in the 1980s also speak, conversely, to the sense that a 'demasculinization' must have occurred in the previous era. The issues of these periods are intimately illustrated by Western films and their exploration of the gender performances of white men. For these reasons, then, the Westerns of the 1950s and 1960s set in the post-Civil War period are considered significant

---

1   Michael Kimmel, *Manhood in America: A Cultural History*, 2nd edn (Oxford: Oxford University Press, 2006) and *The History of Men: Essays on the History of American and British Masculinities* (New York: State University of New York, 2005); E. Anthony Rotundo, *American Manhood: Transformations in Masculinity from the Revolution to the Modern Era* (New York: Basic Books, 1987); and R.W. Connell, *Masculinities*, 2nd edn (Cambridge: Polity Press, 2002).

and are examined throughout this volume. This chapter will examine the important historical shifts within these periods and the impact of these shifts on conceptualizations of ideal masculine gender performance.

Hyper-linearity: Practical Understandings of the Link between Past and Present

Western films of the 1950s and 1960s prove capable of constructing a hyper-linear link between the represented post-Civil War past and the present of their filmic release. This hyper-linear link may emphasize different aspects of the past in order to construct a national history that infers a variety of relationships with the present. Overwhelmingly, this historical relationship is one that is mediated through the white, male central protagonist of these films and, therefore, gender construction becomes a central and historical category for understanding hyper-linear links. This hypothesis relies on the notion that there are indeed recognizable historical parallels between the post-Civil War and Civil Rights Movement eras. Such parallels need to be constructed on screen using cues that are understood by the audience and that are relatable to the audience's own understandings of American history and their own contemporary identities. Such cues are provided in Western films, ranging from explicit historical references regarding personages, events and technologies, and the impact of these historical phenomenon on society and individuals, to less tangible or specific cues including filmic techniques that emphasize a sense of historicity. The historical cues in these films go towards creating a picture of both represented past and filmic present as one of enormous and transformative change with a white hegemonic masculinity under siege from a variety of angles. These films facilitate a fundamental questioning of the value of exclusionary forms of identity and the patriarchal social values such an identity embodies. The narrative devices of this genre may undertake this historical relationship in three main ways. Firstly, the narrative may emphasize a positive historical continuity, suggesting that white masculinity has, should and will

16

CHAPTER I

continue to find ways of resolving social crisis and therefore it is a valid form of gendered identity and a solid foundation for social institutions. Secondly, the narrative may emphasize a negative continuity that highlights the detrimental impacts of the hegemonic masculinity both on individuals and on social structures but cannot envision an alternative form of identity or a way for men to extricate themselves from this trap. These films envision a historical relationship where men, through their gender aspirations, and broader American institutions are doomed to repeat the mistakes of the past. Thirdly, these films may emphasize a discontinuity between past and present, which explores hegemonic masculine standards but proposes an alternative way of being or suggests an alternative vision for the future separate from the issues of the historical past.

Certainly, the majority of Westerns are set in the post-Civil War environment and it is not surprising that the pre-eminent historical genre in American cultural forms would be situated in this temporal locale. Indeed, as Robert Penn Warren asserts, the Civil War marked the beginning of American history

> in the deepest and most inward sense [...] The Civil War is our only 'felt' history – history lived in the national imagination. This is not to say that the war is always, and by all men, felt in the same way. Quite the contrary. But this fact is an index to the very complexity, depth and fundamental significance of the event. It is an overwhelming and vital image of human and national significance.[2]

Warren's perspective points to several key acknowledgments in constructing this argument: the first being the sense that a hyper-linear history does not intend to essentialize notions of the Civil War and its conflicting implications for vastly different regions, groups and individuals within society, nor does it suggest that the representations surrounding Civil War history are received homogenously by spectators. What hyper-linear history does do, however, is reflect the notion of a shared 'national imagination', one that intimately taps into the foundations, and validity, of a shared sense of national identity and experience. For its multitudinous significances

---

2   Robert Penn Warren, *The Legacy of the Civil War* (Lincoln: University of Nebraska Press, 1998 [1961]), 3–4.

and reinterpretations the Civil War is an important arena that allows for a hyper-linear history with the Civil Rights era, one that precisely taps into and exploits the different meanings of the Civil War and the Civil Rights era for different people in different films throughout the 1950s and 1960s. Indeed, Warren points to the significance of the Civil War to Civil Rights era spectators: 'one appeal of the War is that it holds in suspension, beyond all schematic readings and claims to total interpretation, so many of the issues and tragic ironies – somehow essential yet incommensurable – which we yet live.'[3]

The notion of the post-Civil War period and the Civil Rights period as bearing significant historical parallels is not unique to this work. Landmark American race and Southern historian C. Vann Woodward coined the term 'Second Reconstruction' in the 1950s precisely to point to the similarities between these periods. Woodward asserted that although the periods are not identical in terms of issues or reactions, both periods do feature 'ironic contrasts between noble purposes and sordid results, between idealistic aims and pragmatic consequences [which] are characteristic of reconstruction periods', and were particularly manifest in racial policy and foreign affairs.[4] Indeed, to others, such as Maurice Isserman and Michael Kazin the effect of the Second Reconstruction (or even the second Civil War), was not restricted to these areas but, rather, reflected an all-encompassing re-evaluation of American society where 'many Americans came to regard groups of fellow countrymen as enemies with whom they were engaged in a struggle for the nation's very soul.'[5] Certainly the notion of both eras acting to reveal deep tears in the fabric of American social cohesion in its entirety is endorsed here. In such an environment competing interest groups and political ideologies in the Civil Rights era came into conflict in a way that fundamentally shifted the national landscape in an irrecoverable way, much as Americans had perceived a similar shift in national

---

3   Warren, *The Legacy of the Civil War*, 107–108.
4   C. Vann Woodward, 'The Irony of Southern History', *The Journal of Southern History* 19 (1953): 17.
5   Maurice Isserman and Michael Kazin, *America Divided: The Civil War of the 1960s* (Oxford: Oxford University Press, 2000), 4.

culture following the Civil War. Woodward would suggest in the 1950s that as a result of these similarities, and the growing influence of America on the world stage, 'America stands in greater need than she ever did of understanding her own history.'⁶ This scholarly literature regarding the First and Second Reconstructions had its genesis in the 1950s and 1960s; therefore it reflected a broader public sentiment regarding the nature of social change spreading throughout the nation, a sentiment that identified the roots of contemporary problems in Reconstruction-era public policy.

In this context, then, it is little wonder that the Western, with its capacity to reflect on, and inform, audience's perceptions of the connection between the Civil War past and Civil Rights present, its deep links to American ideology and history, and its longevity as an existing medium of cultural communication, rose to the enormous heights of popularity that it did. Indeed, it can be suggested that it is precisely the genre's capacity to undertake a hyper-linear history between past and present during a time of enormous social flux that stimulated its appeal amongst American audiences. These Western films of the 1950s and 1960s used the persona and gender performance of the central male protagonist as a medium through which to engage with these transformative historical conditions. Particularly the protagonist's experiences reflected upon changes to men's status as a result of the fracturing impacts of war, changing women's roles, evolving technologies and economic conditions, and shifts in racialized discourses. It is important to recognize that no one factor was responsible for the re-evaluation of gender performances in both periods but, rather, that all of these factors were compounding and reinforcing, and it is precisely this complexity that caused a fundamental destabilization of white hegemonic masculinity.

Historically, shifts in men's gender roles can be seen as inherent in a society that is participating in war or attempting to reintegrate war veterans into normative peace-time roles and public and private structures. As Paul Cimbala and Randall Miller argue in relation to the Civil War, but is applicable across conflicts, the physical and mental challenges experienced

---

6   Woodward, 'The Irony of Southern History', 18.

by men as a result of war could result not only in personal anguish, but difficulty engaging in former labour roles, and with communities and families who did not understand the wartime experience 'and what new definitions of courage and manhood that war had demanded'.[7] Indeed, the American Civil War itself has been conceptualized by LeeAnn Whites as fundamentally a war relating to definitions of desirable masculine forms and gender relations in all aspects of its outbreak, conduct and subsequent reconstruction efforts.[8] For Whites the complex relationships between Southern and Northern masculinities and the interactions between those masculinities and African American masculinities and rights movements meant that: 'the war presented white men with a crisis for their masculinity, a threat to their manhood as it was socially constructed. Whatever the outcome they could not simply remain as they were.'[9]

This shift in masculinized gender roles was heightened in a post-Civil War environment due to a variety of distinct social factors. The first was the nature of the Civil War, which pitted two distinct ways of 'doing' white American masculinity against each other, as symbolized by the values implicit in Northern industrialism and in the 'genteel patriarchy' of white Southern agrarian land-holding. The sublimation of Southern forms of masculinity in favour of victorious Northern masculinity, and the South's reincorporation into the Union, further exacerbated shifts towards a hegemonic masculinity founded in industrialized capitalist values, identified by Michael Kimmel as the 'self-made man'.[10] More than this, though, for Southern white men it presented a distinct rupture in their performance of masculinity that sat at odds with a national story of inevitable progress and victory culture. Indeed, this was acknowledged by Woodward as the 'irony' of Southern history: with its experiences of 'frustration and failure', poverty,

---

7   Paul A. Cimbala and Randall M. Miller (eds), *The Great Task Remaining Before Us: Reconstruction as America's Continuing Civil War* (New York: Fordham University Press, 2010), xi.

8   LeeAnn Whites, *The Civil War as a Crisis in Gender: Augusta, Georgia, 1860–1890* (Athens: University of Georgia Press, 1995), 3.

9   Whites, *The Civil War*, 3.

10   Michael Kimmel, *The History of Men*, 8–9.

accommodation and submission the South sits distinctly at odds with a national legend that privileges an American identity founded in converse characteristics.[11] One could argue too, that this rupture in the American legend of victory was presented not only by the South as region but also by a vast segment of white Southern men whose illusions of hegemonic gender status were also shattered by loss and Reconstruction as a result of the Civil War.

Aside from the renegotiations of masculinities, both white and African American, among others, that occurred during and after the Civil War, the conflict, like all war, also caused a fundamental re-evaluation of the nature of gender norms for women. In a perceptive article exploring the experiences of Southern women Drew Gilpin Faust argues that the Civil War provided women with shifting ideas regarding female behaviours, for example, a shift from protection of the home to willing self-sacrifice of family, and established wartime archetypes that women challenged in a variety of ways.[12] Faust points to the ways in which archetypal notions regarding women's importance, passivity and willing sacrifice were questioned by women who instead felt purposelessness, discontent and sought active forms of participation in their own lived experiences. She establishes that 'without directly challenging women's prescribed roles, they [women] nevertheless longed for a magical personal deliverance from gender constraints.'[13] Moreover, for Northern women the Civil War also increased the visibility of their public roles, typically in care-taking professions such as teaching and nursing, and provided an opportunity to hone advocacy skills and networks, particularly in abolitionist, anti-slavery and universal suffrage discourses.[14] Further, such arguments mimic longstanding issues relevant

---

11   Woodward, 'The Irony of Southern History', 5.
12   Drew Gilpin Faust, 'Altars of Sacrifice: Confederate Women and the Narratives of War', *The Journal of American History* 76 (1990): 1200–1228.
13   Faust, 'Altars of Sacrifice', 1206.
14   See, for example, Carol Faulkner, "A New Field of Labor': Antislavery Women, Freedmen's Aid, and Political Power', in *The Great Task Remaining Before Us: Reconstruction as America's Continuing Civil War*, eds Paul A. Cimbala and Randall M. Miller (New York: Fordham University Press, 2010), 88–100.

to women's roles in Western states, where women found their traditional gender roles challenged by the demands of Western life and where they often performed a diversity of roles, functions and labour that they attempted to incorporate into an understanding of idealized forms of femininity.[15]

It can be argued that women's experiences of the Civil War and of the West by no means broke gender stereotypes, indeed, the emphasis was on negotiating and reincorporating counter-experiences into existing discourses of femininity, but they did provide a fertile ground upon which the development of first wave feminism in the late nineteenth century would develop. It is important to note that during this time Western states were at the forefront of granting women's suffrage rights.[16] Furthermore, the pressures of women's challenges to hegemonic understandings of femininity coupled with other rights-based movements placed fundamental pressure on the definitions of white hegemonic masculinity and its manifestations in patriarchal institutional structures. As E. Rotundo asserts, men reacted with 'vehemence' to the notion of women's suffrage and its associated implications in undercutting male privilege and the traditional binary of women's domestic and men's public roles.[17]

Although American society in the 1950s and 1960s did not experience a practical, military Civil War, it did experience historical parallels in some sense. Of course, pragmatically, American society was dealing with the impacts of World War II and the struggle to reintegrate its veterans. The difficulties of this reintegration were reflected in the ongoing disparities between the social expectations that men would re-enter the domestic sphere as breadwinner, exhibiting a 'softer' masculinity capable of assuming a collectivist position to meet the needs of wives and offspring, and the realities of a generation of men impacted by the trauma of warfare. The

---

15   See, for example, Julie Roy Jeffrey, *Frontier Women: 'Civilizing' the West? 1840–1880*, rev. edn (New York: Hill & Lang, 1979). These ideas are further explored in Chapter 4.

16   See, for example, Holly J. McCammon and Karen E. Campbell, 'Winning the Vote in the West: The Political Successes of the Women's Suffrage Movement, 1866–1919', *Gender and Society* 15 (2001): 55–82.

17   E. Anthony Rotundo, *American Manhood*, 219.

difficulties of veteran reintegration were also exacerbated by a Cold War atmosphere that privileged 'hard', hawkish political affiliations with a corresponding attainment of hegemonic masculine gender performance.[18] Of course, the term Cold War, ignores the multiple 'hot spots' that involved American military participation abroad, obviously in the Korean War and also in incursions in Cambodia, Cuba and other areas. The nature of Cold War politics continued to send contradictory messages regarding men's capacity to attain hegemonic masculine forms. On the one hand, social factors privileged militaristic, hawkish values in foreign policy and in solidifying capitalist values, whilst, on the other hand, also advocating for a passive masculinity capable of reaffirming the traditional values of the domestic sphere through the suppression of individualistic impulses, and through submission to corporate hierarchies. The experiences of reintegration were also complicated by the experiences of Native American and African American soldiers, many of whom refused to come home to a perceived second-class status of citizenship and actively campaigned for equal rights for their people.[19] Moreover the advocacy of such Civil Rights movements did much to re-emphasize social and regional divisions in such a way that exacerbated the previously established differences of the Civil War. This is particularly evident in the private and political incursions into the South for the purposes of altering segregationist policy. Perhaps the most prominent example of this is the 'sit in' strategy but it this is also evident in the strategies of SNCC, especially in Mississippi, the Freedom Rides of the 1960s and the deployment of Federal troops to support the Little Rock Nine and enforce integration of Little Rock Central High School, Arkansas, despite the segregationist stance of the Arkansas Governor in 1957.[20]

18   K.A. Cuordileone, "Politics in an Age of Anxiety': Cold War Political Culture and the Crisis in American Masculinity, 1949–1960', *The Journal of American History* 87 (2000): 515.

19   Donald L. Parman, *Indians and the American West in the Twentieth Century* (Bloomington: Indiana University Press, 1994), 115, and Isserman and Kazin, *America Divided*, 23, respectively.

20   Isserman and Kazin, *America Divided*, 27–32.

Paralleling the post-Civil War environment, World War II prompted a re-evaluation of women's societal roles but continued to attempt to position this re-evaluation within normative gender constructs throughout the 1950s. This would ultimately dissolve into the second wave feminist movement of the 1960s and 1970s. It is commonly accepted that male participation in World War II forced greater female participation in the labour force and, as a result, caused a fundamental paradigm shift regarding women's capabilities, opportunities and personal desires. As Linda Eisenmann asserts, it is a misnomer to suggest that after the War women stepped aside to allow veterans to assume employment and slotted easily back into domestic life: rather, she argues that women's rates of workplace participation only grew along with women's participation in tertiary education.[21] The participation of women within union, student, peace, and Civil Rights movements at this time arguably sharpened the advocacy skills of women who would later use these to great effect in second wave feminism. Although typically portrayed as a period of domesticity and the re-establishment of traditional normative gender roles, the 1950s was a significant arena for the burgeoning sexual liberation of women prompting fears amongst men that women's sexual awakening would detrimentally impact upon the domestic sphere and upon the existing gender binary that was essential in constructing masculinity itself.[22] Although Betty Friedan's *The Feminine Mystique*, the iconic treatise calling for women to look beyond domesticity for fulfilment, was not published until 1963, other research illustrates the growth in women's discontentment with domesticity as a definer of identity well before this.[23] From 1945 continuing into the second wave of feminism in the 1960s and 1970s, the re-evaluation many women undertook of their public and private roles presented a fundamental challenge to patriarchy and, indeed,

---

21   Linda Eisenmann, *Higher Education for Women in Postwar America, 1945–1965* (Baltimore: John Hopkins University Press, 2006), 3.

22   James Birkhart Gilbert, *Men in the Middle: Searching for Masculinity in the 1950s* (Chicago: University of Chicago Press, 2005), 18.

23   Eva Moskowitz, "'It's Good to Blow Your Top': Women's Magazines and a Discourse of Discontent, 1945–1965', *Journal of Women's History* 8 (1996): 66–98.

to individual men struggling to perform their own masculinity.[24] This can be construed as a challenge due to patriarchy's dependence upon a dichotomous, feminine 'other' for self-definition.

Ultimately, the point here is that certain explicit pre-existing historical parallels occur between men's (and women's) experiences of the post-Civil War and the post-World War II American landscape. Both periods reflected an attempt to reintegrate war veterans into a post-war society, which carried with it a variety of often contradictory codes of masculine behaviour. Similarly, the discourse of men's reintegration often emphasized the importance of archetypal and normative women's roles in re-establishing domestic harmony, yet, underneath the veneer of conformity, women's wartime roles and experiences could not be so easily constrained. Many women found the diversification of their roles, including their labour, the changing social perceptions of gender norms, their increasing participation in the public sphere and the growth in their advocacy for different causes contravened traditional hegemonic conceptualizations of femininity, causing them internalized conflict. These experiences also, arguably, provide a bridge to more radicalized discourse in the form of first and second wave feminism. More than this, men's wartime participation highlighted different ways of being masculine, and caused a fundamental re-evaluation of hegemonic forms both in terms of negotiation between white masculinities and in terms of how minority groups could be integrated into exclusionary, patriarchal masculine forms. Such similarities highlight the enormous pressures placed upon masculine forms, and the re-evaluation of hegemonic masculinity and the values that underpinned it, which is evident in both periods.

Western films reflect this conflict in the sense that they are typically situated in the Civil War/post-Civil War period and are focused on a white masculine narrative. In particular, they focus on American men

24   Of course women's experiences were mediated upon multiple lines of racial, class, political and religious identification, factors which are acknowledged, for example, in Eisenmann's evaluation of women's increasing public participation despite the ideological impetus for a feminine return to domesticity in *Higher Education for Women in Postwar America*.

who were struggling to reconcile competing forms of masculinity into a whole national manhood. Westerns of the 1950s and 1960s reflect this uncertainty in ways of being masculine during the Civil War period and connect it to post-World War II issues in noted subgenres such as the darker, psychological Westerns and in the 'closing of the frontier' Westerns. These subgenres place masculinities at the forefront of self-conscious considera- tion, questioning the values and actions caused by patriarchal standards and behaviours and arriving at a variety of conclusions, rather than natu- ralizing the protagonist's gender performance. Westerns also reflect such shifts in more subtle ways: they do so in the back stories of protagonists who often have military experience and are struggling to reconcile this service with their current situation, and in heroes who are displaced from their properties or who are transients searching for identity through a variety of occupations and interpersonal relationships. The issue of white Southern masculinity and its values are also reflected in post-Civil War Westerns that often vilify representations of the Southern male and the values he represents: the vengeful horseman Abe Kelsey in *The Unforgiven* and the murderously racist Southern posse in *Buck and the Preacher*, both of which are examined in this book, provide interesting case studies that reflect shift- ing privileged masculine norms as a result of the Civil War during this time. These representations are interesting reflections of a hyper-linear history constructed between the gender issues arising out of military service in the Civil War and the post-World War II contexts.

Typically Western films of this period have been classified precisely by their support of gender binaries between masculinity and femininity, where masculinity forms the axis of the plot and femininity is doomed to irrelevance and/or a civilizing force incapable of understanding the true nature of the West or American society and the men who occupy it.[25] A revision of this conceptualization of women's roles is needed for a fuller understanding of the genre and its capacity to reflect historical and gender issues. Indeed, rather than a cast of women who are unaware of the mas- culine world, in distinct subgenres of Westerns, it is actually women who,

25   See in particular Jane Tompkins, *West of Everything: The Inner Life of Westerns* (New York: Oxford University Press, 1992).

acting separately from aspirations of masculine hegemony, are capable of keener insight into the issues impacting the lives of men and the often detrimental connection between personal identity, masculine gender performance and patriarchal institutions. Acting outside of these networks of homosociality and homosocial competition women are also capable of operating between groups otherwise fractured along class, racial, or gendered lines and also demonstrate a self-conscious awareness of how to use aspects of their own gender performance to their advantage when dealing with different social groups and with other women.[26]

While many Westerns may portray women in 'traditional' and peripheral roles it is important to recognize a subgenre of Westerns where women are developed characters who bring to bear their own personal, racial, class and gendered understandings on the narrative and, in turn, on the audience's understandings of the link between gender and history in insightful ways. It is also important to recognize that not all women aspire to or demonstrate an adherence with 'femininity' as it is typically constructed – indeed, significant revisionist Westerns present women with distinctly masculine characteristics who try to compete in, rather than withdraw from, operate outside of, or ultimately submit to, patriarchal power. Although men in Westerns do not all demonstrate an aspiration or capacity to engage with hegemonic manifestations of masculine gender performance, I am yet to consider a Western where such qualities are not either admired or deplored by men who refuse to fully embrace a feminine form of personal identity.

Changing technological and economic norms in both periods also placed pressure upon the hegemonic conceptualization of masculinity and was subject to hyper-linear links in Western films. Although the links between technology and gender construction are not necessarily obvious

---

26   This volume particularly focuses on Amy and Helen in *High Noon*, Rachel in *The Unforgiven*, Cresta Lee in *Soldier Blue*, Etta in *Butch Cassidy and the Sundance Kid* and Ruth in *Buck and the Preacher*. Clearly there is enormous potential to explore the changing depictions of women in Western films over time, the relationships between women along the various lines of their identities and the ways in which women are impacted by patriarchal action in a longer study.

it is important to note the inherent interconnections between the two: 'scholars have written of a "mutual shaping" of the social and the technological: each shapes the other. In times of technological change, then, we can expect contests over social categories such as gender.'[27] Such changes fundamentally altered the ways in which white men derived their masculinity from their labour and skills, causing a re-evaluation of privileged hegemonic gender forms. Indeed labour and technology can be seen as a primary driver of masculine identity; as David Gilmore asserts in his sociological study of manhood: 'the data shows a strong connection between the social organization of production and the intensity of the male image [...] this correlation could not be more clear, concrete, or compelling.'[28] Although Gilmore suggests that it is the scarcity of resources that heightens the vigorousness with which masculinity is displayed, I would suggest that in these historical contexts and in Western representations a vigorous contestation regarding masculine identities occurs not necessarily because resources are scarce but because capitalist structures intrinsically pit men against each other in competition over resources and also because times of technological change intrinsically require the elevation of masculine forms capable of investing in and using such technology over other masculine forms that cannot.

Historically, Michael Kimmel suggests that the post-Civil War period, which he defines from approximately 1870 to 1900, saw a five hundred per cent increase in American industrial output, which was marked particularly by a decline in farm holdings and self-employment.[29] This shift in the industrial landscape saw a move away from privileging agrarianism, artisanship, and the connection between individual, labour and the

---

27 Nina E. Lerman, Ruth Oldenziel, and Arwen P. Mohun (eds), *Gender and Technology: A Reader* (Baltimore: John Hopkins University Press, 2003), 2. For a discussion of the intersections between social construction, technology and capitalism see David F. Noble, *America By Design: Science Technology and the Rise of Corporate Capitalism* (Oxford: Oxford University Press, 1977), xvii–xxvi.

28 David D. Gilmore, *Manhood in the Making: Cultural Concepts of Masculinity* (New Haven: Yale University Press, 1990), 224.

29 Michael S. Kimmel, *Manhood in America*, 57.

formation of masculine identity, and towards urbanization, increased use of technology and associated mechanization of labour, and a lack of control over production, which created an enormous transformation in privileged masculine gender identities.[30] This new masculine identity founded firmly in capitalist values and practices privileged homosocial competition, pitting men against each other in hierarchical corporate structures and requiring the subservience of less skilled labour to entrepreneurial capital and 'self-made' men.[31] This white homosocial competition was compounded by the increased labour competition posed by freed slaves, immigrant populations, and by the increase in women's participation in the paid workforce and in education.[32]

This transformation of privileged masculine gender forms and the associated implications for men's status, identity and relationship with each other was resisted by white men in both passive and aggressive ways. Ultimately this resistance suggests that transformation in privileged forms of gender identity is not seamless or painless; rather it involves enormous negotiation and personal struggle to reconcile one's own sense of identity into broader social patterns of privilege, power and status. Passively, white men demarcated the time between work and leisure pursuits and used leisure as a means to recover seemingly 'lost' masculine virtues. For example, this period saw an enormous rise in 'physical culture', which emphasized the importance of exercise and physical strength as a means to develop men's character and virtues.[33] This was supplemented by men's participation in fraternal lodges and elite sports groups that allowed for homosocial bonding and, through the exclusion of women and racial minorities, allowed for the solidification of gender dichotomies and inter-masculine hierarchies that privileged white masculinity at the same time that differences and competition between white men became more apparent.[34] Indeed, the outright oppression of minority groups and the embracing of Social

---

30   Kimmel, *Manhood in America*, 58.
31   Michael S. Kimmel, *The History of Men*, 9, 44.
32   Kimmel, *Manhood in America*, 59.
33   Rotundo, *American Manhood*, 223.
34   Rotundo, *American Manhood*, 200–204.

Darwinism could be construed as an attempt to paper over the growing cracks in a solidified white masculinity.[35]

The West as region also became an important signifier of lost masculinities for those in the East, and the concept of journeying overland as part of the rite of passage for wealthy young men and as an icon of toughness to be used to supplement one's political ambitions became well established.[36] Such a conceptualization of the West was ironically made possible by the spread of the railroad as a result of the Civil War. Railroads were the 'paramount agents of change' in the region, bringing new technologies, investment, markets and labour to the region that fundamentally altered its character.[37] In addition, the proliferation of print technologies allowed for the reproduction and distribution of dime novels that mythologized the region even as it was changing, modernizing and arguably 'closing'.[38]

More aggressively, it is important that far from painting a picture of technology and industrialization leading to inevitable and harmonious progress in white American life, the post-Civil War period saw the rise of national labour organizations such as the Knights of Labor and the American Federation of Labor and a growth in the number, significance

35   Kimmel, *Manhood in America*, 62.
36   Rotundo, *American Manhood*, 228.
37   Stewart L. Udall, 'The 'Wild' Old West: A Different View', 68. Indeed it is integral to point to the importance of the railroad in opening national markets and facilitating distribution in the post-Civil War period which in turn caused enormous ructions in labour habits and men's identities, whilst also acknowledging, as Udall does, that some Western regions were not serviced by railroads until the 1920s and the effects of the rail were diverse within the region homogenously referred to as 'the West'; Udall, 'The 'Wild' Old West', 66, 64–71. See also for example, Richard White, *Railroad: The Transcontinentals and the Making of Modern America* (New York: W.W. Norton & Co, 2011) and Paul Mitchell Taillon, 'Casey Jones, Better Watch Your Speed!: Workplace Culture, Manhood and Protective Labor Legislation on the Railroads 1880–1910s', *Australasian Journal of American Studies* 30 (2011): 20–38.
38   See, for example, Philip Durham, 'A General Classification of 1,153 Dime Novels', *Huntington Library Quarterly* 7 (1954): 287–291 and Warren French, 'The Cowboy in the Dime Novel', *The University of Texas Studies in English* 30 (1951): 219–234.

and violence of strikes across a number of industries.[39] As Troy Rondinone
asserts in his analysis of the use of Civil War language in framing the Great
Railroad Strike of 1877, following the Civil War changes in workplace
relations including growth in the size of workplaces, widening gaps in
employee/employer relations and the dangers technology posed to some
traditional skill bases heightened the concerns of labour and of the broader
public who were now increasingly aware that 'the foundations upon which
the republic rested were fragile and possibly contradictory.'[40] The proliferation of guns at relatively cheap prices following the Civil War and the
innovative forms of marketing used to convince men of the importance
of gun ownership to supplement their sense of identity can be seen as a
factor contributing to the sometimes violent eruptions between men along
class, race, gender or even personal lines.[41] Of course, the actual instances of
violent and fatal shootings remains an area of contestation, particularly in
relation to Western historiography.[42] Ultimately though, the resistance to
what Kimmel dubs the 'proletarianization' of the male workforce should
not be under-estimated: 'everywhere, cultural critics observed masculinity to be in crisis.'[43]

Of course, in part, definitions of masculinities also attempted to
accommodate for the displacement of traditional forms of hegemonic

39   Troy Rondinone, "History Repeats Itself": The Civil War and the Meaning of Labor
      Conflict in the Late Nineteenth Century', *American Quarterly* 59 (2007): 412.
40   Rondinone, "History Repeats Itself", 410–411.
41   See, for example, George M. Stantis, 'Rifles and Revolvers', in *Icons of the American
      West: From Cowgirls to Silicon Valley*, ed. George M. Bakken (Santa Barbara, CA:
      Greenwood Reference, 2008), 277–292.
42   For different perspectives in this debate see, for example: Michael A. Bellesiles,
      Arming America: The Origins of a National Gun Culture (New York: Alfred A.
      Knopf, 2000), Robert R. Dykstra, 'Quantifying the Wild West: The Problematic
      Statistics of Frontier Violence', *The Western Historical Quarterly* 40 (2009): 321–347,
      Clare V. McKanna, Jr, 'Alcohol, Handguns, and Homicide in the American West:
      A Tale of Three Counties, 1880–1920', *The Western Historical Quarterly* 26 (1995):
      455–482, and Stewart L. Udall, et al., 'How The West Got Wild: American Media
      and Frontier Violence, A Roundtable', *The Western Historical Quarterly* 31 (2000):
      277–295.
43   Kimmel, *The History of Men*, 10.

power. This could be undertaken through social understandings of the association between failure and masculinity, whereby failure was often seen to be a result of the failings of the individual rather than endemic of a society structured around homosocial capitalist competition. However, the constant fear of failure, the notion of fortune as a factor mediating success and the capacity for one to incorporate failure into a sense of self resiliently and to recover, kept men enfranchised within patriarchal systems and allowed for an exclusive, competitive, hierarchical hegemonic masculine standard to flourish.[44] New definitions of masculinity also relied on shifting the blame for men's alienation onto women; in this sense men may undertake labour they considered devaluing but did so for the sake of allowing women to maintain their femininity as defined by their engagement with the domestic realm. This reconceptualization of men's roles meant that 'it [manhood] was no picnic of power and privilege; it was dirty and demanding, and men went through it because they loved their wives and children.'[45] Of course, rejection of capitalist accumulation as a measure of manhood and nostalgia for previous times similarly echoes the competing and often contradictory impulses involved in masculine transformation and the genuine flux experienced by white men of this era.[46]

It can be argued, then, that white men's relationship to labour and technology in the Reconstruction period underwent significant change that fundamentally shifted the power base for hegemonic masculine forms. The solidification of the 'self-made' masculine identity saw the displacement of previously hegemonic forms of masculinity. Men coped with hierarchical shifts in a variety of ways that both attempted to solidify a sense of white masculine sameness that maintained white men's collectively high status over the perceived threats posed by women and minorities, whilst also struggling to reconcile increasing homosocial competition within a

---

44 Rotundo, *American Manhood*, 179–183.

45 Kimmel, *Manhood in America*, 67. Of course the focus here and throughout this volume is on hegemonic expectations of women's behaviour; an understanding that ignores the realities of women's participation in paid and unpaid labour, especially those women of low socioeconomic status and women of colour.

46 Kimmel, *Manhood in America*, 72.

hierarchical male identity. Such a conclusion supports Judith Bennett's conceptualization of a 'patriarchal equilibrium', which refers to patriarchy's capacity to accommodate enormous and potentially transformative historical changes, in so doing maintaining men's collectively high status with various impacts individually.[47]

The 1950s and 1960s represented a period of similar technological and economic transformations in America that called into question the ongoing validity of the 'self-made man' as an ideal form of hegemonic masculinity and caused a fundamental re-evaluation of masculine identity. Typically 1950s America is portrayed in such a way that omits the negative or tumultuous effects of these changes and emphasizes instead the growth of: wages and disposable incomes; purchase of consumer goods and the associated impact of this on leisure and lifestyle; citizens possessing a tertiary education and an associated expansion of white-collar work, which outstripped blue collar work by 1956; and, an expansion of suburban housing.[48] Underneath the veneer of ideal suburban domesticity, however, lay an increasing disquiet amongst social commentators regarding the masculinity being stimulated by such an environment. As Thomas Andrew Joyce observes, although a masculinity that derived its identity from white-collar labour was becoming the norm in the 1950s, there was a concern that such labour was in fact emasculating.[49] Such commentary emphasized that, unlike mid-late nineteenth century ideals, the norm was becoming a masculinity that privileged the capacity to submit to managers and the larger corporation, to conform to standards dictated by others, and a retreat into domesticity with its feminine and 'soft' connotations. This reinterpreted ascendant masculinity required renegotiation to ensure that it fit within the parameters of hegemony.[50]

47 Judith M. Bennett, *History Matters: Patriarchy and the Challenge of Feminism* (Manchester: Manchester University Press, 2006), 77–81.
48 Isserman and Kazin, *America Divided*, 15.
49 Thomas Andrew Joyce, 'A Nation of Employees: The Rise of White-Collar Workers and the Perceived Crisis of Masculinity in the 1950s', *The Graduate History Review* 3 (2011): 27.
50 Joyce, 'A Nation of Employees', 24–25.

Just as in the First Reconstruction this period saw many white men perceive a threat to their status in the form of labour competition from African Americans and women.[51] In particular, African American migration to industrial cities, prominently in the North and West, concentrated their political power giving them greater electoral sway and, moreover, greater employment prospects.[52] Certainly the notion of the Civil Rights Movement as one tactically founded in the exercise of African American consumer power (that is, through the use of boycotts and sit-ins) is well founded. However, as Gavin Wright asserts, many gains of the Civil Rights Movement were economic in character and relate fundamentally to the ties between white men's labour, economic exclusion and hegemonic gender identity. Specifically, the desegregation of interstate travel and accommodation, allowing African Americans greater freedom of movement, the demand for equal access and paying employment and, for example, the desegregation of the textiles industry as a result, all signify the real-world economic expectations of African Americans in the labour market.[53] This is not to suggest by any means that African American experiences were ones of permanent, ongoing or equitable economic uplift; it is to suggest, however, that the gains made by African American rights movements in the economic arena and the growing illustration of African American

51   Of course it should be acknowledged that many white men in both periods supported African American emancipation and Civil Rights goals respectively and/ or women's liberation efforts. It is interesting to note, though, that many African American groups maintained deeply entrenched traditional gender ideologies. This, in fact, supports Judith Bennett's conceptualization of a patriarchal equilibrium that maintains men's high status collectively relative to women. In this sense movements ostensibly about racial inequality are also about gender: that is, these movements do not challenge patriarchy but rather seek to renegotiate the parameters within which men can access patriarchal power bases regardless of differences along other lines of identity.

52   Gary A. Donaldson, *The Second Reconstruction: A History of the Modern Civil Rights Movement* (Malabar: Krieger Publishing Company, 2000), 4–5.

53   Gavin Wright, 'The Civil Rights Revolution as Economic History', *The Journal of Economic History* 59 (1999): 267–289. See also Robert Korstad and Nelson Lichenstein, 'Opportunities Found and Lost: Labor, Radicals and the Early Civil Rights Movement', *The Journal of American History* 75 (1988): 786–811.

resentment at ongoing economic disadvantage posed a threat to white hegemonic conceptualizations of their gender identity as derived from their place in, and ideas surrounding, the capitalist market at this time. It also called into question a national identity that privileged white economic domination and the notion that economic abundance was available to all by suggesting that certain social groups were excluded from equitable competition and suffered disadvantage that reflected not upon their own skills and character but rather was a systemic problem with racist institutions, policies and employment practices.

Certainly other minority groups, particularly Native American rights organizations, also questioned white economic power. Although, as Donald Parman asserts, 'Indians remained impoverished compared to non-Indians', World War II created for Native Americans greater job opportunities, especially in industrial cities, higher wages, a higher standard of living and a growing resentment of poverty and economic exclusivity.[54] Following this the fights for eligibility and access to welfare and government-funded health and education services in some States, as well as Native American land claims, heightened white sensitivity to Native American economic conditions.[55] Again, this is not to suggest that Native Americans had a homogenized experience of racial interaction or that Native Americans collectively experienced anything akin to economic uplift in this extremely fraught period of federal legislative reform.[56] It is to suggest, however, that Native American rights groups were increasingly engaged with economic rights discourse in such a way that challenged a white male hegemony founded in capitalist competition that justified exclusive access to resources amongst some of the population to the detriment of others. More than this, such protest also provided significant counter-narrative to the American

---

54   Donald L. Parman, *Indians and the American West in the Twentieth Century* (Bloomington: Indiana University Press, 1994), 117 (also 108 & 122).

55   Parman, *Indians and the American West*, 127–128.

56   See, for example, Alison R. Bernstein, *American Indians and World War II: Toward a New Era in Indian Affairs* (Norman: University of Oklahoma Press, 1991) and Kenneth R. Philp, 'Termination: A Legacy of the Indian New Deal', *The Western Historical Quarterly* 14 (1983): 165–180.

story of continued linear 'progress' that privileged white patriarchal understandings of race and identity.

Just as post-Civil War society resisted the transition in masculinity demanded by industrializing workplaces, so too did post-World War II America struggle with a renegotiation of masculine norms. As with the Reconstruction, men sought the reclamation of hegemony through nostalgia for previous ways of being; indeed the enormous popularity of the Western in this period has typically been read as symptomatic of the desire to return to 'simpler' ways of being, although perhaps it should instead be read as a desire amongst men to explore masculinities and the relationship between changing gender norms and history.[57] More than this, though, what James Gilbert refers to as the essentializing of categories of identification, in particular the rigorous reinforcement of boundaries between male hetero- and homo-sexuality, communist and capitalist, hawk and dove can be seen as further evidence of the desire to contain potentially destabilizing gender discourses by the maintenance of rigorous binaries in other areas of identity.[58] In a sense this can be seen as an evolution of the nineteenth century fear of failure applied to a modern context: Michael Kimmel asserts that contemporary manhood is defined by its homophobia, meaning 'the fear that other men will unmask us, emasculate us, and reveal to us and the world that we do not measure up.'[59] This concept is reflected in the rigorous maintenance of dichotomies that reinforce exclusionary gender forms and the stimulation of a fear-based identity that defines itself precisely by what

57   For complete breakdowns of Hollywood Western output see Edward Buscombe (ed), *The BFI Companion to the Western* (London: British Film Institute, 1988), 426–428.The popularity of the Western genre being linked not only to Hollywood film output but to television, radio serials, books and merchandizing; see, for example, William Boddy, 'Sixty Million Viewers Can't Be Wrong': The Rise and Fall of the Television Western', in *Back in the Saddle Again: New Essays on the Western*, eds Edward Buscombe and Roberta E. Pearson (London: British Film Industry, 1998): 119–140.

58   Gilbert, *Men in the Middle*, 18.

59   Michael Kimmel, 'Masculinity as Homophobia: Fear, Shame and Silence in the Construction of Gender Identity', in *Theorizing Masculinities*, Harry Brod and Michael Kaufman (eds) (London: Sage Publishing, 1994), 131.

it is not. This fear maintains the links of patriarchy despite the potentially negative impacts of hegemonic gender ideology and patriarchy on the individual lives of men.

Western films of this era reflect the crisis in masculinity stimulated by changing economic and technological norms in a multitude of ways. It is interesting to note the perception of the Western protagonist as divorced from employment, consumer capitalism or ownership; as Robert Warshow suggests, the Westerner is a 'man of leisure [...] he appears to be unemployed', with material goods only playing a role as moral signifiers rather than as actualities; an arrangement that goes unquestioned by the audience.[60] It is telling, however, the number of Westerns that feature a central protagonist who is or was gainfully employed, typically in agricultural or military pursuits, but is facing the loss of such employment in a time of great transition in workplace norms. The idea of this being a negligible component of his identity is thoroughly refuted by narrative devices centred on: land disputes and contestations between ranchers and capital; the demythologizing of the gunfighter as a form of legitimate employment and mythic character; the increasingly mercenary conceptualization of the protagonist's employment prospects; and criminality and ageing masculinities unable to find gainful employment in a changing West.[61] Indeed it can be argued that one of the great dichotomies of the Western – the separation of civilization and wilderness – and its great symbol – the gun – play on important themes

60   Robert Warshow, 'Movie Chronicle: The Westerner', reprinted in *Film Theory and Criticism: Introductory Readings*, 4th edn, eds Gerald Mast, Marshall Cohen, and Leo Braudy (Oxford: Oxford University Press, 1992), 455.

61   In the central films analyses within this volume only one, *High Noon*, contains a central protagonist who does not fall easily within these categories, although it could be said that the film does demythologize the gunfighter due to the difficulty Kane faces in raising a posse. It could also be argued that Kane's submission to Amy's wishes that he becomes a shop-keeper rather than a sheriff also problematizes his relationship to labour. For a discussion of men's employment in Westerns related to 1950s history see: Robert D. Leigninger, Jr, 'The Western as Male Soap Opera: John Ford's Rio Grande', *Journal of Men's Studies* 6 (1998): online. Available from <http://o-search. proquest.com.library.newcastle.edu.au/docview/222635949/13B1B698DC4247A7 299/1?accountid=10499>.

of access to resources, technology and the capacity to gain entrance into exclusionary spaces through the demonstration of appropriate forms of gendered performance and social status, such as employment.

Along with a fracturing along class lines the historical parallels between the First and Second Reconstruction reflect a further confrontation between white patriarchal institutions and peoples of colour. In both eras this confrontation reflected a re-evaluation of the very cornerstones of American ideology: the notions of a country founded on available land and freedom, equity and democracy. The most obvious and well documented connection between the First and Second Reconstruction for scholars has surrounded the place and rights of black Americans in American society. For such scholars the connection here relates to the gap between American promises and reality as relevant to the role of the Civil War in emancipating, empowering and incorporating blacks. Ultimately for these scholars the reality for blacks following the Civil War was a 'dismal failure' in public policy resulting in their economic, political and social disenfranchisement.[62] Despite this failure African American experiences at this time encouraged a growing rights-based discourse and the development of black and black-orientated religious organizations that provided a channel for race consciousness and for tactics that would ultimately feed into the Civil Rights Movement of the 1950s and 1960s.[63] For black migrants to Western states it can be argued that this was particularly the case. The West provided blacks with opportunities: to build independent communities; establish religious and personal networks, despite, or perhaps strengthened by, some white resistance; for economic self-advancement; and, treatment that was often mediated by their consumer spending power.[64] Of course this is not to say that the West was a race-less or equitable space, but ultimately the West was distinctive as a multi-ethnic place whose citizens were of varying racial origins and backgrounds forced into co-operation and competition

---

62   Donaldson, *The Second Reconstruction*, v.

63   Bruce A. Glasrud and Charles A. Braithwaite, *African Americans on the Great Plains: An Anthology* (Lincoln: Bison Books, 2009), 8.

64   Glasrud and Braithwaite, *African Americans on the Great Plains*, 7–10.

with each other.[65] As such, Quintard Taylor asserts, black experiences in the West demonstrates both the region's 'distinctiveness and its continuity with the legacy of African American history in the rest of the nation'.[66]

The nature of the Civil Rights Movement in the 1950s and 1960s hardly needs extrapolation to illustrate the immensely transformative effect it had on white social institutions, patriarchal authority and the nature of hegemonic gender standards. As Gary Donaldson suggests, 'blacks, after 1945, would stand at the center of many of those [broader social, political, and economic] changes.'[67] Fundamentally, the movement challenged American society, in terms of legislative and practical discrimination against minority groups and called for a dismantling of exclusionary legal, educational, employment, and other social policies and practices. It did so whilst celebrating a diversity of modes of being that refused to be assimilated into white modes of understanding. Ideologically, such a movement required a re-evaluation not only of specific practices but a white patriarchal institutional foundation, broader social attitudes and individual behaviours. Regardless of the success of the movement in implementing all of its goals, especially when moving from a legalistic framework to addressing economic inequalities, the diverse reactions to the movement and the overarching challenge it provided placed enormous fracturing pressure upon patriarchal institutions and upon the exclusionary nature and values of hegemonic masculine gender forms which would require renegotiation throughout the period.

Of course, although black experiences of both Reconstructions have formed the foundation of many scholarly works, these periods also featured racialized pressures from other minority groups.[68] The issue of black

---

65   Quintard Taylor, *In Search of the Racial Frontier: African Americans in the American West, 1528–1990* (New York: W.W. Norton, 1998), 18.

66   Taylor, *In Search of the Racial Frontier*, 19.

67   Donaldson, *The Second Reconstruction*, 3.

68   Although there is a potential here to explore the experiences of South Americans, Asian Americans and other groups whose experiences impact the nature of the historical West in particular, this volume focuses on Native American experiences in these time periods.

emancipation as a result of the Civil War raised important questions regarding white society's treatment of Native American peoples. However, as Brian Dippie points out, concerns for Native American policy and rights were often complicated by contradictory racial philosophies regarding the capacity for Native American assimilation, the nature of claims by and attitudes towards other racial groups, the nature of tribal society, and competing social and economic policy impetuses of government.[69] Nevertheless, it is important to conceptualize the racial issues surrounding the Civil War as not distinctly related to black experiences; after all this was a period when white institutions were faced with enormous challenges on a multitude of racial fronts. Such challenges caused re-evaluation of American institutions and ideology, with associated social divisions that impacted significantly on conceptualizations of ideal, hegemonic gender forms. The issue of Native American rights would again become prominent during the post-World War II era, prompted by Native American military contributions, migration and changing living standards for some Native Americans during the War and a growing Pan-Indian sensibility.[70] The establishment of important organizations such as the National Congress of American Indians, the National Indian Youth Council, American Indian Movement, and Americans for Indian Opportunity were vehicles in a broader 'Red Power' movement that expressed Native American demands and dissatisfaction with legislative reforms in this period.[71]

It is little wonder that in periods of racialized pressures placed upon hegemonic conceptualizations of white masculinity and its manifestation in patriarchy, the West as a multi-racial frontier would be called upon to explore and renegotiate the role of race in American ideology. These themes are reflected most obviously in Western films of this era in the 'pro-Indian' Western cycle. This 'cycle' of films can be characterized as a sub-grouping of

---

69   Brian W. Dippie, *The Vanishing American: White Attitudes and US Indian Policy* (Middletown, CT: Wesleyan University Press, 1982), 77–97.

70   See, for example, Peter Iverson, 'Building Towards Self-Determination: Plains and Southwest Indians in the 1940s and 1950s', *The Western Historical Quarterly* 16 (1985): 169.

71   Parman, *Indians and the American West in the Twentieth Century*, 152–154.

overall Western films that gave more substantial roles to Native American characters and attempted to delve into Native American experiences of white/Native American interaction more deeply. Scholars have raised important issues regarding the subversive impact of these films and their capacity to present a true challenge to patriarchy and the white hegemonic gender performances that support it. In particular they have suggested that representations of Native Americans lack true textual or historical legitimacy because they and their plight act as signifiers for racial issues surrounding black rights discourses and the experiences of Vietnamese citizens relevant to American participation in the Vietnam War.[72] Moreover the use of non-Native American actors to fulfil Native American roles further complicates the intersections between identity, historicity and legitimacy in these Western films.[73] The assertion that Native American roles act only as 'stand ins' for other groups, however, neglects to emphasize the important discourse surrounding Native American rights undertaken in the post-Civil War and the Civil Rights contexts as a response to major legislative reform and other rights-based movements. A consideration of the hyper-linear connections between past and present established in these films allows for insight, though, into the long-standing issues regarding white attitudes to Native American affairs, and to perceived free land and justifiable interventionism. Moreover, to suggest that white treatment of Native Americans is used as a way to illustrate then contemporary issues regarding American involvement in Vietnam does not necessarily de-legitimize Native American experiences but rather problematizes a history of governmental landed occupation. The representation of Native American issues can be used to

72   For example, Steve Neale, 'Vanishing Americans: Racial and Ethnic Issues in the Interpretation and Context of Post-war 'Pro-Indian' Westerns', in Edward Buscombe and Roberta E. Pearson (eds), *Back in the Saddle Again: New Essays on the Western* (London: British Film Industry, 1998), 9–10.

73   See, for example, Edward Buscombe, *'Injuns!' Native Americans in the Movies* (Cornwall: Reaktion Books, 2006), 154–155 and Nicolas G. Rosenthal, 'Representing Indians: Native American Actors on Hollywood's Frontier', *The Western Historical Quarterly* 36 (2005): 339.

illustrate important historical continuities in American policy, which is particularly important in a Vietnam War context.

In addition, to suggest Native American representation acts only as a stand-in for black experiences exorcises from history the Westerns of the 1950s and 1960s that do feature black characters, a phenomenon which follows on from the black audience Westerns of the 1930s.[74] Of course this is not to suggest that there is a correspondence between racial discourse in society and a positive image of racial minorities in Western films. It is to suggest though that African Americans are not entirely absented from Western representations, although they are still sparsely represented. When black characters are present in Western texts they can raise important questions about the American past, the nature of American identity at a national level, and the nature of hegemonic masculinity and gender behaviour at a personal level. Such representations may imply a variety of different reactions to racial difference, but rarely are these reactions over-simplified; rather, they are complicated by racial and historical discourses and are mediated by both intra- and extra-diegetic factors.

Ultimately, there are important historical links between post-Civil War and 1950s and 1960s America, links that are represented in Westerns released in this time frame. Such links are pre-established by scholarly works on the First and Second Reconstructions, and includes the social impacts of war, the transformative effects of technological and economic change, and the nature of women's and racial movements. These changes caused fundamental fractures in the conceptualization of white men's gender identity, resulting in a renegotiation of privileged masculine gender forms and a re-evaluation of the patriarchal institutions and values upon which American society and hegemonic masculinity rested. Western films of the 1950s and 1960s explored the historical connections between these two periods and the impacts that social change had on American manhood, in so doing telling a hyper-linear history that situated then-contemporary crises in American society and gender within an historical past that informed audience's understandings of history in a multitude of ways.

---

74   Julia Leyda, 'Black-Audience Westerns and the Politics of Cultural Identification in the 1930s', *Cinema Journal* 42 (2002): 46–70.

The research for this work supports the idea that there are important historical parallels between the represented past, typically the post-Civil War environment, and the time of filmic release. In particular, both periods were times of immense change in privileged masculine gender forms, stimulated by transformative social, economic, and technological shifts in broader American society. The Western, by virtue of its generic conventions, historical connections and ideological underpinnings was an extremely apt vehicle by which society could explore its history and the nature of previous historical shifts in gendered understandings. Indeed, it can be argued that the enormous popularity of the Western in this period reflects a society struggling to understand itself and its history in the face of paradigm shattering social change.

The following chapters will explore the nature of hyper-linear history in Western films of this period. In particular, the nature of economic and technological shifts, women's rights movements, Native American representation, American interventionism, and black rights movements will be examined with a view to understanding the ways in which such representation reflected past and present historical conditions. These representations reflected historical conditions that fundamentally challenged understandings of hegemonic white masculine identity and the nature of capitalistic and patriarchal American ideology, institutions and attitudes. In so doing these films use the past to inform audience's understandings of their own present in a multitude of ways that are far from uniform or homogenized and that reinforced the centrality of gender as an analytical tool. They all suggest the important place that film occupies in informing public understandings of the historical past and illustrate the ongoing impetus for theoretical refinement of conceptual understandings regarding how history is constructed on film and how this can be successfully harnessed to enhance, rather than hinder, our scholarly understandings of the nature of the medium and its usefulness as history.

'He's not a man! He's a sack of money!': Corporatism and the Male Breadwinner

In his landmark studies of the history of masculinities Michael S. Kimmel clearly points to the intractability of the relationship between hegemonic masculine gender performance and existing economic conditions. For Kimmel, along with social and political context, the economic sphere is the prime vehicle by which men define and change the parameters of desirable gender behaviour and values, and establish conditions that lead both to homosocial competition amongst men and men's justification of continued patriarchal oppression of other groups.[1] From the changing economic conditions of the nineteenth century emerged 'a masculinity defined, tried and tested in the marketplace'; a 'self-made man', whose desirable gender manifestations would meet and adapt to changing circumstances and crisis over the coming two hundred years.[2] Indeed, to take this point even further, Robert T. Schultz argues in his comparison of representations of white masculinity and resistance across time, that the academic focus on the crisis points in masculinity occasioned by various rights movements, diverts attention from a more meaningful dialogue with the structural forces of power and resistance brought to bear by economic arrangements.[3] For Schultz, 'at the centre of the white guys' unfulfilling lives [...] lie their

---

1   Michael S. Kimmel, *The History of Men: Essays on the History of American and British Masculinities* (New York: State University of New York, 2005); Michael S. Kimmel, *Manhood in America: A Cultural History*, 2nd edn (Oxford: Oxford University Press, 2006).

2   Kimmel, *The History of Men*, 8.

3   Robert T. Schultz, 'White Guys Who Prefer Not To: From Passive Resistance ('Bartleby') to Terrorist Acts (*Fight Club*)', *The Journal of Popular Culture* 44 (2011): 603.

relationships to the industrial or postindustrial economies that shape their opportunities, their work routines, their personal and social relationships, and their cultural assumptions.'[4]

This chapter extends upon existing works that connect constructions of masculine gender performance and the demands of the marketplace by examining representations of masculinity in the Western, in particular the 1953 Robert Mann film *The Naked Spur*. This chapter explores the ways in which an emasculated version of masculinity is represented. This film locates the root of emasculation in economic arrangements along with other compounding factors.

In undertaking this analysis the chapter will highlight the ways in which many Westerns of the 1950s and 1960s parallel, in hyper-linear fashion, the then contemporary crisis of masculinity resulting from economic shifts in the post-war economy, centred around corporatism and the emergent corporate, 'group man', and the crisis in masculinity associated with industrialization in the late nineteenth century. Some Westerns of this era point to capitalism as one of the key causes in alienating men from themselves and each other as well as locking white men into increasingly detrimental competition, rather than simply enacting oppressive dominance over other groups. The Westerns of the 1950s (and other non-Western films such as *Rebel Without a Cause* [Nicholas Ray, 1955]) generally present the challenges posed to men reintegrating into society and their familial roles as meaningful but surmountable.[5] However, by the end of the 1960s, Westerns often connected the disenfranchisement of men seemingly unable to adapt and integrate into an industrializing society due to their lack of necessary skills and personal alienation from their labour, with a sense of a wholesale challenge to their sense of self that fundamentally undermines traditional patriarchal values.

---

4   Schultz, 'White Guys Who Prefer Not To', 587.
5   For a general discussion of the representation of masculinities in 1950s American film, including but not exclusive to the Western, see Harry M. Benshoff and Sean Griffin, *America on Film: Representing Race, Class, Gender and Sexuality at the Movies*, 2nd edn (Oxford: Wiley-Blackwell, 2009), 274–276.

In illustrating this alienation through a hyper-linear connection with the past this film points to important areas of contestation with existing literature. Firstly, whilst Kimmel points to the tendency to represent the past as a 'happier, easier and more stable time' in response to contemporary gender crises, Westerns of the 1950s and 1960s illustrate that a connection with the past can be made that reflects upon disturbing continuities and patterns of crisis over time. *The Naked Spur*, for example, conveys an ongoing frustration with capitalist structures as both a symptom and driver of detrimental gendered behaviour.[6] These films also contest Shultz's notion that current generations are disconnected from history and from crisis, which is seen by them as a result of the folly of previous generations, by pointing to the deeply historical, linear, indeed almost causal, connections between the represented past and the present experience of the audience.[7] In so doing these films make a deeply historical statement that identifies the underlying and ongoing issue with a capitalist economy that forces men into hegemonic and mutually destructive gender performances with negative impacts on their social relationships. Further, while Shultz highlights an important issue by pointing to the significance of long term structural (economic) issues in maintaining the privilege of patriarchy and hegemonic masculinity, I argue here that the importance of particular rights-based movements cannot be divorced from a discussion of these structural forces, entwined as rights-based movements are with challenging structural prejudice. Ultimately, challenges posed by women's, sexuality and racial liberation movements in the 1950s and 1960s are important in compounding the economic disenfranchisement and emasculation perceived by men at this time and which featured in representations of the Western male.

In light of these aims and relationship with existing literature the chapter is presented in three sections: the first examines the representation of emasculated men in one film in particular, *The Naked Spur*. The second component considers the hyper-linear connection between economic conditions in the late-1800s and the 1950s and 1960s. Finally, the third component focuses on other factors that contributed to the emasculating

6   Kimmel, *Manhood in America*, 173.
7   Schultz, 'White Guys Who Prefer Not To', 596.

of men in this period such as the breakdown, and difficult reconstruction of, homosocial relationships between men and the increased competition posed by women's participation in the labour force. In doing so this third component will presage the chapters to follow, which will examine other factors contributing to a crisis in white masculinity in these time periods.

'Money splits better two ways instead of three': Economic Disenfranchisement in *The Naked Spur*

The film under consideration here, *The Naked Spur*, exemplifies the ways in which hegemonic masculinity began to erode in Westerns of the 1950s, an erosion that would deepen during the 1960s. This film does this by connecting, in a hyper-linear fashion, social and personal fears regarding men's status in post-Civil War American society to similar attitudes during the 1950s post-war reintegration; a hyper-linear connection that emphasizes negative continuity between both temporalities, with a particular focus on the impacts of men's alienation from their labour over time. The film is set in 1868 and features James Stewart as Howard Kemp who is pursuing wanted murderer Ben (Robert Ryan), with the aid of two misfits he meets along the way, Jesse (Millard Mitchell), an ageing, failed gold prospector, and Roy (Ralph Meeker), a dishonourably discharged cavalry man. As the pursuit unfolds, however, it is revealed that Kemp is not the law officer he appears to be but, rather, a bounty hunter intent on claiming the five thousand dollar reward for the capture of his ex-friend, dead or alive. Kemp needs the bounty to repurchase his ranch, which his ex-fiancée, Mary, sold out from under him while he was fighting in the Civil War in order to elope with another man. After his capture, Ben, realizing that Kemp needs the whole of the reward money for this aim, not the share he would get if the money was divided amongst the posse, begins a cat-and-mouse game of manipulation, attempting to appeal to each member of the posse's greed, mutual distrust and desire for his female companion, Lina (Janet Leigh), in order to engineer an escape. Meanwhile, Roy is revealed as having raped a Native American woman, and as a result the posse must survive a revenge attack by Blackfeet. Kemp, injured in the Indian attack, is increasingly both attracted to Lina and uneasy about profiteering from murder.

Ultimately Ben's plan to divide the posse works through Jesse, lured as he is by Ben's false 'revelation' that he owns a profitable gold claim which he would share with Jesse in exchange for freedom. After aiding in Ben and Lina's escape, Ben kills Jesse and lays in wait for the pursuing Roy and Kemp on a steep cliff top ravine. With the aid of Lina, however, the pair kill Ben and his body falls into the river below. In the attempt to reclaim the body and, in turn, the reward money, Roy drowns. Torn between the money and Lina's expectations, Kemp emotionally breaks down before finally finding redemption through Lina's love and acceptance of him. The film ends with Kemp digging a grave for Ben, intent on beginning a new life with Lina in California without the reward money. In all, there is an overwhelming, taut sense of menace in the film as the group slowly unravels due largely to greed, and Kemp's psyche disintegrates under the weight of unnatural actions forced upon him by economic imperatives, a sense hardly alleviated through the reconciliation of Kemp and Lina.

At the core of the film, then, is the notion of meaningful homosocial friendships between men as a fallacy in the face of economic mechanisms that force men into competition with each other and force them to assume 'hard' masculine characteristics that alienate them from themselves. Each of the men presented here possesses both fatal flaws in character and, despite apparent justifications for them, they prove incapable of bonding over them or illustrating a deeper understanding of how their motivations and flaws have led them into the position where they are either hunted or hunting for the sake only of a monetary reward without any illusions that they are performing a more idealistic service. Indeed, in this film men are not only alienated from a sense of identity distinct from their economic purposes but acknowledge that they have no masculinity separate from it. As Jesse asserts regarding Ben: 'He's not a man! He's a sack of money!' Unlike traditional perceptions of the moral functions of the posse, Kemp never suggests that his purpose has a moral edge or is a service to the community. Indeed Kemp acknowledges that he and Ben did play cards together, and Ben may be innocent, but that, ultimately: 'I don't care about anything but the money, that's all I care about. That's all I've ever cared about [...] Maybe I don't fit your ideas or meet with em. That's the way I am.' In making this assertion, regardless of the motivation for wanting the reward money, Kemp repudiates the central values of the classic Westerner, a fact he seems conscious of by allowing the men to think him a lawman – the only morally viable occupation to justify the hunt for Ben.

The other members of the posse are similarly fractured by economic pressures and an alienation from normative institutions. The prospector Jesse is most obviously motivated by economic circumstances and the desire to get rich quick: his occupations have never provided him with a financially secure future and he is under no illusions of the morality in aiding Kemp. This is illustrated by his comment immediately upon meeting Kemp when, even under the deception that Kemp is a legitimate lawman, he states: 'helping you don't put money in my pocket.' For his part, the disgraced ex-soldier Roy has been alienated from social structures that allow him to earn an income and demonstrate a socially viable form of hegemonic masculinity. The fault for this, he asserts, lies not with his own behaviour but rather with the institutions themselves, stating: 'The army never did understand me.' Similarly, Ben's criminality can be read as a symptom of his alienation from broader social institutions. His self-consciousness of this fact leads to his ability to play on the insecurities of the other men, who lack such an understanding of their own situations. For example, Ben's statement to Kemp that death is not the quandary but rather 'choosing how to live, that's the hard part', implies that Kemp should do better than be motivated by betrayal to blindly seek out blood money. This illustrates the outlaw Ben's greater capacity for insight into the nature of men. Even Lina is not exempt from the impacts of this economic competition and the disenfranchisement of, and deadly competition between, the men who take part in it: her father was killed in a bank robbery and it is this that led her to be in Ben's company.

In this film the emasculation experienced by the central protagonist and other men under the weight of economic pressures is not only inherent in the plot but compounded through Kemp's characterization, Stewart's performance, and the use of landscape, which subverts traditionalist notions of the Western as the domain of hegemonic masculinity. It should be noted that these elements were tools used generally throughout the Mann-Stewart collaborations: this film was one of the eight Mann-Stewart features made in the 1950s, of which five were Westerns, and represents the continuation of Stewart's shift away from his all-American persona to more complex and emotionally fraught roles.[8] Stewart's performance of Kemp has been variously acknowledged as a 'cowboy on the brink of a nervous breakdown' in a 'demonic Western', 'unbalanced', and as a man consumed with masochism and hysteria bordering on psychosis.[9] Kemp's character from the beginning is signalled as emasculated by two main cues. The first comes from his back story, in the revelation that he has been economically and emotionally undone by his former fiancée, examined more fully later in the chapter. This indicates that he lacks the Western hero's masculine capacity to attract and hold female loyalty or reject the feminine on one's own terms. The second arises from Kemp's masquerade as a law enforcement officer rather than disclosing his true status as a bounty hunter. This acknowledges that his actions lack the moral compass of the quintessential Western hero.

His emasculation progresses through his literal and metaphorical competition with other men. This is apparent when Kemp is unable to scale the rope up a cliff in pursuit of Ben and is forced to forfeit his place to Roy, who is physically capable. The dominance of Roy in this sequence is reinforced by Roy's ability to similarly emasculate Ben by asking him to 'open your gun belt and let it fall'; the forced and protracted removal of others' gun being a commonly acknowledged symbol of masculine dominance.[10] Kemp's emasculation is completed by his wounding in the

8   For an overview of the Mann-Stewart collaborations see Howard Hughes, *Stagecoach to Tombstone: A Filmgoers' Guide to the Great Westerns* (London: I.B. Taurus, 2008): 68–77, and Robert Horton, 'Mann & Stewart: The Two Rode Together', *Film Comment* 26 (1990): 40–47.

9   Howard Hughes, *Stagecoach to Tombstone*, 70; Jim Kitses, *Horizons West: Directing the Western from John Ford to Clint Eastwood* (London: British Film Institute, 2004), 143; Dennis Bingham, *Acting Male: Masculinities in the Films of James Stewart, Jack Nicholson and Clint Eastwood* (New Brunswick, NJ: Rutgers University Press, 1994), 56.

10   Such moments of obvious emasculation were repeated in other Mann-Stewart collaborations, most notably in *The Man From Laramie* (Anthony Mann, 1955) where

battle with the Blackfeet, which results in his immobilization and hallu-
cinations, where he lies, hysterical, screaming and calling for Mary, presumably his lost fiancée. As Dennis Bingham asserts, throughout the film
Stewart appears in a state of hysteria, a phenomenon typically coded as
feminine, which culminates in this scene. Moreover, this performance
embodies Freud's notion of moral masochism, wherein an individual creates situations that lead to the temptation of immoral conduct which, in
turn, requires punishment in order for absolution to be granted.[11] In this
sense the active play on psychological conditions in this film can itself
be seen as another historical hyper-link, a reflection of the contextual
popularity of psychology and psychiatry, and the attribution of perceived
women's issues such as hysteria to men in the post-war environment.[12]
Apart from the contextual links to this mental state, though, the notion
of the Western hero as defined by his hysteria and masochism is a major
departure from conventional perceptions of the Western hero, yet it is
definitely not a departure from representations in this era. John Wayne
became the obsessive, murderous hunter in *The Searchers* (John Ford,
1956), Paul Newman as the Freudian Billy the Kid in *The Left-Handed
Gun* (Arthur Penn, 1958), and Audie Murphy as the doomed gunfighter
in *No Name on the Bullet* (Jack Arnold, 1959), among others demonstrate
this.[13] The point being made here is that the performance given by Stewart
impresses the deep sense of emasculation occasioned by economic pressures through his failure as a prospective husband and landowner, his lack
of a clear identity, homosocial competition and the psychologizing of his
reactions (see Figure 1).

Stewart's character is literally dragged through fire by the villain (see: Horton, 'Mann
& Stewart', 46).

11   Bingham, *Acting Male*, 64.

12   James Birkhart Gilbert, *Men in the Middle: Searching for Masculinity in the 1950s*
(Chicago: University of Chicago Press, 2005), 20–21.

13   Paul Newman's efforts in Westerns including that of the alienated youth in *Hud*
(Martin Ritt, 1963) and the man trapped between racial worlds in *Hombre* (Martin
Ritt, 1967) are considered psychological, as are Anthony Mann directed Western
films of this era, for example.

Figure 1: Howard Kemp (Jimmy Stewart) awakening in hysteria in *The Naked Spur*.

Of course, in evaluating the impact of Stewart's performance, it is necessary to acknowledge the role of his star persona in influencing the reception of this potentially gender destabilizing performance. 'Jimmy' Stewart
came to embody the 'average' man in films pre-dating World War II. With
a background famously grounded in small-town Pennsylvania, where his
family owned a hardware store, a family history of military service and
a high quality tertiary education, Stewart embodied both all-American
values and the aspiration for class mobility. His lanky, physical awkward-
ness and his earnest, stuttering delivery, whilst hardly symbolic of hard
masculinity, was redeemed through the moral fortitude of his characters
in iconic films such as *Mr Smith Goes to Washington* (Frank Capra, 1939).[14]

14   *Mr Smith Goes to Washington* (Frank Capra, 1939) was an exploration of the nature
      of political corruption in the United States with Jimmy Stewart's, Jeffery Smith, the
      triumphant idealist.

By the end of World War II, however, perceptions of Stewart's masculinity had hardened. Despite being eligible for exclusion from war service on the grounds of both weight and age Stewart enlisted in 1941, becoming a flight instructor before serving overseas from 1943, a factor given greater credence because Stewart himself refused to publicize or capitalize on his war service.[15] Stewart also became a husband and step-father for the first time in 1949, at the age of 41, later becoming a biological father to twin daughters in 1951.

In all, it could be argued that these publicized events in Stewart's personal life, coupled with his existing oeuvre, acted to cement his own identity as a heterosexual man and a subscriber to the values and practices of hegemonic masculinity, thereby allowing him to experiment with and destabilize gender on-screen whilst simultaneously containing this subversion within the audience's knowledge of his private life.[16] For example, as Robert Horton suggests, Stewart may play almost psychotic characters in these Westerns, but because it is Stewart 'an audience is going to watch sympathetically.'[17] Certainly Western films are populated by recognizable stars (Wayne, Murphy, Stewart, Eastwood, to name a few) whose reel and real personas have appeared inextricably bound within the genre, raising potential issues with the audience's reception of them, particularly should they seek a diversity of roles. In many ways, however, the role of the Western star is important particularly in that it provides a financial incentive to fund risky, subversive additions to the genre that otherwise would not be made, and presents information that challenges without alienating audiences. Certainly this had heightened impetus for Stewart who transitioned from the studio system to the modern system and was

---

15   Although he did narrate or appear in a number of propaganda films supporting the
      US Air Force, and appeared in *Strategic Air Command* (Mann, 1955) as a former
      World War II pilot recalled to duty, as well as *The Spirit of St Louis* (Billy Wilder,
      1957), where he played Charles Lindbergh, and *The Flight of the Phoenix* (Robert
      Aldrich, 1965), where he appeared as an aeroplane designer and crash survivor.
16   Bingham, *Acting Male*, 11.
17   Horton, 'Mann & Stewart', 41.

the first star to work for a percentage of film profits.[18] On the other hand, many Western stars act both for and against type, making it difficult to categorize them as either subversive or commercial. Stars such as John Wayne, representing the past forms of hegemonic masculinity in *The Man Who Shot Liberty Valance* (John Ford, 1962), and Clint Eastwood, as the ageing pig farmer in *Unforgiven* (Clint Eastwood, 1992), arguably had a more subversive impact precisely because they acted against type. Ultimately to conclude that the off-screen life of an actor greatly influences the audience to feel comfortable with the material they see on screen dramatically reduces the complex processes of audience reception whereby audience members bring to bear their own unique contexts and are capable of reading against the grain.[19]

The sense of Kemp's emasculation is emphasized by the costuming of his character, which, in the Mann-Stewart Westerns, tends to be uniform and in adherence to the conventional costuming of the archetypal Western hero: a beaten jacket, jeans, chaps, and a neckerchief that adds some dandyish colour. Traditionally these costuming elements are seen to make man part of the landscape, associating him with its hard virility, and connecting this to a sense of historical authenticity.[20] However, the notion of this costume as indicative of hard masculinity is self-consciously inverted in the Mann-Stewart Westerns in a number of ways. Firstly, in all of the Mann-Stewart Westerns, Stewart used the same horse and the same stained off white hat, a symbol of the character's own moral stains,

18   Bingham, *Acting* Male, 52. See also, Mike Wilmington, 'Small-Town Guy: James Stewart interviewed by Mike Wilmington', *Film Comment* 26 (1990): 33–34 for Stewart's reflections on Hollywood's 'golden age'.

19   See, for example, Steve Neale, 'Masculinity as Spectacle: Reflections on Men in Mainstream Cinema', in *Screening the Male: Exploring Masculinities in Hollywood Cinema*, eds Steven Cohan and Ina Rae Hark (London: Routledge, 1997), 9–20.

20   For a discussion on the role of costuming in creating an illusion of historical authenticity whilst also eroticizing the male, and therefore positioning him effeminately as the object of the male gaze, see Jane Marie Gaines and Charlotte Cornelia Herzog, 'The Fantasy of Authenticity in Western Costume' in *Back in the Saddle Again: New Essays on the Western*, eds Edward Buscombe and Roberta E. Pearson (London: British Film Institute, 1998), 172–181.

in a way that creates continuity between the performances given in these Westerns.[21] Through the continuity of visual symbols Mann highlights for the audience the similarities between these characters, calling to the fore the neurosis and failings of characters in previous performances, thereby allowing the audience to draw connections between and impressing upon them the cumulative failures of the masquerade of hegemonic masculinity, which creates a deeper sense of men's emasculation. Secondly, in this film Kemp is outfitted in chaps that tend to frame the groin in moments of vulnerability, such as when he falls attempting the cliff climb, emphasizing that Kemp's falling results from his being less of a man.[22] Moreover the ritualistic forced removal of the gun-belt does much to demonstrate the self-consciously constructed connection between costume and emasculation in *The Naked Spur*. By emphasizing that this is in fact costume, which can be removed or added to create the illusion of hard masculinity, rather than a natural extension of the body, this film highlights the constructed nature of gender and positions masculinity as spectacle, a position typically coded as feminine.[23]

Lastly, the film itself is named after an article of clothing: the spur on the boot typically worn in Westerns by cowboys, but in this Western is worn by Jesse. This is given status in the title as, when Ben kills Jesse, he uses his boots for target practice and it is the shot off spurs that Kemp finds and uses to wound Ben, leading to his downfall. The juxtaposition of the word 'naked', a state rarely seen in a cowboy because it is vulnerable, feminine and soft, with 'spur', typically symbolic of hard masculinity, denotes the central gender play of the film: a masculinity eroded, feminized and laid bare and vulnerable whilst attempting to regain some form of hegemonic status. Ultimately then Mann uses costume ironically, taking the signifiers of hard masculinity and inverting them, highlighting that they are in actuality empty signifiers in men's masquerade of hard masculinity.

21   Bingham, *Acting Male*, 57. See Wilmington, 'Small Town Guy', 50–52 for Stewart's reflection on 'Pie', the horse used throughout his Western films.
22   Bingham, *Acting Male*, 57.
23   Steve Neale, 'Masculinity as Spectacle'; see also Laura Mulvey, 'Visual Pleasure and Narrative Cinema', *Screen* 16 (1975): 6–18.

Similarly, in *The Naked Spur*, Mann also tends to subvert the archetypal use of landscape. Traditionally Westerns are seen to present a monumental, dry, masculinized landscape from which the hero emerges and proves his gender in juxtaposition to the feminized qualities of civilization. However, this film takes place on the trail, traversing mountains, rivers, cliffs and ravines, far removed from civilization and any of its symbols. In so doing the landscape has the monumental qualities of traditional Westerns but Kemp's relationship with it is far different. By not relating the film to civilization, the traditional moral impetus – that justifies the use of violence amongst men as a means to protect and maintain social order – is removed and what is left is Kemp's personal motivation.[24] In removing morality and civilization the film destabilizes the notion of necessary and justifiable violence as a way to prove or maintain one's gender identity and, in turn, at the macro-level to prove nationhood. This destabilization of justifiable violence as a tenet of American society more broadly is also suggested by the barbarity of conflict between the Blackfeet and the posse accompanied by the poignant tone of its conclusion. This scene illustrates the amoral nature of conflict, which defies the notion of violence as a purely defensive action, or victory as an indication of Manifest Destiny and as associated with righteousness of cause or with glory.[25]

More than this, though, Mann was noted for requiring a high level of physicality in performances, using the landscape as an indication of the central protagonist's inner state of mind and also as a method of punishment that keys into their masochism.[26] Whilst Western heroes are traditionally perceived as being strengthened from their relationship with the land, which tests and solidifies their hegemonic masculine status, in *The Naked Spur*, Kemp is 'literally beaten' by his struggle against the landscape; the landscape being a symbol of broader structural forces and his own

---

24 Bingham, *Acting Male*, 56.

25 Diane M. Borden & Eric P. Essman, 'Manifest Landscape/Latent Ideology: After images of Empire in the Western and 'Post-Western' Film', *California History* 79 (2000): 31. This article also discusses the broader demythologizing of the hero within the landscape taking place at this time.

26 Kitses, *Horizons West*, 159–160; Horton, 'Mann & Stewart', 41.

conscience.[27] It is important to note that the settings here are not those coded as masculine such as open desert terrain contrasted to monumental monoliths but are, rather, closed in, and associated with moisture through their display of forestry or water. These are settings typically associated with the feminine and that lends itself to the 'atmosphere of anxiety and dementia' of the film and its context.[28] In this representation the use of landscape in this film moves away from the simple dichotomy of civilization/feminine and wilderness/masculine to a more sophisticated model. This model sees landscape as a source of suffering rather than strength, as a reflection of a conflicted psyche, and as composed of different gender components (both dry and wet, the masculine and the feminine). This incorporation of different gender signifiers into the landscape can itself be read as a profoundly subversive statement when connected to the notion of landscape as a symbol of psyche, as it implies that all people have elements of masculinity and femininity inherent in their identities.

Certainly many films reflect the boundary between civilization and frontier, femininity and masculinity, as easily traversed, such as in *The Man Who Shot Liberty Valance* (John Ford, 1962), and *Butch Cassidy and the Sundance Kid* (George Roy Hill, 1969), among others.[29] Indeed, even those films that show a clear demarcation between the two tend to lament the loss of either the wilderness or civilization in such a way that raises implications for how the hero will cope without respectively the masculinized or feminized elements of his own character (*Shane* [George Stevens, 1953], for example).

---

27   Kitses, *Horizons West*, 145.

28   Horton, 'Mann & Stewart', 46.

29   The capacity to maintain or breach the dichotomy of civilization and wilderness is one of Will Wright's primary lenses through which to analyse the Western, and he suggests that by the development of the 'professional Western' – including films such as *Rio Bravo* (Howard Hawks, 1959), *The Professionals* (Richard Brooks, 1966), *True Grit* (Henry Hathaway, 1969), and *The Wild Bunch* (Sam Peckinpah, 1969) – the opposition of civilization and wilderness is no longer strong. Will Wright, *Six Guns and Society: A Structural Study of the Western* (Los Angeles: University of California Press, 1975), 121.

Contextualizing the Emasculated Western Protagonist in the Capitalist Arena

An analysis of *The Naked Spur* reveals the deep emasculation and search for identity undertaken by men in Western films of this period. At the root of emasculation in this film are economic structures that alienate men from themselves and each other. However, Robert Warshow's iconic essay 'The Westerner', which classified the essential characteristics of the Western hero, suggested that this genre does not place emphasis on occupation; in some films he may appear as a lawman or, more rarely, a rancher, but this aspect of identity is mentioned only in passing and is typically superfluous. He writes:

> the Westerner is *par excellence* a man of leisure [...] he appears to be unemployed [...] yet it never occurs to us that he is a poor man. There is no poverty in Western movies, and really no wealth either. Those great cattle domains and shipments of gold which figure so largely in the plots are moral and not material quantities [...] Possessions too are irrelevant.[30]

Although the extent to which this is practicable at any time is questionable, certainly in the Western films of the 1950s and *The Naked Spur* in particular, we see a reversal of this trend, where occupation and men's relationship to institutional structures assumes paramount importance and is identified as a key source of conflict between men.[31] This conflict would devolve over time, presenting characters completely alienated from a sense of self, from their

---

30 Robert Warshow, 'Movie Chronicle: The Westerner', reprinted in *Film Theory and Criticism: Introductory Readings*, 4th edn, eds Gerald Mast, Marshall Cohen, and Leo Braudy (Oxford: Oxford University Press, 1992), 455.

31 See, for example, Peter Stanfield's analysis of the 1930s singing cowboy where he suggests that although the cowboy may lack ties to place and labour, he typically acts in aid of landed interests in opposition to the big end of town in a reflection on both industrialization and, I would suggest, the Depression-era context. Peter Stanfield, 'Dixie Cowboys and Blue Yodels: The Strange History of the Singing Cowboy', in *Back in the Saddle Again: New Essays on the Western*, eds Edward Buscombe and Roberta E. Pearson (London: British Film Institute, 1998), 104.

labour, and from themselves as social beings. This is a point well illustrated by the prevalence of films showing ageing cowboys who, with no social relevance or marketable skills, must die to make way for a new generation of men who possess different skills and perform a different form of hegemonic masculinity. This is illustrated in films beginning most obviously with *The Man Who Shot Liberty Valance* (John Ford, 1962), where John Wayne's character must die to make way for James Stewart's brand of masculinity founded in the capacity to negotiate and compromise. Other films such as *Butch Cassidy and the Sundance Kid* (George Roy Hill, 1969) and *Ride the High Country* (Sam Peckinpah, 1962) express similar sentiments with varying degrees of nostalgia for past times and gender manifestations associated with those times. It is also demonstrated in 'revisionist' Westerns that question what value exists in exclusionary, violent hegemonic standards, a questioning that reaches its most iconic pinnacle in Peckinpah's *The Wild Bunch* (Sam Peckinpah, 1969).

Perhaps the most profound statement of the social disenfranchisement occasioned by economic competition can be witnessed in the lesser known 1966 film *The Shooting* (Monte Hellman), which has many structural parallels to *The Naked Spur*.[32] In this film the central character, Willet Gashade (Warren Oates), an ex-bounty hunter turned unsuccessful goldminer, is one of a small group of mercenaries employed by a woman to guide her to the town of Kingsley. It is clear that the woman, whose name and purpose is never revealed, has her own agenda and is actually in pursuit of another man and plans to kill him. What follows is a mysterious, aggressive and nihilistic pursuit across the desert with all individuals incapable of basic civility towards each other, the men unaware of their purpose or the knowledge that other men (or women) possess, and seemingly incapable of undertaking any alternative course of action despite the knowledge that their current course will inevitably lead them to death, either at the hands of their prey, another member of the posse, or to the desert conditions as they quickly

---

32   *The Shooting* has various release dates as it was not theatrically released except for limited festival showings. It was originally made as one of two films with Jack Nicholson under the direction of Monte Hellman (the other being *Ride in the Whirlwind*) in 1965/66 and was released to television in 1968.

run out of water, food, and horses. The only motivation Willet had is monetary and ultimately it is revealed that their pursuit all along has been for a man called 'Coin', Willet's twin brother. The name of this character and of the destination 'Kings'-ley cannot be seen as coincidental in this context. Ultimately this existential film presents men forced into violent confrontation with each other due to forces they cannot understand and do not control, having given up any illusion of morality or deeper understanding for the futile, unfulfilling quest of coin, both literal and metaphorical, in a critique of capitalist structures and its impact on men.

However, the most obvious evolution of these issues is witnessed in Sergio Leone's 'Dollars' trilogy. These films present men pitted in competition against each other where money is the central object of each film. As Christopher Frayling asserts in relation to the 'Dollars' trilogy: 'The primary motivation is money, the dollar [...] but there is no suggestion that he *will* spend the money. Dollars are not currency, not associated with conspicuous consumption – but something that must be grabbed before the next man [...] money is the prize, and the gun the arbiter' [original emphasis].[33] In making this observation Frayling taps into important issues regarding the relationship between capitalism and masculine gender identities. That is, that the competition provoked by capitalist economic structures is not primarily about competition for access to resources such as money, as much as it is competition for a way to access dominance via forms of exclusionary identity. In this way the centrality of gender and the formation of gender identities themselves can be seen to underwrite economic structures. In particular it can be argued that the privilege placed on masculine identity as exclusionary and inherently geared towards competition and oppression of non-hegemonic groups creates an outlet through capitalist practices rather than capitalist practices themselves inherently leading to this expression of competitive identity. Thus, patriarchal values both drive and are enforced by economic structures.

More than this, though, Frayling points to the seemingly inescapable nature of the men's plights in the 'Dollars' trilogy, suggesting that 'they are

33   Christopher Frayling, *Spaghetti Westerns: Cowboys and Europeans from Karl May to Sergio Leone* (London: Routledge & Kegan Paul, 1981), 160–161.

brutal because of the environment in which they exist. And they make no attempt to change that environment. They accept it, without question.'[34] This is one of the primary tenets of a negative hyper-linear historical relationship: a sense in which men are inextricably bound to behaviours and institutions without a conscious understanding that they are and therefore possessing an inability to change their behaviours or challenge existing institutions regardless of the detrimental impacts they may have at a personal, interpersonal or societal level. Certainly, Frayling's acknowledgment of the importance of gun violence as a method of regulating competition, particularly at moments of crisis, taps into the ways in which patriarchy works to distract oppressors of the ways in which they too are disadvantaged by structural mechanisms. This is, as gender theorist, R.W. Connell points out, a measure of gender's instability; 'violence is part of a system of domination, but it is at the same time a measure of its imperfection. A thoroughly legitimate hierarchy would have less need to intimidate.'[35]

This is not to suggest that all films of this era necessarily demonstrate the dissolving of homosocial bonds under the pressure of economic competition. Often, though, films that promote the homosocial bond between groups of men in this era tend to be classified as professional Westerns such as *The Magnificent Seven* (John Sturges, 1960). In these films men may express positive bonds towards each other, yet their value in the group is predicated upon their possession of unique skills rather than inherent identification between men. These 'professional Westerns', as categorized by Will Wright, feature men who exercise their skills in the pursuit of money rather than an inherent sense of justice. Ultimately, they may come to see the worth of society; itself a critique of the ways in which men are positioned to view relationships through the prism of exploitative capitalist systems.[36]

34 Frayling, *Spaghetti Westerns*, 160.
35 R.W. Connell, *Masculinities* (Sydney: Allen & Unwin, 2005), 84.
36 Will Wright, *Six Guns and Society: A Structural Study of the Western* (Berkeley: University of California Press, 1975), 85–131; Noel Carroll, 'The Professional Western: South of the Border', in *Back in the Saddle Again: New Essays on the Western*, eds Edward Buscombe and Robert E. Pearson (London: British Film Industry, 1998), 47.

The precarious homosocial bonds between these groups is highlighted in nihilistic Westerns such as *The Wild Bunch* where these militaristic groups are bonded together and ruthlessly turn against each other based on economic interest regardless of the implications for broader society or for the other (male) members of the group.

These representations of manhood fractured under the pressure of economic competition that alienates men from each other and also from themselves, reflects upon many of the contextual concerns of their post-World War II and Cold War context. As Cuordileone asserts, in a study of the intersections between Cold War culture and gender, this period can be characterized as a crisis of masculinity for men in that 'there was a growing disparity between the ideal itself [of hegemonic masculinity] and the avenues available for white middle-class men to realize that ideal.'[37] In part this was occasioned by the reintegration of men into society following the end of World War II and the associated shift in measuring masculinity through aggressiveness and physicality to a masculine ideal defined by one's capacity as a breadwinner and by their capitalist accumulation, a measure given heightened importance in the context of the perceived communist threat to American capitalist values.[38] For men the attainment of this status was made complex by the contradictory notions that to attempt to gain breadwinner status, one must forfeit one's individuality to a corporatized group mentality, whilst simultaneously the only way to avoid this fate would be to shun the responsibilities of domesticity, itself an act of non-conformity that does not adhere to patriarchal standards.[39] The option of non-conformity may be seen as particularly unviable in a Cold War context that privileged oppositional values of conformity and subservience to authority, values similarly contradicted by the demands of a home front militarization to protect against communist subversion.[40] These films identify through their narrative

37   K.A. Cuordileone, "Politics in an Age of Anxiety': Cold War Political Culture and the Crisis in American Masculinity, 1949–1960', *The Journal of American History* 87 (2000): 528.

38   Kimmel, *Manhood in America*, 148.

39   Kimmel, *Manhood in America*, 156–157.

40   Cuordileone, "Politics in an Age of Anxiety", 527.

structure alone the deep contradictions of masculine gender performance expected of men during this period and the resultant loss of identity at an individual level and a loss of cohesion and identification between men at a broader social level. In *The Naked Spur* Kemp himself demonstrates this anxiety regarding both his capacity to physically demonstrate hegemony in the spirit of traditional patriarchal values, whilst also proving to be incapable as a breadwinner and domestic arbiter.

By situating Kemp within a particular historical context using both explicit and implicit historical cues, the film connects the issues in the filmic context to similar past issues in American history. The mid-to-late nineteenth century similarly presented men with the difficulties of post-war reintegration and with associated changes brought about by an industrializing economy. That is, the decline in an agrarian economy, self-employment and a masculinity grounded in the notion of the yeoman farmer, increased urbanization, loss of the means of production and control of labour, and the sense of labour as mechanical, brought about a wholesale re-evaluation of what it was to be a man and how hegemonic masculine forms could be demonstrated.[41] Such re-evaluation often highlighted the contradictions and complexities in idealized hegemonic forms in a way that is similar to the contradictions of the 1950s and 1960s: industrialization required the creation of subservient workers, whose masculinity was simultaneously cemented and eroded by the submission of their labour to capitalistic mechanisms. In creating this connection a long history of men's alienation emerges, encouraging a critique of the underlying structures that continually put forward hegemonic standards that are detrimental at both a personal and societal level.

It is little wonder that in both of these temporalities men turned to Western symbolism as a method of reflecting upon the values and ideology underpinning masculine gender performance. This was seen in the nineteenth century in the mythologizing of the West through dime-store novels and performances such as Buffalo Bill Cody's Wild West Show (1883–1916) and in popular movements that espoused the importance of exposure to the West as a positive influence in shaping the character of

41 Kimmel, *Manhood in America*, 58.

young boys, and necessary in providing a counter-balance to the smother-
ing influence of mothers, a factor evidenced in the establishment of the
Boy Scouts movement and National Parks, for example.[42] Of course this
was espoused politically by Theodore Roosevelt, who used his exaggerated
connections with the West as indicative of his character and capacity for
effective leadership. Kennedy would also use the imagery of the frontier
in justifying ongoing interventionism in Southeast Asia and the funding
of the space program.[43] In the 1950s television Westerns dominated primetime; the 1958–1959 season devoted 26 per cent of primetime viewing to
Westerns or the equivalent of 400 feature films, with their popularity
allowing for spin-offs, radio serials and merchandizing rights.[44] Fifty-four
feature film Westerns were made in 1958 alone.[45] Whilst these films are
themselves products of a capitalist social structure, and therefore one must
inherently question the extent to which they can ever truly come to stand
for subversive social values, it is deeply ironic that at their most profitable,
some Westerns also went about critiquing those same structures that led to
their success. At a more fundamental level its success in both temporalities
says something more about the function of the genre and its connection
to the historical past. Beyond simply attributing this success to a need for

---

42   See, for example, Gaylyn Studlar, 'Wider Horizons: Douglas Fairbanks and the Rise
      of Nostalgic Primitivism', in *Back in the Saddle Again: New Essays on the Western*, eds
      Edward Buscombe and Robert E. Pearson (London: British Film Industry, 1998),
      63–76, and R.W. Connell, *Masculinities*, 195; for a brief discussion of the gendered
      and class associations of the National Parks and camping holidays, beginning with
      the establishment of Yellowstone in 1872, see Laura Woodworth-Ney, *Women in the
      American West* (Santa Barbara, CA: ABC-CLIO, 2008) 207–209.

43   Many have written on the links between Roosevelt and subsequent political lead-
      ers, the West and the construction of a political persona; see, for example, Karen R.
      Jones and John Wills, *The American West: Competing Visions* (Edinburgh: Edinburgh
      University Press, 2009), 87–117, and Richard Slotkin, *Gunfighter Nation: The Myth
      of the Frontier in Twentieth Century America* (New York: Harper Collins, 1992),
      29–65, 489–559.

44   William Boddy, '"Sixty Million Viewers Can't be Wrong': The Rise and Fall of the
      Television Western', in *Back in the Saddle Again: New Essays on the Western*, eds Edward
      Buscombe and Robert E. Pearson (London: British Film Industry, 1998), 119–120.

45   Michael Kimmel, *Manhood in America*, 165.

nostalgic escapism amongst audiences, it could be argued that the historical bridge between past and present provided by the Westerns allows the audience to make sense of their present, providing a context for contemporary issues by re-examining the past, particularly past moments that also exhibit features of a crisis in masculinity.

By representing these issues within a deeply historically rooted genre and, by using distinct historical cues (in the case of *The Naked Spur* positioning the film in distinct time and place with reference to the Civil War), Westerns of this period inherently connects the audience to their past and in so doing, prove capable of providing a deeper, structural critique of the capitalist values that underpin patriarchal American society. These films position the audience in such a way that they are encouraged to look to history, view the connections between the historical past and the contextual present and, from this, develop a new understanding of the ways in which the past has shaped the present and the ways in which this relationship can shape future understandings. In many ways the relationship that is created here is one that is destabilizing to then contemporary relationships of power. At their most subversive (such as in *The Shooting*) these films can be read as illustrating that it is in the interests of capitalistic institutions to keep men alienated from each other and from themselves in such a way as to deny them knowledge of their own dissatisfaction with existing power arrangements, therefore denying them any meaningful way to challenge that system. These films argue that capitalistic arrangements pit men against each other creating an intractable competition between men that is detrimental to the achievement of any real or lasting happiness and that allows for the suppression of other minority groups for a masculine ideal that is not achievable. This presents a challenge not only to a society founded on the principles of capitalism but also to patriarchy itself, as it exposes as false the notion of masculinity founded in unchanging permanency, truth, and unity in favour of multiple masculinities that change and adapt over time to meet new demands.[46]

---

46   Martin Pumphrey, 'Why to Cowboys Wear Hats in the Bath? Style Politics for the Older Man', in *The Movie Book of the Western*, eds Ian Cameron and Douglas Pye (London: Studio Vista, 1996), 53, 61.

I suggest that although many of these films imprint socially positive or redemptive endings, as is often seen as the case in films such as *The Naked Spur*, this does little to relieve the audience of the underlying themes of the film; themes of loss, competition and struggle for survival in a changing world.[47] *The Naked Spur*, for example, positions Kemp as basically a 'good man' forced into action that is distasteful to him. His capacity to recognize the sins of his action, repent, and be prepared to adapt to meet his changed circumstances, allows for him to survive whereas Jesse and Howard, still intent on receiving a payday, die. This understanding suggests that for Kemp the problems he encounters are largely attributed to factors external to himself, relating to the incapacity of society to reintegrate war veterans and fulfil its own promise of economic security and, subsequently, to the lack of understanding of men's wartime experiences and sacrifices shown here, for example, by his runaway fiancée. The denouement reflects that whilst he may not be able to alter these structures, he can alter his reaction to them. This marks a differentiation between the sources of male suffering between Westerns of the 1950s, where it is more likely that obstacles faced by the protagonist are imposed by societal structures but his inherent character allows him to resolve these differences and integrate or align himself with positive social forces, and Westerns of the 1960s, which are more likely to position the obstacle or problem both within institutions and within the protagonist himself.[48] In the 1960s the seeping away of hegemonic masculinity had occurred and the Westerner no longer has the tools or desire to resolve societal differences or meaningfully engage with broader structures. For example, *The Naked Spur* would transition into films such as *Butch Cassidy and the Sundance Kid*, where life revolves around the next big score and the characters are incapable of change, and the positivism surrounding redemptive violence when exercised by the right individual in *Colt .45* and *Shane* turns into the vivid, pointless, nihilistic violence of *The Wild Bunch*.

---

47 A similar argument regarding the ending of *The Naked Spur* doing little to relieve the themes of the film is made in: Jim Kitses, *Horizons West*, 145 and Robert Horton, 'Mann and Stewart', 46.

48 See, for example, Richard Whitehall, 'The Heroes are Tired', *Film Quarterly* 20 (1966/67): 18

However, in acknowledging the redemptive intention of the conclusion, Kemp finishes the film in a state of emotional and physical exhaustion, sobbing, vulnerable, torn between money and Lina, before ultimately capitulating. In this sense 'entry into the community can thus feel like a defeat.'[49] The impression here is not of a recovery of a hegemonic form of masculinity, or a discovery of an alternative form of identity, but rather a submission to the power of the feminine and recognition of the limitations and problems associated with attempts to attain gender hegemony.

'Won't ya do me?': White Men Competing with Women and Minorities

Of course this film illustrates not only the broader sense that men's emasculation results from economic pressures but also provides evidence of the fracturing of masculinity brought about by the pressures created by women and minority groups both in terms of their increasing societal participation (including economic participation) and also in posing an alternative, challenging narrative of American history. The film does this briefly through the interactions between the posse and the Blackfeet but more soundly through the phantom presence of Kemp's lost fiancée and the relationship between Lina, Ben, Kemp and Roy. In looking at these causes of male emasculation this section will illustrate the ways in which economic pressures were compounded by other rights-based movements in this period, as connected hyper-linearly to the past, to create a wholesale challenge to patriarchal values and their associated privileged forms of gender manifestation. Moreover, a discussion of these other pressures cannot be extricated from the economic sphere considering the centrality of economic enfranchisement as both a driver and aim of most rights-based movements.

---

49   Kitses, *Horizons West*, 145. See also Horton, 'Mann & Stewart', 46.

The first way in which this is demonstrated is through the portrayal of frontier violence in a deromanticized and competitive way, rather than as inevitable or beneficial. The concept of ongoing frontier violence is intro-duced to the audience through Roy, who states that he was a member of the sixth cavalry and 'Indian fighter extraordinary', but whose papers reveal that he was dishonourably discharged and considered 'unsatisfactory. Morally unstable.' Both his demeanour and the information provided about him, including the later revelation that he raped a Native American woman, provides an immediate challenge to the traditional Western presentation of cavalrymen as moralistic saviours in the face of white society under threat from a violent and 'savage' Indigenous population. Roy both attacks Lina – which she uses to actively challenge the notion of violent oppression as a method of maintaining masculine dominance, stating 'You're a big one for beatin' up women' – and attempts to bribe her with the promise of steak as a way to ingratiate himself to her for his potential sexual gain. Ultimately, the battle between the posse and Blackfeet, who are seeking revenge for Roy's rape of a 'squaw' was, as Bingham notes, 'one of the first to suggest that Indian fighting was slaughter.'[50] Moreover, the suggestion of rape as a motivating factor for this assault alludes to the notion that armed resist-ance by Native Americans was justified and moral. Kemp is not exempt from this, with his dramatic bludgeoning of a warrior, which continues far beyond the fatal blow, suggesting that no character is morally exempt from the senselessness of violence, a violence which does not carry the illusion of the moral high ground.

This, and many other films of this period that deal explicitly with frontier violence, reflect a society increasingly aware of postcolonial move-ments throughout the Asian and South American region, and undergoing the process of questioning its own role in imperialist expansion through-out the developing world. The emergent African American Civil Rights Movement in the 1950s and 1960s also resulted in a deeper questioning

---

50   Bingham, *Acting Male*, 65. I would stress that Bingham states it is 'one of' the first – certainly Stewart's own 1950 film *Broken Arrow* (Delmer Davis) stands as a pertinent (albeit complex and largely tentatively integrationist) example of early sympathetic portrayals of Native Americans.

of the tension between American ideals and practice, as did a legitimate growth in awareness of First Nation issues. In using the Western genre to express these concerns, these issues are paralleled quite clearly with America's colonial foundations and the persecution of First Nation Peoples through frontier settlement. This hyper-linear relationship between past violent oppression signalled in this film through frontier conflict, and contemporary contextual issues surrounding postcolonial rights movements domestically and around the world, occasions a profound re-evaluation of the notions of justifiable violence, Manifest Destiny and divine right – that is, the cornerstones of American patriarchal society, its foreign policy, and its associated individual manifestations in the form of hegemonic masculinity.

The film more profoundly reflects upon the attitudes of women and the role they have played in the ongoing emasculation of men. Most obviously, Kemp is betrayed by his fiancé who uses his money to elope with another man, a betrayal echoed when Lina distracts him into a potentially romantic conversation to facilitate Ben's escape attempt. In many ways these women and their reaction to circumstance can be seen as a reflection of concerns, expressed in Friedan's *The Feminine Mystique*, for example, that beneath the veneer of domesticity women were increasingly discontented with life sequestered in the private sphere and searching for a sense of belonging and identity outside of marriage and motherhood.[51] This was further exacerbated economically, through the competition posed by increased female participation in paid labour following gains brought about by World War II as well as increases in women's participation in tertiary education.[52] This film reveals these anxieties through the impact of Kemp's abandonment on his continued behaviour, which connects then contemporary issues to the destabilization of gender roles in a post-Civil

---

51   Daniel Horowitz, 'Rethinking Betty Friedan and *The Feminine Mystique*: Labor Union Radicalism and Feminism in Cold War America', *American Quarterly* 48 (1998): 1–42.

52   For a discussion on the relationship between gender ideology and women's participation in education in this period see Linda Eisenmann, *Higher Education for Women in Postwar America, 1945–1965* (Baltimore: Johns Hopkins University Press, 2006).

War context where women increasingly sought opportunities for public participation.

Whilst the characterization of Lina may in part demonstrate a reconciling of these anxieties with the idea that there are still women who crave domesticity and marriage, this reading is tempered somewhat by the nature of the group as symbol of domestic family structures and by the film's awkward portrayal of sexuality. As Kitses suggests the composition of the posse mirrors that of 'a malignant family bent on murdering each other at the first opportunity.'[53] By structuring the posse in such a way that it does resemble a 'malignant' (some would suggest incestuous) family Mann goes about pointing to anxieties regarding men's place within the domestic sphere but, more tellingly, questions an ideology that in these particular time periods presents men's place as patriarch of the domestic sphere in an untainted and functional way.

These concerns were not only reflected most obviously in the 1950s context, with its widely acknowledged cult of domesticity, but also during an industrializing economy that increasingly removed men from the home and left women with greater influence over the domestic realm and child rearing.[54] Certainly the strangely presented sexuality in this film, where the nature of Lina's relationship with Ben is never revealed, although his continual requests for a back rub, suggestively phrased 'won't ya do me?', grate on the relations amongst the posse. In conjunction with Kemp's asexual wooing of Lina and Roy's sexual aggression the film reveals an anxiety regarding men's roles and capacity for functional potency in a heterosexual relationship. This, in turn, reflects on destabilized gender manifestations in both temporalities and an associated anxiety regarding this destabilization. The roles of women in Westerns will be explored in the next chapter with a specific focus on the 1952 film *High Noon* (Fred Zinnemann, 1952), another film that explicitly uses gender to create hyper-linear historical relationships between temporalities.

53   Kitses, *Horizons West*, 158.
54   Studlar, 'Wider Horizons', 63–76.

Conclusion

This chapter has undertaken an examination of the film *The Naked Spur* in order to illustrate the multitude of ways in which men are portrayed as emasculated, and the ways in which this is connected to the represented historical past and the historical present of the filmic context. Such an analysis reveals the ways in which narrative arcs, characterization, star performance, costume and landscape in this film, with reference to other Westerns of the 1950s and 1960s, play on and subvert archetypal conceptualizations of 'hard' masculinity to reveal white masculinities fractured and alienated from each other, a sense of self and a means of attaining hegemonic status. In large part this fracturing of masculinity finds both an expression and driver in capitalist economic structures. Moreover, Westerns, by virtue of their inherent historicity and specific historical cues, do much to establish a hyper-linear connection between economic conditions and their effects on gender in the represented past and in the present of the filmic release; in this instance connecting the corporatism and post-war restructuring of the 1950s with industrialization and post-Civil War restructuring represented on screen. This is not to say that these are the only sources of destabilized gender norms; rather, rights-based movements did much to compound this alienation and further complicate the patriarchal values upon which American society is based, a factor connected hyper-linearly to first wave feminism and frontier violence in the represented past.

CHAPTER 3

'Back home they think I'm very strange. I'm a feminist': Re-Evaluating the Feminine Other

Western films, many theorists have pointed out, position men and the hegemonic masculinity they embody at the centre of the narrative structure. Further, this centrality of men's experiences has been linked to broader constructions of national identity, ideology and policy practices at both the domestic and international level. As we have seen in relation to *The Naked Spur*, and as we will continue to see throughout this volume, men's gendered identities in the Western genre are positioned as not only personal manifestations but also manifestations of macro-level identity issues that operate within a distinctly historical juncture in this grouping of films. On the other hand, it is generally seen that masculine centrality occurs through the marginalization of women's roles in Western films. For many women are juxtaposed to men, sitting on the margins of the narrative as little more than symbols of the civilization that the male protagonist will ultimately protect and embrace (through the institutions of marriage and the family), or relinquish in favour of maintaining his own rigorous identity in the ongoing quest for the next frontier. Westerns of the 1950s and 1960s, however, mark a subtle repositioning of the role played by women that contributes to, reflects and re-enforces the re-evaluation of hegemonic masculinity undertaken in these films. These Westerns illustrate the ways in which changing ideas regarding women's roles and self-identity occasioned the slow seeping out of notions of the ideal hegemonic masculinity (and patriarchal society) in both the represented historical past and the present of the filmic release. This chapter will explore the discourse surrounding women, the West and the Western before turning to an analysis of the representations of women in the Westerns of this period, in particular the iconic Western *High Noon* (Fred Zinnemann, 1952).

This chapter argues that conceptualizing women as peripheral beings in Westerns of this period underplays the importance that women's characterizations and relationships to each other, to men, and to patriarchal institutions had in destabilizing hegemonic notions of gender identity. This is not to say that women's experiences were the focus of Western films; clearly in most Western films of this period female characters were not the narrative focus nor did they carry the majority of screen time. Yet screen time is not necessarily a measure of textual impact and, ultimately, although many Westerns may continue to marginalize women's experiences, a more complex analysis of these Westerns is needed. Certainly a distinct subgenre of Westerns existed in this period that places women in a more prominent role, indeed, even a central role to the main narrative structure. These roles, however, tend to be overlooked in the homogenizing discourse surrounding the alleged gender dichotomy of Westerns, with notable exceptions such as the analysis of the rival female leaders in *Johnny Guitar* (Nicholas Ray, 1954).[1] However, even those films that may provide little screen time for female characters do not necessarily relegate women to unimportant roles, or deny them development beyond that of signifier. Often women render these roles complex, performing their gender identities in ways that play upon gender stereotypes, reflect a deeper understanding of men's motives and women's capacity to react within and to overarching patriarchal structures. Indeed, at times women's place outside of competitive intra-masculine hierarchies grants them a liminal status that allows them to traverse multiple roles and relationships that are inaccessible to those aspiring to hegemonic masculine performances.

Moreover, it would seem extremely removed from the historical experience of the post-Civil War West, or of the 1950s and 1960s, if Western

---

1   This binary is articulated, for example, in Pat Kirkham and Janet Thumin (eds), *You Tarzan: Masculinity, Movies and Men* (London: Lawrence & Wishart, 1993), 20, and also in Jane Tompkins' premise that Westerns arise from threats posed by women to men's dominance and therefore Westerns enact fantasies of masculine dominance – *West of Everything: The Inner Life of Westerns* (New York: Oxford University Press, 1992). It is important to acknowledge that Tompkins' own perspective on women's roles in Westerns, 'when push comes to shove ... they crumble' (61), is very different to that put forward throughout this work.

films did not seek to incorporate women or grapple with gender relations. This is the case because both periods were characterized by increased confusion surrounding men's gender identities and roles, an issue that was partly stimulated by a rise in women's public participation that defied traditional, hegemonic gender norms. These films illuminate hyper-linear historical relationships between the represented past and their present in terms of ideas surrounding women's roles. In particular Western films reflect upon changes to gender norms in the post-Civil War era including: the rise of women's suffrage movements and political participation in temperance and public morality movements, racial and labour movements, economic shifts and the rise of the 'New Woman', which stimulated associated concerns about the ways in which changes to women's roles would impact upon men's identity.[2] These issues are connected to changing gendered attitudes occasioned by women's increasing public participation in labour, education and in multiple rights-based movements that culminated in second wave feminism in the post-World War II period. Overall, these films construct hyper-linear links between the first wave feminist movement (which also had its roots in women's participation in other rights-based discourses) and the second wave feminist movement (which likewise was also stimulated by other contextual issues). This is not to say that either period marked a major revolution that permanently altered a balance of gendered power in a patriarchal society. Both periods, however, were significant in their attempts to mask fissures in hegemonic masculinity by reinstating a gender order that was increasingly crumbling under the pressures of social change.

2   The rise of all male groups that particularly emphasize men's physical prowess and the 'cult of the body' can be seen as symptomatic of this. The establishment of the Boy Scouts at this time can also be seen as symptomatic of male anxiety. See Lee Clark Mitchell, *Westerns: Making the Man in Fiction and Film* (Chicago: University of Chicago Press, 1996), 115.

Women's Roles in Real West and Reel West

It is not surprising that Western films would become a vehicle through
which to tell a hyper-linear history regarding men's and women's gender
roles. Laura Woodworth-Ney suggests that the American West in the late
nineteenth and early twentieth century 'more than any other region at
any other time in US history [−] became a geographic laboratory for federal policies aimed at defining the American home, the family, woman-
hood and masculinity.'[3] However, such a perspective has not always been
prevalent in Western scholarship: as Glenda Riley asserts, a large part
of Frederick Jackson Turner's legacy has been in the conceptualization
of the frontier as a masculine space, an academic 'tunnel vision' that has
resulted in, at worst, the silencing of women's voices, particularly Latin
American, Native American and black women's voices.[4] At best, this legacy
has resulted in scholarship that has incorporated women only in so far as
they are connected and confined to the domestic sphere, and seen as little
more than 'dolls, vassals and drudges.'[5] From this, 'new Western' historians have discussed the importance of incorporating a diverse and complex
array of women's experiences in order to gain a fuller picture of Western,
and American, life.

These 'New Western' perspectives reveal the enormously changeable,
diverse and complex nature of gender ideology, constructions and relationships in Western women's experiences. Perhaps the most prominent
scholarship has sought to examine the factors that resulted in Western
states being at the forefront in granting women's suffrage rights, and the

3   Laura E. Ney-Woodworth, *Women in the American West* (Santa Barbara, CA: ABC-
     CLIO, 2008), 180. Importantly, though, Ney-Woodworth does define this trans-
     formative period more broadly than this volume does: 1877–1920.
4   Glenda Riley, 'Frederick Jackson Turner Overlooked the Ladies', *Journal of the Early
     Republic* 13 (1993): 217.
5   Riley, 'Frederick Jackson Turner Overlooked the Ladies', 219; T.A. Larson, 'Dolls,
     Vassals and Drudges – Pioneering Women in the West', *The Western Historical
     Quarterly* 3 (1972): 5.

associated roles of suffragettes and other rights campaigners in the West.[6] This development, though conceptualized as a universal step forward for women was mediated, of course, by women's racial and class based identities, by individual motivations to harness women's voting power and the intentions of particular states.[7] This does not detract from the advocacy, community building and other rights-based movements undertaken by a diverse array of Western women.[8] It is, however, to suggest that the West was a site of gender contestation, with varying results individually compounded by other aspects of identity and circumstance and across regions. Along with this practical rights development was the passage of the *Homestead Act, 1862*, which opened up the possibility for some women classed as heads of household to claim and operate land independently, thereby reshaping ideology relevant to women's relationships to property and to the household.[9] These scholars have also sought to uncover the multi-ethnic West by examining women's voices through multiple methodologies and to seek to understand relationships between women, including between women of differing ethnic identification.[10] Others have sought to understand the impact of new technologies and consumer ideologies in reshaping women's access to power and their performance of their gender.[11]

6   See, for example, Holly J. McCammon and Karen E Campbell, 'Winning the Vote in the West: The Political Successes of the Women's Suffrage Movement, 1866–1919', *Gender and Society* 15 (2001): 55–82; and, John Markoff, 'Margins, Centers and Democracy: The Paradigmatic History of Women's Suffrage', *Signs* 29 (2003): 85–116.

7   Ney-Woodworth, *Women in the American West*, 191–193.

8   Ney-Woodworth, *Women in the American West*, 183 & 193.

9   Joan M. Jensen and Darlis A. Miller, 'The Gentle Tamers Revisited: New Approaches to the History of Women in the American West', *The Pacific Historical Review* 49 (1980): 183; Ney-Woodworth, *Women in the American West*, 187.

10   Jensen and Miller, 'The Gentle Tamers Revisited', 173–213.

11   Ney-Woodworth, *Women in the American West*, 193–198. Ney-Woodworth particularly points to transport technologies (the railroad) as a transformative, and generally positive, development in women's experiences though I would also point to the increased availability of gun technologies after the Civil War as also highly transformative for women. Jensen and Miller, for example, suggest that comparisons of women's experiences of warfare across ethnic lines would be particularly illuminative; Jensen, 'The Gentle Tamers Revisited', 197–198. The impact that increased

Importantly 'New Western' historians have sought to examine the
ways in which all women enacted their gender performances in relation to
patriarchal structures and existing gender ideologies. Seminal to this femi-
nizing project of 'New Western' history has been Julie Jeffrey's 1979 work
Frontier Women: 'Civilizing' the West? 1840–1880, in which she argued that
the frontier experience had the potential to transform positively the roles
and expectations of white women, which they reconciled within traditional
gender ideology.[12] For Jeffrey the journey West provided a testing ground
of the pervasiveness and rigidity of traditional nineteenth century conceptualizations of femininity, which are seen as a confinement of women to
the domestic sphere where, away from the corrupting influences of public
life, they acted as guardians of social and moral values. White feminine
gender performance during this period was marked by the ideas that 'they
[women] devoted themselves naturally to others. As feeling rather than
thinking creatures, lacking egotism and pride, women were uniquely able
to perceive and act upon moral truth. Their physical charms and affection-
ate nature provide them with useful advantages.'[13]

Ideologically, then, women's power in the domestic sphere was predicated on contradictory notions of innocence, capacity for self-sacrifice and
submission to masculine knowledge of external affairs. Although women
continued to use this ideological framework as a measure of their experience and the expectations placed upon them (indeed, for many, women
were seen as a necessity on the frontier as 'civilizing' agents), the trials of
the journey and subsequent settlement made gender norms highly flexible. While women operated from a base of traditional gender norms, the

---

availability of gun technology had on women's experiences in terms of individual
and domestic violence can be added to this; see, for example, Clare V. McKanna, Jr,
'Alcohol, Handguns, and Homicide in the American West: A Tale of Three Counties,
1880–1920', *The Western Historical Quarterly* 26 (1995): 461–462. The role of gun
technology is further explored in Chapter 6.

12   Julie Roy Jeffrey, *Frontier Women: 'Civilizing' the West? 1840–1880* (revised edition)
      (New York: Hill & Wang, 1998). See also: Annette Kolodny, *The Land Before Her:
      Fantasy and Experience of the American Frontiers, 1630–1860* (Chapel Hill: University
      of North Carolina Press, 1984).

13   Jeffrey, *Frontier Women*, 14.

practical impact could be subversive where women, Jeffery asserts, were active decision-makers, choosing to emigrate for a variety of financial, religious, health and personal reasons. They also performed a variety of different types of work both inside and outside the home, including work typically classed as men's and for financial profit. Jeffrey also found that Western women exerted influence over their husbands' decisions, whether indirectly or through direct confrontation.[14] It is precisely this flexibility of individual gender performance, which sees the West as a liminal space within which to enact such performance, and it is precisely this diversity of women's experiences, compounded by factors such as race, class, political identification, sexuality, and marital and family status, that have been emphasized in contemporary literature.

These historical developments in women's experiences point both to the diversity of women's experiences but also to the post-Civil War period in the West as an enormously transformative one for women. This transformation was ultimately a challenge to patriarchal gender norms and a challenge to the ways in which individual men formed a masculine gender identity. The multi-ethnic nature of the West meant that increasingly white women were in contact with the differing experiences of other women, with a variety of impacts. White women were increasingly allocated political power, independence, and public roles through suffrage and land rights reform, along with other forms of advocacy in temperance, religious, and racial movements. The nature of Western settlements meant that labour roles were also increasingly flexible and many women no longer found their work to be entirely in the home or in accordance with traditional gender roles. In this context, white women may have attempted to reconcile practical changes to their circumstances with traditional gender ideologies but clearly these changes had dramatic impacts upon gendered understandings and on individual gender performance that resisted such easy reconciliation. This attempt to reconcile ideology with the reality of changing historical circumstances clearly parallels America's experiences of gendered norms in the 1950s and 1960s.

---

14   Jeffery, *Frontier Women*, 46–47.

This post-World War II period has popularly been conceptualized as a reassertion of rigid gender binaries and a separation of spheres that returned women to the home and domesticity. However, practically, the concept of women returning to the domestic sphere in uncomplicated ways is problematized by the fact that many women simply did not return to domesticity. Ruth Milkman notes, for example, that 'despite the postwar resurgence of an ideology of domesticity, by the early 1950s the number of gainfully employed women exceeded the highest wartime level. And as early as 1948, the labor force participation rate of married women was higher than in 1944, the peak of the war boom.' These rates would only grow and, Milkman argues, this public and paid workplace participation permanently altered women's connection to paid labour.[15] During this time numbers of women, spurred on by the loosening of gender boundaries during the war, achieved tertiary qualifications and became politically active in Leftist and Socialist organizations, in the Civil Rights Movement, and in the Union Movement.[16] Certainly it could be argued that this process accelerated after the McCarthy era when greater freedoms of self-expression became possible. In participating in these causes many women became aware not only of the disadvantages they faced due to their social, political, class and racial identities but also the ways in which this was compounded by gender bias.[17] As

---

15   Ruth Milkman, *Gender at Work: The Dynamics of Job Segregation by Sex during World War II* (Illinois: University of Illinois Press, 1987), 100.

16   Eisenmann, *Higher Education for Women in Postwar America*, 44–45. Eisenmann suggests that the absolute number of women enrolled in college rose, so that one in five women between the ages of eighteen and twenty-one were students in 1957 and one million more women receiving a tertiary education in 1963 than in 1948 (1.7 million compared to seven hundred thousand). As a proportion of the student body, however, women's numbers only had a significant impact on campus life by the 1960s. As was noted earlier in this volume it is important to acknowledge that this discussion is about the collision of hegemonic standards of feminine behaviour with realities; the reality is also that many women through paid and unpaid labour never experienced cloistering in the domestic sphere.

17   Daniel Horowitz, 'Rethinking Betty Friedan and *The Feminine Mystique*: Labour Union Radicalism and Feminism in Cold War America', *American Quarterly* 48 (1998): 1–42.

the Reverend Dr Pauli Murray, the Civil Rights and women's activist who coined the phrase 'Jane Crow' to refer to the double disadvantage faced by black women, stated in reflection of her time at Howard University Law School beginning in 1941: 'I had entered law school pre-occupied with the racial struggle [...] but I graduated an unabashed feminist as well.'[18]

For other women who may not have become politically active the dissatisfaction many felt in the confines of suburban femininity during this time was reflected in Betty Friedan's best-selling book *The Feminine Mystique*, which was published in 1963.[19] Indeed, as Eva Moskowitz argues, a 'discourse of discontent' regarding women's status and confinement to the domestic sphere was clearly evident in the immediate post-war era from 1945. Moskowitz examines women's magazines of the Cold War period, typically held as symbols of women's fulfilment with traditional gender roles. She argues that women's magazines specifically sought to combat women's dissatisfaction with life as housewives and to help them to reconcile feelings of unhappiness, even depression, with social expectations placed upon them.[20] Other women did not find limitation in their status as wives and mothers but empowerment to influence public discourse. Applying Jeffery's argument that frontier women operated within the confines of patriarchal norms to effect gender change, it should be pointed out that many women in this post-war context arrived at political activism not by refuting but by embracing patriarchal standards of traditional femininity. For example, Amy Swerdlow observed in analysing the victory of the Women Strike for Peace [WSP] organization against the House Un-American Activities in 1962 that such a victory could only be achieved because the accused consciously used gender performance and the juxtaposition of gender difference to impress

18   Pauli Murray (1956) as quoted in *Women's America: Refocusing the Past*, 6th edn, eds Linda K. Kerber & Jane Sherron De Hart (Oxford: Oxford University Press, 2004): 537.

19   Horowitz, 'Rethinking Betty Friedan and *The Feminine Mystique*', 1–42. Despite the publication date in 1963 Friedan's research was undertaken in the 1950s. Moreover, the central feminist treatise Simone de Beauvoir's, *The Second Sex*, had already been published in 1949.

20   Eva Moskowitz, "Sometimes It's Good to Blow Your Top': Women's Magazines and a Discourse of Discontent, 1945–1965', *Journal of Women's History* 8 (1996): 66–98.

that, as mothers, they would always have the moral and patriotic high-
ground. In doing so 'the WSP women were not concerned with transforming the ideology of femininity but rather with using it to enhance women's
political power. But in so doing they were transforming that ideology and
foreshadowing the feminism that emerged later in the decade.'[21] Clearly
a parallel can be found here in Jeffery's argument regarding the diversity
of frontier women's experiences, from operation within the boundaries of
hegemonic standards of femininity to express power, as well as women's
active participation in suffrage, abolition and education movements, particularly from the 1880s.[22]

The interesting aspect of this historiographical development is the way
in which, despite enormous changes in historical understandings of the
role of women in the West and in the 1950s and 1960s, this has not been
matched by a deeper exploration of women in the Western film in representational studies. Understandings of the women's role in the Western
are typically conceptualized as archetypal: the 'good', pure (Caucasian)
Madonna-esque, representative of civilization, contrasted with the sullied,
sexualized Eve (usually a prostitute or racial minority). This limited and
one-dimensional conceptualization of the feminine in representational
studies labels the portrayal of Western women as 'weak and unworthy' and
whose primary narrative function is 'basically as the catalyst bringing men
together.'[23] When it is acknowledged that women's roles have relaxed and
become somewhat more complex over time, as in Philip French's reflections on then-contemporary 1960s Westerns, this is generally attributed
to changing censorship regulations and the collapse of the studio system,
not the changing ideas of women's contributions in the Western past or to
contemporary society.[24] Indeed, the concept that these archetypes possess

---

21   Amy Swerdlow, 'Ladies' Day at the Capitol: Women Strike for Peace versus HUAC',
      Feminist Studies 8 (1982): 515.
22   See, Jeffery, *Frontier Women.*
23   Joan Mellen, *Big Bad Wolves: Masculinity in the American Film* (London: Elm Tree
      Books, 1978): 178–179.
24   Philip French, *Westerns: Aspects of a Movie Genre* (London: Secker & Warburg,
      1973): 62–63.

'historical actuality' (that is, that archetypal representations are an accurate depiction of women's experiences of the frontier and West) is put forward in an uncontested way, despite the changing historical understanding of women's roles.[25] At the extreme, the result of these images is, for Jane Tompkins, that the Western 'worships the phallus', encouraging audiences to identify with and aspire to become the Western hero to the exclusion of female characters. Indeed, even feminine-identifying audience members become so alienated from the representations of their gender on-screen they come to identify with the masculine lead.[26] Tompkins argues in relation to the portrayal of women: 'there's nothing *to* them. They may seem strong and resilient, fiery and resourceful at first, but when push comes to shove, as it always does, they crumble' [original emphasis].[27] However, the inherent historicity of all gender performances negates the idea of women's roles as unchanging and homogenous. Moreover, whilst Western films may often position women in minor roles, these roles are not necessarily insignificant foils. Indeed the argument here is that by the 1950s and 1960s, women's roles in some Western films signalled major contextual shifts in gender spurred on by emerging second wave feminism, amongst other challenges, to the existing gender order, and a heightened awareness of how this historical present related to the challenges and shifts of the past. This is certainly illustrated in the film *High Noon*.

High Noon, released in 1952 at the beginning of these transformations, does not clearly suggest or endorse a distinctly feminist discourse for all the female characters. It does explore the roles of women, the interaction between women, and the ways in which women learn a gender performance that works for them within a patriarchal system. It highlights both the commonalities of women's experiences and the disjunctions between them in a way that reflects the diversity of women's experiences in an historically

25   French, *Westerns*, 62–63. For an exploration of censorship and the collapse of the studio system see, for example, Bill Mesce, Jr, *Peckinpah's Women: A Reappraisal of the Portrayal of Women in the Period Westerns of Sam Peckinpah* (Lanham, MD: Scarecrow Press, 2001): 13–39.

26   Tompkins, *West of Everything*, 28.

27   Tompkins, *West of Everything*, 61.

meaningful way that, in a hyper-linear fashion, connects both the past and the present of its filmic context. *High Noon* is important for this discussion precisely because it does not endorse a particularly feminist stance, a perspective that would certainly place it as a fairly unique Western of this period. Rather, it has been critically received as a Western that places men at the centre stage and a contest between men and their capacity to engage with society in a meaningful way as the pivot of the narrative structure. Yet, it is the presentation of women's gender performances and the relationship between them that forms both a substantive sub-plot in the film and whose actions actually mould and shape the narrative form in insightful ways.

High Noon, often acknowledged as an 'iconic' Western, is set in the small town of Hadleyville on the wedding day of the town marshal, Will Kane (Gary Cooper). Indeed Kane is introduced to us as he is being married to Quaker Amy Fowler (Grace Kelly), who we learn has insisted that he retire and leave the town to commence business as a store owner. As they depart, however, Kane learns that gang leader Frank Miller, whom he had caught in Hadleyville and who had been sentenced to hang, had his sentence commuted and is now being released. The Miller gang are back in town and waiting for Frank's arrival on the noon train to exact their revenge against Kane and to take over the town again. Despite Amy refusing to stay with him Kane will not leave Hadleyville to its fate in order to save himself, especially as his replacement has not yet arrived. Kane systematically and unsuccessfully seeks the aid of the townspeople to gather a posse and realizes that he must face the gang alone. In the meantime, Amy, with the guidance of Kane and Miller's ex-mistress, businesswoman Helen Ramirez (Katy Jurado), realizes that, bonded by marriage, she must support Kane. She rushes to his aid, killing one gang member. She is taken hostage by Miller but scratches his face, injuring and distracting him for long enough to allow Kane to shoot him dead. The film concludes here, with the townspeople spilling back onto the street, helping to load up the wedding carriage, as Kane throws his tin star into the dusty street.

This film has been attributed many meanings, most commonly as the ultimate anti-McCarthy tale. The script writer, Carl Foreman, was a former Communist Party member who, in 1951, while working on the *High Noon* script, was brought before the House Un-American Activities

Committee. He was blacklisted and has openly admitted since that the script was a parable of his treatment by Hollywood and the atmosphere brought about by McCarthyism more broadly.[28] It was this interpretation of the film that prompted an outraged John Wayne and Howard Hawks to respond with the film *Rio Bravo* (Howard Hawks, 1959).[29] The film has also been interpreted as a commentary on America's involvement in the Korean War and, by Howard A. Burton, theorizing in literary studies, as a new incarnation of the morality play *Everyman*.[30] *High Noon*'s director, Fred Zinnemann, however, rejected that his intention was to make an explicit political statement, suggesting rather that *High Noon* conveys a universal theme: 'of conscience as against compromise: how far one can follow one's conscience before having to compromise – just that, nothing else.'[31] It is worth noting, however, that Zinnemann was clearly conscious of the film's contemporary connotations and that it, in some way, tapped into contemporary social issues, stating: 'there was something timely – and timeless – about it [*High Noon*], something that had a direct bearing on life today.'[32] Certainly the element of time and historicity were used self-consciously throughout the film, connecting the viewer not only to then contemporary issues such as McCarthyism but also encouraging the viewer to see these as part of a long-standing (hyper-linear) set of issues. This occurs not simply through the sense of urgency imparted upon the audience by the visual image of the ticking clock, counting down to noon, but also through the historical references made by supporting characters in their justifications for refusing to aid Kane, be they real or imagined.[33]

---

28   Neil Lerner, "'Look at That Big Hand Move Along': Clocks, Containment and Music in *High Noon*', *South Atlantic Quarterly* 104 (2005): 157.

29   Stephen Prince, 'Historical Perspective and the Realist Aesthetic in *High Noon*', *Film Criticism* 18/19 (1994): 59–60.

30   Lerner, "Look at that Big Hand Move Along", 157; Howard A. Burton, "'High Noon': Everyman Rides Again', *The Quarterly of Film, Radio and Television* 8 (1953): 80–86.

31   Arthur Nolletti, Jr, 'Conversation with Fred Zinnemann', *Film Criticism* 18/19 (1994): 11.

32   Neil Lerner, "'Look at That Big Hand Move Along", 157

33   It is important to note that the idea of historicity inherent in this film is contested: Barsness argues, for example, that Hadleyville is 'a town with no past-and no reason

These justifications, given below, connect a nihilistic view of history with a disempowered masculine gender performance to communicate the ways in which men are trapped within a negative and destructive gender performance that they do not understand and that is incapable of effecting meaningful, positive and lasting change.

For the townsmen the decision to refuse Kane's aid comes from their personal historical experiences, importantly conceptualizing the individual as an historical subject and the personal as public. Judge Mettrick (Otto Kruger), who sentenced Miller to hang, has been in this situation before, and escaped only with the aid of a woman and his mother's diamond ring, and, after all, 'nothing that happens here is really important'; he recounts the story of an Athenian city in the fifth century whose citizens received back their former tyrant, even as he executed members of the legal government to add weight to his justification for fleeing. The former Marshal, Martin Howe (Lon Chaney, Jr), physically wearied by age and emotionally scarred from too many convicts being released, as well as a lack of community appreciation, refuses to die 'for nothing. For a tin star.' The male portion of the church congregation appeals to historical precedents set in towns where gun fights have reduced business investment, as well as to the Biblical Commandments. It is important to note that Amy's initial refusal to help also relies on historical precedent: she refuses because she has witnessed first-hand the impact of violence (as a form of masculine regulation) in the murders of her nineteen year old brother and her father through gun violence.[34] Added to this sense of historicity, both Zinnemann and photographer Matthew Brady sought inspiration from Civil War photography 'in order to impart a grittier, more realistic flavour to the film, to make it appear as though it were a newsreel from 1870.'[35] For Stephen Prince the nature of the film then is to answer the nihilism of the town, the sense that

---

for existence ... completely outside of history ... its marshal is equally nonhistorical'. John A. Barsness, 'A Question of Standard', *Film Quarterly* 21 (1967): 34.

34   Stephen Prince makes similar observations in relation to the historicity of the personal character narratives in this film in 'Historical Perspective and the Realistic Aesthetic in *High Noon*', 66–69.

35   Lerner, 'Look at That Big Hand Move Along', 155.

history does not matter, with Kane's response that: 'history does matter and that individual decisions and behaviour are important because they are a measure of a state's health. The micro and macro levels are linked.'[36]

The historicity of this film, which links the Cold War context to a longer history of American struggle at the domestic and international level between, as Zinnemann terms it, 'conscience and compromise', is aided by a further gender analysis. In this film, as masculine gender performance embodies the state, the ineffectiveness of men in this film juxtaposed with active, effective women, reveals underlying shifts in the gender order; in particular it questions the role of women's empowerment in contributing to or emphasizing men's emasculation. Such an analysis in this film highlights the ways that women's roles become central in creating a political climate of paranoia and erosion of community values, which reflects the demasculinization of men in the 1950s. Further it connects this development to a longer history of gender adjustment caused by women's changing roles and rights.

To elaborate on this demasculinization, it is necessary to state that the rejection of Kane and his ideals of community, and the necessary use of restorative violence, occurs solely by male characters until the finale of the film. Men's history in this film is one of negative continuity; as the Judge states, a similar dilemma has been posed to society since the ancient world and there is nothing that Kane or any other man can do that can effect meaningful change. This is not simply an abstract notion but one that has been personally enacted by the men in the film, a fact especially highlighted by the jaded ex-Marshal, who states: 'You risk your skin catching killers, and the juries turn them loose so they can come back and shoot at you again. If you're honest, you're poor your whole life, and in the end you wind up dying alone on some dirty street. For what? For nothing but a tin star.'

36   Prince, 'Historical Perspective and the Realistic Aesthetic in *High Noon*', 69. From this perspective it could be argued that moralism and the intent to explore moralism in this film precludes its capacity to present a nihilistic history. This response complicates such a perspective through an exploration of women's gender roles through an historical lens.

Prince suggests that it is ultimately in Kane's bravery that an answer to nihilism is found. However, I argue that the textual support for this conclusion is somewhat lacking: just as the ex-Marshal has experienced, there is no appreciation of his actions by the townsmen who are just as quick to bustle him out after the battle as before. Indeed, the only reason Kane did not die 'alone on some dirty street' was due to the dedication of a woman. Kane acknowledges the futility of his decisions by throwing down his star, the symbol of hope, law and the notion that meaningful leadership can effect change. He has already demonstrated knowledge of this ultimate futility and the intractability of his performance of hegemonic masculinity by stating to Amy earlier: 'if you think I like this, you're crazy.' Although he does not like it, neither Kane nor anyone else in the film is able to articulate why Kane must fight or what forces compel him to continue his quest. In this light, an examination of the role of the women in *High Noon* is telling, providing a central insight into how this process of demasculinization – evident here in the nihilism of negative historical continuity – takes place and, moreover, the way in which Westerns can and do present complex and challenging female characters that link the concerns of the past with the issues of the time of filmic release.

The Women of *High Noon*

In contrast to masculine nihilism the townswomen of Hadleyville, including Amy and Helen, pose challenging, even subversive, questions for the men and their failures and reflect upon how gender meaningfully informs their understandings of the domestic order. While the responses of the women to the men facing this crisis of morality are not uniform, they do suggest both the commonality of women's concerns and the diversity of women's experience, gender performance and methods of coping with patriarchal norms. The following looks at the women in *High Noon* in three main ways: firstly, as the broader grouping of townswomen that voice their opinion in relation to the defence of the town; secondly, in the central figure of Amy

Fuller and her relationship with Kane; and lastly, in the figure of Helen Ramirez and her relationship with Amy as well as with the dominant male figures of Kane, Miller and Harvey (Lloyd Bridges), Kane's Deputy.

Although the film opens with images of the Miller gang the audience is unaware of their criminal nature until they encounter a woman: an elderly woman on the street in Hadleyville crosses herself as they pass. Although throughout the film references are made to the danger that the gang poses to women, and the townsmen reflect on a time when it was not safe for women to walk the streets, it is the townswomen, beginning with the elderly woman, who demonstrate an understanding of the critical nature of the situation and a desire for action. Indeed, in almost every situation that a man denies Kane aid, this denial is interceded in some way by a countering feminine perspective. The Judge recalls that he owes his life to a woman, who helped him escape from a similar situation, and to his mother, whose diamond ring he used as a bribe. Deputy Harvey's refusal is mediated by Helen who repeatedly laughs at his cowardice and his excuse that he resents being passed over as Kane's replacement – she openly tells Harvey in separate scenes that he needs to 'grow up' and that Kane 'is a man. It takes more than big, broad shoulders Harvey and you don't have it. I don't think you'll ever make it.' When the men at church list reasons not to come to Kane's aid, it is a woman that stands up and appeals to their sense of justice and the gendered expectation that they should protect the women of the town. Kane's friend, Sam Fuller (Harry Morgan), makes his wife answer the door to Kane and lie about his whereabouts despite her moral and practical objections and, overcome with shame, he lashes out at her judgement by asking whether she wants to be a widow. Another townsman, Herb (James Millican), who initially agrees to fight with Kane, backs down using his wife and children as an excuse; and the ex-Marshal's housekeeper is in the room listening to their exchange, although tellingly the ex-Marshal has no significant other, positioning him as Kane's mirror – the honest lawman, who will die alone. The capacity of women rather than men to understand the grave nature of the situation they face and to respond assertively that Miller cannot be allowed to return, sits directly at odds with the traditional notion that women are unconcerned with, and incapable of understanding, the nature of masculine public affairs.

Moreover, it suggests the capacity for women to play on and with gendered expectations to achieve outcomes they consider desirable: the townswomen play with the concept of feminine inability in order to attempt to goad men into the defence of the town, in so doing revealing their depth of understanding of men and their self-conscious deployment of gender ideology. This reflects women's capacity to use the power available to them within a patriarchal, hegemonic framework in order to serve their own interests.

The relationship between men and women in Westerns has been portrayed as one where 'men have the deeper wisdom and the women are children'; however, in this film, the townswomen demonstrate a deeper wisdom: they are able to see the end result of allowing Miller to return to the town.[37] The role of women in this broader sense reflects upon women's capacity to participate in public affairs, to comprehend and defend the links between their personal lives and the public sphere, and the power of women to impact and question the patriarchal order, all of which reflect historical issues. These issues revolve around the ways in which to participate and enact meaningful change whilst positioned within traditional power bases. However, in many ways the relationship between men and women here conveys men's confusion regarding women's expectations: the women can articulate a deeper understanding of the issues (there is no confusion of the outcome of Miller's return for them) but they are unable to enforce or consistently articulate a resolution. Simultaneously women desire men to act as their protectors, to make the town safe for them, but when pressed about whether they are prepared to forfeit their status as wives to be widows they are unprepared, or unsure whether, they can fully commit. Ultimately the message conveyed here is of men's uncertainty regarding the nature of their roles and the ways in which to perform their own gender, divided as they are between economic, occupational, gender, moral and ideological factors which have fractured their idea of what hegemonic masculinity is and how it can be demonstrated.

---

37   Robert Warshow, 'Movie Chronicle: The Westerner', in *The American West on Film: Myth and Reality*, ed. Richard A. Maynard (Hasbrouck Heights, NJ: Hayden Book Company Inc., 1974), 65.

In this narrative a distinctly historical gender bind is conceptualized: a masculinity torn between violent confrontation and breadwinning for its self-definition. Men in this narrative use women as an alibi for their non-performance of violence in favour of breadwinning and the threat the townsmen pose to women, widowhood, is primarily an economic one. The women are able to understand the political situation, they do want moral action even if it does entail violence, but their capacity to act is limited by the patriarchal structures within which they are sustained and from which they derive ideological power: the family. Michael Kimmel asserts that definitions of masculinity in the post-World War II period were marked by the struggle between breadwinning and maintaining a sense of personal autonomy and ultimately it can be argued that it is this struggle that *High Noon* presents.[38] Finding this gender balance for men was compounded contextually both by the attempted reintegration of war veterans, who were forced to sublimate the privileged values of violence during wartime in favour of breadwinning, along with the continued privileging of 'hawk' values associated with the Cold War and military action in Korea.[39] To the extent that breadwinning also relies on the feminine retreat into domesticity and financial dependence this gender bind also exists for women. This film reflects upon a context wherein the reality of women's experiences of greater public participation in economic, political and educative arenas, and their disillusionment with gender restrictions, collided within ideological expectations regarding appropriate forms of their gendered behaviour.[40] *High Noon*, then, represents the complex gender contestations occurring in the Western past regarding men's and women's roles in order to create connections with its present, in so doing rendering complex historical understandings of both periods.

Amy attempts to dissuade Kane from his task even though she is sure of which status she would rather: she 'will not wait an hour to find out if I

---

38   Michael Kimmel, *Manhood in America*, 156–157.
39   See, for example, K.A. Cuordileone, "Politics in an Age of Anxiety': Cold War Political Culture and the Crisis in American Masculinity, 1949–1960', *The Journal of American History* 87 (2000): 515.
40   Cuordileone, 'Politics in the Age of Anxiety', 527–528.

am a wife or a widow.' She would rather leave and, just as she cannot sway Kane, neither will she be swayed. Much has been made of Grace Kelly's portrayal of Amy as being negative and stereotypical: 'with her hysterical fears and her womanish mores', Amy presents a story of woman's inability to comprehend masculinity and ultimately she capitulates to man's superior knowledge.[41] Indeed, when questioned on the subject of *High Noon* being a film 'with strong women and weak men' Zinnemann confessed to 'never [having] thought about that before [...] she [Amy] was quite blank as a human being. Like a piece of paper that had not been written on yet.'[42] Criticism surrounding women's roles in the film tends to centre around two 'problems' with Amy's characterization: the idea of her lack of knowledge and her ultimate capitulation to Kane. In particular theorists have pointed out that, aside from the stereotypical garb of virginal white wedding gown, suggestive of her inexperience and her place within the stereotypical virgin Madonna representation, Amy lacks deeper, masculine knowledge necessary to comprehend the true situation facing the town. This is demonstrated in her repeated questioning of, and failure to understand, why Kane must fight despite never actually receiving an explanation from him. This in turn frames her as a woman unable to comprehend the public responsibilities of men. However, Amy reveals to the audience via a conversation with Helen, who advocates but never demonstrates an intimate knowledge of gunplay, that she has seen the impact of such violence. It was witnessing the murder of her father and teenaged brother that spurred her to become a Quaker. By sharing her past Amy demonstrates that she does have a deeper knowledge and this deeper knowledge has highlighted for her the incompatibility of her own ideals with the patriarchal system in operation around her. Ultimately her experiences have impressed upon her that, although she cannot escape patriarchy, she must minimize her engagement with its destructive forms, in this case the enactment of hegemonic masculinity through violence (see Figure 2).

41   Barsness, 'A Question of Standard', 33.
42   Alan Marcus & Fred Zinnemann, 'Uncovering an Auteur: Fred Zinnemann', *Film History* 12 (2000): 55.

Figure 2: Amy Kane (Grace Kelly) and Helen Ramirez (Katy Jurado), planning to leave town together in *High Noon*.

It should be mentioned that Amy is not the only person to express his or her lack of understanding of Kane's commitment to action: Deputy Harvey confronts Kane about why he did not recommend him to be the next Marshal. To this Kane responds that 'if you don't know I ain't got time to tell you.' The response parallels Kane's earlier responses to Amy, but the audience has learned that Amy is aware of why Kane is pursuing his quest, her questioning is a deeper one regarding why Kane feels so entrenched within his current predicament seeing violent confrontation as the only solution and himself as the only person capable of enacting it. Harvey is simply unreflexive and, as Helen acknowledges, childish. It is the juxtaposition between these two types of questioning that highlights Amy's deeper understanding of the situation.

It is also important to acknowledge that the portrayal of Amy highlights the capacity to translate deeper knowledge into personal identity and political philosophy. Reference is made frequently to Amy's Quakerism and its impact: Amy will require Kane to leave his profession and become a storekeeper; when Kane seeks aid from churchgoers Amy's choice of a civil rather than church service for their wedding on that very day is highlighted and an added reason for his marginalization; and, more broadly, the frequent reference to her pacifism alludes to her political choices. Most telling of all, when Amy discusses the reasons for her Quakerism with Helen (revealing her family tragedy), the script actually included the line, which was omitted from the final cut: 'back home they think I'm very strange. I'm a feminist.'[43] By compounding gender and political identity in this way the film alludes to the disparity and diversity of gender performance. The film also connects this gender performance with history: Amy's 'feminism' connects peace movements and women's rights movements of the past with then contemporary 1940s and 1950s peace and rights movements, and the struggle to establish authentic women's voices within rather than external to existing gender orders. The compounding nature of Amy's political and gendered identity also renders complex the notion that white women in Western films embody the same values and are automatically accepted within white settlements.

Moreover, a number of other Westerns of this period point to this greater knowledge amongst women. For example, in *The Fastest Gun Alive* (Russell Rouse, 1956), Dora (Jeanne Crain), the wife of the title character, George Temple (Glenn Ford), is the only person (including George) who anticipates George's behaviour and the underlying anger and fear that motivates him, and is also prepared to leave him for his own lack of insight and commitment to meaningful change of his desire to obtain a hegemonic (violent) masculinity. In *Butch Cassidy and the Sundance Kid* (George Roy Hill, 1969), Etta acknowledges the inevitability of the title character's death entrenched as they are within their gender performance and elects to leave them. Rachel Warren (Inger Stevens), in *Hang 'Em High* (Ted Post, 1968), ultimately recognizes the nihilism of her own quest for revenge in direct contrast to the central character, Jed (Clint Eastwood) who continues his all-consuming and meaningless pursuit of his attackers.

---

43   As noted by Gwendolyn Foster, 'The Women in *High Noon*: A Metanarrative of Difference', *Film Criticism* 18–19 (1994): 79.

Finally Cresta (Candice Bergen) from *Soldier Blue* (Ralph Nelson, 1970) is the vehicle chosen to expose Indigenous experiences and suffering during the period of white landed conquest and frontier settlement, which results in her voluntary exile from white society.[44] The argument here is that women in Western films do no simply act as signifiers, rather they often present a deeper understanding of societal issues, a deeper understanding that is usually attributed to the masculine realm.

Tellingly it is their self-conscious gender performance that is expressly indicative of this understanding. This is because such self-conscious gender performance requires an understanding of hegemonic power bases and expectations and a capacity to exploit or subvert these expectations, which in turn requires an understanding of the ways in which power operates within society. This deeper understanding typically reveals the inadequacy of patriarchal institutions and the inadequacy of men to enact meaningful change, trapped as they are within the hierarchy of masculine gender performance and lacking critical reflection regarding these hierarchies and what they mean for the individual lived experience.[45] For these women, then, the option becomes how either to perform their own gender so as best to meet their own needs or to withdraw from the power play of hegemonic and self-regulating masculinity, rather than how they themselves may change this system. Historically, these films connect the ideas surrounding women's rights movements during the filmic context and the represented time to reflect on the ways in which they highlight the inadequacy of patriarchal institutions and the embodiment of these ideas in personal masculinity and in the construction of a state. However, they do not present a true alternative to this system, rather reflecting a 'patriarchal equilibrium' by which

---

44   Of course this carries questionable implications regarding the capacity of a white woman to truly represent Native American experiences.

45   It is interesting to consider the ways in which class consciousness typically occurs in those who are disadvantaged within the class system while class is invisible to those privileged by it. In a similar way it could be argued that those men who have found themselves privileged by their gender identity find gender an invisible category until they find their status threatened in some way. Women, inherently situated outside of patriarchal authority may have developed greater gender consciousness precisely because of this.

patriarchy maintains its dominance despite the transformative potential of mass change.[46]

Amy's 'capitulation' at the end of the film – where importantly it is she who saves Kane and the town – suggests that she has simply come to the conclusion that the patriarchal system binds her too, particularly if she elects to participate in normative institutions such as marriage. This capitulation is not one sided, however: the ballad of *High Noon*, 'Do Not Forsake Me' (incidentally, the first theme song ever released before the film itself),[47] played throughout the film, is an ode to Kane's emotional reliance on Amy. Consider, for example, the lyrics: 'Do not forsake me O my darlin'/ On this our wedding day/ [...] O to be torn 'twixt love and duty/S'posin' I lose my fair-haired beauty! [...] I'm not afraid of death, but O'/What will I do if you leave me?' It is not the rejection of the town that causes Kane anguish but rather it is Amy exercising her right to forsake him.

Nevertheless, the notion of capitulation has been a long-standing issue related to women's roles in Western films more generally. For example, a negative critique regarding capitulation has also been made of Barbara Stanyck's character, Jessica Drummond, in the 1957 film *Forty Guns* (Samuel Fuller). Adding to Stanwyck's oeuvre of challenging female roles and a reputation for performing her own stunts in Westerns, *Forty Guns* (originally – and tellingly – to be called 'Woman With A Whip'), Drummond is presented as a fiery and independent cattle baron and leader of forty hired guns.[48] Her domination of Cochise County, Arizona, and the illegal activities of her brother, Brockie (John Ericson), bring her into conflict with the marshal, Griff (Barry Sullivan), with whom she ultimately falls in love. The film ends somewhat ambiguously: Griff shoots Jessica when she is taken hostage in order to kill Brockie, who has become violently out of control, and the film finishes with Jessica, recovered from her wounds, telling Griff that she could not be with the man that murdered her brother. When Griff

---

46   Judith M. Bennett, *History Matters: Patriarchy and the Challenge of Feminism* (Manchester: Manchester University Press, 2006), 77–81.

47   Lerner, "Look at That Big Hand Move Along", 153.

48   See, for example, Sandra Schackel, 'Barbara Stanwyck: Uncommon Heroine', *California History* 72 (1993): 40–55.

departs, however, she chases after his wagon and he stops, allowing her to board. Her capitulation to Griff, complete with white costume in contrast to her black riding garb, is seen as confirmation of the theme song of the film, 'High Ridin' Woman': 'she's a high ridin' woman with a whip […] but if someone could break her and take her whip away, someone big, someone strong, someone tall, you may find that the woman with a whip is only a woman after all' (see Figure 3).

Figure 3: Jessica Drummond (Barbara Stanwyck) is a woman with a whip in *Forty Guns*.

However, this ignores Jessica's central observation to Griff when they discuss their mutual love: 'the frontier is finished. There are no more towns to break. No more men to break. It's time you started to break yourself.' For Fuller, to love is analogous to breaking and it is love, not gender, that changes behaviour. For example, the farmhand Logan, whose love is spurned by Drummond, immediately commits suicide; a wedding becomes a central scene for a gun battle, and it is Jessica and Griff's love for both of their brothers that limits and controls each of their actions. The point here is that although some Westerns may feature the capitulation of female characters to love, or to the will of the central male character, this does not equate simply to a feminine weakness or lack of knowledge or understanding of the public realm and the man's duty within it. Indeed, often it can point to the opposite, or an encompassing mutual reliance between characters, that is not gender specific. Ultimately, by placing these Western films in a hyper-linear context we can see that they attempt to provide resolution in gendered crisis points in the American past and provide insight into then-contemporary gender issues. Some films may attempt to resolve this conflict by establishing a positive hyper-linear relationship that sees women willingly capitulate to men's needs and reaffirm traditional ideas of a gendered dichotomy, for others such as *High Noon* though such capitulation is rendered complex or impossible and the historical connections between past and present far murkier.

The other central female character in *High Noon* is Helen Ramirez who, as a Mexican attired in a black corset, is visually stereotypical of the negative female archetype. Other attributes quickly supplement this perspective: we are introduced to Helen in the company of her lover, Deputy Harvey; we learn of her previous sexual liaisons with both Kane and Miller; and, Helen's ethnicity is strongly accentuated by her accent and her displays of Latino passion. Yet, despite this, Zinnemann goes about subverting this stereotype. For Zinnemann the character of Helen was: 'strong alright [...] [possessing] tremendous vitality, great dignity above everything else [...] she was Mother Earth.'[49] Firstly, Helen is capable of demarcating and enforcing the boundaries around her in both a physical and metaphorical sense. Physically, Helen explicitly asserts her control of her own body, telling Harvey when he attempts to grab her arm after they separate that: 'I don't like anyone to put his hands on me unless I want him to and I don't want you to anymore.' Moreover access to Helen is constantly monitored by the hotel clerk and an assistant and she can thereby control who has contact with her with the sole exception being the threat posed by Miller when he returns and discovers her liaisons with both Kane and Harvey. She refuses to have control placed upon her either through male protection offered by Harvey or through Miller himself, stating 'I can take care of myself', and, ultimately, her decision to leave the town is one of business rather than fear for her body. Metaphorically, the relationship between Helen's ability to maintain boundaries between her body, men, business and the town more broadly highlights the inherent contradiction embodied in many gender performances of an earlier period (for example,

49   Marcus and Zinnemann, 'Uncovering an Auteur', 55.

the conflict in *She Wore a Yellow Ribbon* [John Ford, 1949]). Specifically, this contradiction is the idea that racial 'others' are simultaneously exiled or segregated from the mainstream of society but still desire acceptance from that society and usually strive for this through competition for the male lead, a competition they inevitably lose. In contrast Helen embodies a gender performance that, intersecting with her race, does not accept that society imposes restrictions upon her; rather, she maintains boundaries between herself and society, and she refuses to engage combatively for acceptance within society presented in the form of Kane's love or desire. That is, she openly tells Amy that Kane is not hers (provocatively inverting the concept of male ownership over the feminine) and she will not fight with or for him; indeed she reveals that she has had no contact with Kane since their separation.

Secondly, just as Amy acknowledges the way in which her political affiliation impacts upon her gender performance, Helen is conscious of the compounding nature of different facets of her identity. For example, Helen states: 'I hate this town [...] to be a Mexican woman in a town like this.' Helen understands that her relationship with the town has always been mediated not by her gender alone but also by her race and economic status: she is a financially independent Mexican woman and a 'fallen woman' and as such is situated outside of normative feminine ideals; she would not be accepted by other white women in a small town. Subsequently, this denial of insight into the private domain has afforded her an understanding of the public domain and the men that inhabit it, a view supported by her business partner who, when she sells him her share for two thousand dollars in an efficient and decisive manner, bids her farewell with the comment that at the beginning of their business partnership 'you know my wife thought ...' He trails off, recognizing the sensitivity of the issue, and concludes that Helen had always been fair and good to him. Ultimately, then, Helen must leave town, not because she is a woman and due to her previous relationships with Kane and Miller may be harmed, but because as an unwed Mexican woman she has been forced to maintain her financial independence and, with the threat posed by Miller to the financial viability of the town and her stake in the public realm gone, she has no reason to stay.

The portrayal of femininity and the notion that it contributes to a demasculinization of men is not made solely through the characterization of these women, but also through the relationship between them. The interaction between Amy and Helen begins when Amy decides to wait for the noon train in the foyer of the town hotel, considering it to be safer than the station where the Miller gang had made veiled comments about her. As she waits she witnesses her new husband visit Helen's room and, through a conversation with a belligerent clerk who holds a grudge against Kane, the nature of their previous association, of which Amy was unaware, is revealed. Rather than reacting negatively Amy visits Helen to ask whether Kane is staying for her. Her interest is not how a relationship between Helen and Kane impacts on her situation but rather how it will impact on Kane's safety and from a desire to truly understand a motivation for violence. In asking this question Amy acknowledges the power of female gender performance to both subversively stimulate male violence (to shape masculine gender performance itself) and to contain subversion by feeding into hegemonic standards of masculinity. What Amy is asking, in effect, is whether Helen is 'that kind of woman', a question that Helen explicitly returns when she questions why Amy would not stay and fight with Kane: 'What kind of woman are you?' It is important to note that the first and primary way in which Helen and Amy assess each other is through their performance of gender and the differences in their perspectives on gender are elaborated on and explained through personal experience. In so doing Helen and Amy both acknowledge the foundational nature of gender and their commonality as women even whilst acknowledging differences in identity, performance and experience. Through sharing their personal accounts these women are able to accommodate difference into their shared identity as women, and to use this to build a gendered bond that allows them to leave the town together on the noon train. It is this bond, rather than the bond of marriage alone, that provides Amy with a model of alternate feminine gender performance that allows her to flee the noon train and save Kane's life.

Gwedolyn Foster ultimately concluded in her evaluation of the intersections of race and gender embodied in Amy and Helen's relationship, that the 'possibility for consistent sisterhood across racial lines is an impossibility.'[50] However, it can be argued that the converse is true: this relationship explores the possibility for sisterhood by the way in which the characters explore the links between race, gender performance and personal relationships. This particularly occurs in the sense that both characters acknowledge the connection between race and gender as intertwined, that is, that their race allows them to perform their gender in different ways. In this way gender and race are not distinct categories but mutually informing. *High Noon* is not the only film in this era to deal with the intersections of feminine gender performance and race, issues which are further explored in Chapter 4. It does, however, go some way to illustrating the diversity of women's attitudes, experiences, forms of identity and methods of performing gender identities in ways that meet their needs in a distinctly historical way.

Conclusion

Ultimately despite the dissimilarities between Amy and Helen in *High Noon*, most prominently racial and visual, these are matched by the similarities in their understandings of the ways in which they perform gender: both find their gender identity compounded and complicated (and their place within Hadleyville jeopardized) by other factors, namely political identification and race; both recognize that the relationships they have with men do not detract from their autonomy; both recognize that they need to perform different types of femininity depending upon the context and that such performance is necessary to meet their needs; and, importantly, both are able to reach an understanding of their gender unity despite any differences, an understanding that verges upon sisterhood. They do so in the face of men who exhibit only confusion regarding desired gender forms and who are stifled by indecisiveness and ineffectiveness.

50   Foster, 'The Women in *High Noon*', 79.

An exploration of the roles of women in Western films of this period, with a focus on the film *High Noon*, provides a great deal of insight into the way in which emergent gender movements destabilized hegemonic understandings of what it is to enact hegemonic masculinity, with a resulting demasculinization of men. Examining women's representations in this period reveals female portrayals that are more complex and varied than the usual archetypal labels applied to women in these films. It reveals a repositioning of women that reflects then contemporary changes to the gender order and connects these to women's movements in the American West in a hyper-linear fashion. However, *High Noon* reveals a structure of negative continuity with neither men nor women able to successfully pose an alternative to destructive, hegemonic gender forms.

'You're the party done all the suffering': Representing Stereotypes of Native Americans in the 'Pro-Indian' Western Cycle

While Mexican characters populate Western films, perhaps the most visible and recognized Western subgenre to explore the intersections between race and gender are those films that feature relations between Native Americans and European Americans. This analysis will focus on the representations of Native Americans and 'native–white' relations in the so-called 'pro-Indian' Western cycle, with a particular focus on two films: *The Unforgiven* (John Huston, 1960) and *Soldier Blue* (Ralph Nelson, 1970). On the surface it appears these films have little in common except for the central theme of how white society copes with 'Indian issues' and for their placement within the broader cycle of films centred on relations between Native Americans and European Americans. However, both films do use similar devices to express vastly different racial ideas, and as such they are extremely pertinent to a discussion of the historicity of stereotype and the capacity of racialized representation to pose a challenge to patriarchal social structures. Both films use strategies such as female characters to mediate between Native American and white societies; 'the man who knows Indians' stereotype either used or subverted in the portrayal of the central male protagonists; an older male figure who is a harbinger of different societal attitudes and a catalyst for change; violence and its significance at both the individual and governmental level; the questioning of who and/or what is 'unforgiven' in society; and, most significantly, the connections between race, belonging and gender identity. This chapter suggests that these films present stereotypes that are deeply historical and chart developments in US racial attitudes. In particular, *The Unforgiven*, released in 1960, adopts a 'colour blind' approach to race relations, suggesting that racial prejudice can be overcome by individuals and, therefore, that white masculinity can adapt to survive racial challenges. Such an attitude aligned with then-contemporary answers to pressing racial challenges. However, by *Soldier Blue*, released in 1970, the redemption of white masculinity became increasingly impossible and the portrayal of a violent, landed conquest of Native Americans is brought to the fore in order to parallel a discourse of racial difference at home and an increasing disillusionment with American policies and practices abroad. In particular many rights-based groups were pointing not to assimilationist approaches but rather to cultural practices, identity and power separate from white attitudes, an approach also stimulated by the impacts of the Vietnam War.

This chapter discusses the ways in which these films convey different approaches to race and how these films draw upon the past experiences of racial policies in order to gain insight into contemporary racial issues. It examines how both films use similar themes and stereotypes with a particular view to understanding the ways in which they reflect a white hegemonic masculinity adapting to the demands of racial minorities over time. In particular, these films construct hyper-linear links between their present and the represented past (post-Civil War and the Sand Creek massacre of 1864 respectively) in order to impress the long-standing links between racial policy, gender identity and patriarchy over time. The challenge posed by racial minorities, in this instance Native Americans, can be seen as one factor in the broader process of men's demasculinization in the 1950s and 1960s, which these films connect in hyper-linear fashion to the represented past. There are three sections in what follows: the first provides an overview of literature regarding the Native American stereotype in the pro-Indian Westerns of this period; the second examines the nature of representation and stereotyping in *The Unforgiven* and *Soldier Blue* with a view to analysing change and continuity over time; and the third relates this representation to the intricacies of historical context.

Interpreting the Pro-Indian Western Cycle

The 1950 film *Broken Arrow* (Delmer Davies) is generally seen as the start of the so-called 'pro-Indian cycle' of Westerns. *Broken Arrow* starred James Stewart as Tom Jeffords, a man trying to broker peace between whites and Cochise Native Americans in a post-Civil War context. It was marked by a seemingly increased sympathy to the plight of Native Americans and by greater screen time and character development of Indigenous characters, characteristics of the broader 'pro-Indian' Western subgenre of this period that lasted until the most iconographic 'pro-Indian' films: *Little Big Man* (Arthur Penn, 1970) and *Soldier Blue* (Ralph Nelson, 1970). This thematic cycle had a mini-resurgence in the early 1990s with the production of films such as *Dances with Wolves* (Kevin Costner, 1990), *Last of the Mohicans* (Michael Mann, 1992), *Geronimo: An American Legend* (Walter Hill, 1994) and *Dead Man* (Jim Jarmusch, 1995). Rick Worland and Edward Countryman argue in their analysis of American historiography that 'New Western' history is centrally characterized by the acceptance of the frontier as an already occupied space and, certainly, this theme and its occasional acknowledgement, with associated moral complications also characterized so-called 'pro-Indian' Westerns. Native Americans are shown to occupy and use the land distinctively and to resist white settlement and conquest of the continent.[1] Such a theme subverts traditional conceptualizations of the Western as an uncomplicated site of white male conquest of the savage land and the 'savage Other'. However, the extent to which such a cycle actually functions in a subversive manner to effectively challenge notions of Manifest Destiny, divine right and the inevitability of white conquest, or, moreover, to represent the diversity of Native American experiences, lifestyles and cultures, is contested.

1   Rick Worland and Edward Countryman, 'The New Western Historiography and the Emergence of the New American Westerns', in *Back in the Saddle Again: New Essays on the Western*, eds Edward Buscombe and Roberta E. Pearson (London: British Film Industry, 1998), 185.

John A. Price, writing in 1973, perceived the pro-Indian cycle of the
1950s and 1960s as a major rupture in the history of the Western film in the
sense that such films sought to break down existing negative stereotypes of
Native Americans. Price qualifies this perspective, stating that this cycle put
forward other negative stereotypes regarding Indian-hating whites pitted
against 'the Indian-wise hero', and the continuing problems of white casting in Indigenous roles, as well as the fictionalization of Native American
cultural practices. However, for Price, *Broken Arrow* signalled the recognition of Native Americans 'as people with a legitimate culture, [and that]
cases of stupidity and bigotry [occurred] on both sides in cultural conflict'
justifying the title of a truly 'pro-Indian' cycle.[2] In contrast some critics
suggest that the pro-Indian cycle acts to reflect upon contextual concerns
regarding the African American Civil Rights Movement, anti-Vietnam
movements, and a growing awareness of anti-colonialism and American
interventionism abroad. From this perspective pro-Indian films actually
have little to do with Native Americans or with the represented historical
past; rather Native American representations simply function as a 'stand in'
for other marginalized racial groups and their then-modern group politics.[3]
Obviously such a perspective raises a number of questions. How is it that
one racial group can simply be substituted for another without causing
the audience to connect with and question the experiences of the group
actually represented? Is there something unique about Native American
stereotype that allows representations of this group to function only as
signifiers of the present?[4]

2   John A. Price, 'The Stereotyping of North American Indians in Motion Pictures',
     Ethnohistory 20 (1973): 161, 160.
3   See, for example: Richard Maltby, 'A Better Sense of History: John Ford and the
     Indians', in *The Movie Book of the Western*, eds Ian Cameron and Douglas Pye
     (London: Studio Vista 1996), 36; John H. Lenihan, *Showdown: Confronting Modern
     America in the Western Film* (Chicago: University of Illinois Press, 1980), 55–89.
4   For a comprehensive overview of the intricacies of this debate see Steve Neale,
     'Vanishing Americans: Racial and Ethnic Issues in the Interpretation and Context
     of Post-war 'Pro-Indian' Westerns', in *Back in the Saddle Again: New Essays on the
     Western*, eds Edward Buscombe and Roberta E. Pearson (London: British Film
     Institute, 1998), 8–28.

Others, while sympathetic to the notion that the 'pro-Indian' cycle genuinely attempted to critique white/Native American interactions, representations and understandings, highlight the difficulty of any film being able to do so adequately considering both that they participate in the dominant discourse which inherently privileges white patriarchal perspectives and, also, that a film only seems revisionist in the context of previous filmic contributions and are soon outmoded by new contributions.[5] Mary Katherine Hall asserts:

> There is a long history of Westerns positioning themselves against previous Westerns, claiming to present a newly sympathetic and realistic view of Indian culture and new condemnation of white conquest, only to find themselves a generation or two later the traditional Western against which new ones are positioned.[6]

Reinforcing this argument, filmographical representations mirror the ways in which historiographical orthodoxies are established and subsequently superseded by new knowledge, understandings and modes of comprehension. Therefore, just as Western films have moved away from uncomplicated examinations of white men's experiences to a narrative structure more inclusive of different perspectives and more critical of hegemonic masculinity and patriarchal structures, so too have 'New Western' histories superseded Turnerian exclusivity. It is pertinent here to consider film as not only a mimic of this historiographical process but as an active participant in it. Film, as social barometer, has the capacity to stimulate and shape historiographical trends as well as to reflect changes in academic thought.

Hall's argument regarding the nature of Westerns, though, suggests that the subversive potential of such films is curtailed by the fact that their point of view is mediated through white experiences and therefore they do little to upset existing stereotypes of Native Americans but add new

5   See, for example, Mary Katherine Hall, 'Now You are a Killer of White Men: Jim Jarmusch's *Dead Man* and traditions of revisionism in the Western', *Journal of Film and Video* 52 (2001): 3–14.

6   Mary Katherine Hall, 'Now You are a Killer of White Men', 3.

stereotypes of white men.[7] In this instance, stereotypes of Native American culture as vanishing, of perfect and noble Indians doomed to loss, of the white hero who knows Indian culture and transcends the racism of white culture to mediate between Native Americans and the audience, and the stereotype of prejudiced white settlers, populate the pro-Indian cycle in ways little different from previous or future films centred on Native American experiences.[8] To extend upon this perspective it could be argued that the term 'pro-Indian' is fallacious in that it does not reflect the ways in which potential subversion is limited by the dramatic, commercial and political considerations of the mainstream film-making industry, wherein the primary aim is to appeal to the sentiments of a predominantly white movie-going audience. In this way stereotypes may be replaced or modernized to cater to majority audience tastes but they cannot be divorced from the white, capitalist, patriarchal structure from which they are produced and, therefore, can never truly represent the interests or perspectives of a minority group.[9] Ultimately, despite a cycle of films that focuses to a remarkable extent on the interactions between whites and Native Americans, often in new ways, scholarly discourse surrounding these representations has focused overwhelmingly on either Indian as allegory (and therefore essentially absent or empty of intrinsic meaning) or on the representations of

7   Hall, 'Now You are a Killer of White Men', 3–14.
8   For works containing examinations of some or all of these stereotypes see: Ralph E. Friar and Natasha A. Friar, *The Only Good Indian … The Hollywood Gospel* (New York: Drama Book Specialists/Publishers, 1972); John E. O'Connor, *The Hollywood Indian: Stereotypes of Native Americans in Films* (Trenton, NJ: New Jersey State Museum, 1980), 8–13; Price, 'The Stereotyping of North American Indians in Motion Pictures', 160–161; Hall, 'Now You are a Killer of White Men', 8–12; Maryann Oshana, 'Native American Women in Westerns: Reality and Myth', *A Journal of Women Studies* 6 (1981): 47–48.
9   See, for example, O'Connor, *The Hollywood Indian*, 3–13. It is important to note that some see the possibility to challenge dominant discourse through independent Native American filmmakers, more employment opportunities for Native Americans in a diversity of film-making positions, and through the vehicles of documentary and independent film-making. See, for example, S. Elizabeth Bird, 'Gendered Construction of the American Indian in Popular Media', *Journal of Communication* 49 (2006): 77–78.

minority groups as fundamentally flawed and stereotypical (and therefore largely ahistorical).

'Say something pretty': Representation, Stereotypes and Race Relations in *The Unforgiven* and *Soldier Blue*

While accepting the fundamental notion that the portrayal of Indians is couched in terms of stereotype and mediated through white, patriarchal discourse, this chapter extends the discussion in two major ways: firstly, it historicizes stereotypes – that is, it examines the ways in which stereotypes can and do evolve over time in a way that is fluid and reflective of changing historical understandings of the past and the ways in which that past relates to present experiences. By examining stereotypes in their complexity, deployed in a range of ways for a variety of purposes that can be both conservative and subversive, and intimately connected with history, the analysis contributes to a greater understanding and deconstruction of stereotype in general.[10] Specifically this chapter explores the ways in which stereotypical representations of Native Americans and whites are deployed in *The Unforgiven* (John Huston, 1960) and *Soldier Blue* (Ralph Nelson, 1970). Although both films use stereotypes regarding the 'vanishing Indian' and the 'hero who knows Indians', these stereotypes are used in different ways and to express very different racial ideas. The first advocates for the possibility of an integrationist and colour-blind approach to race

10   It should be noted that this aim of historicizing stereotypical representations of racial minorities has already been explored by the author in a co-authored article regarding African American stereotypes in two 'social message' films of the Civil Rights era. See: Emma Hamilton & Troy Saxby, "Draggin' the Chain': Linking Civil Rights and African American Representation in *The Defiant Ones* and *In the Heat of the Night*', *Black Camera* 3 (2011): 75–95, which was subsequently re-printed in Ian Gregory Strachan and Mia Mask (eds), *Poitier Revisited: Reconsidering a Black Icon in the Obama Age* (New York: Bloomsbury, 2015), 73–96.

relations by appealing to a discourse of racial sameness whilst the second clearly sees this as an impossibility. Certainly this example demonstrates then-contemporary shifts in racial ideas surrounding the African American Civil Rights Movement but it also, significantly, connects to shifting policies regarding Native American rights in the same era, which are also discussed. More than this, representations are connected to a long view of conflict over racial ideas regarding both Native Americans and other racial minorities in the Civil War context. In creating this hyper-linear connection between policies of the Civil War context and the Civil Rights era these films make complex and often subversive statements regarding the disparity between American ideals of equality and their practical implementation over time.

Secondly, and interconnectedly, this chapter examines stereotypes largely in terms of how they reflect upon the changing nature of white masculinity during periods of clear pressure on hegemonic, racialized and patriarchal institutions manifest in individual gender performances. Clearly these films are mediated by discourses of white male power and to frame the examination of stereotype in such a manner seems a logical extension of the films themselves. When examined in this context these films reveal the ongoing struggle of white masculinities to adapt to changing ideas of race and racial oppression, and its associated questioning of the capacity of America to truly enact its values, in both the represented past and the contemporary social setting of the film's production context.

There are several important reasons for specifically including *The Unforgiven* and *Soldier Blue* here. Despite starring several of the most iconic stars of its era in Burt Lancaster, Audrey Hepburn and Audie Murphy, *The Unforgiven* has largely been overlooked both popularly and in academic analysis in favour of *The Searchers* (John Ford, 1956), which examines similar themes of race, family and inter-racial captivity narratives.[11] Moreover

---

11   This theme is however inverted, with *The Unforgiven* framed around a Native American woman raised by white settlers and *The Searchers* featuring a white woman raised by Native Americans, a man of 'mixed blood' raised by whites and a white-Indian marriage that is intended for comedic effect, though the execution of this is extremely unsuccessful. Both films are based on novels by Alan LeMay. See: Brian Henderson, "The Searchers': An American Dilemma', *Film Quarterly* 34 (1980–1981):

The Unforgiven has largely been conceptualized as extremely conservative and difficult to incorporate into any 'pro-Indian' sensibility. Indeed, this understates the vehemence with which some commentators have responded to the film, for example, Maryann Oshana suggested that 'the negative racial and sexual overtones of this film are overwhelming', and Ralph and Natasha Friar argue that it is 'probably the most anti-Native American film ever made.'[12] It is also a film that keenly illustrates the contrasting impetuses of commercial and production spheres and directorial intent. By the time *The Unforgiven* was released, director John Huston was already a noted liberal, as were several other key players including Lancaster and scriptwriter Ben Maddow.[13] Ultimately, however, Huston denounced *The Unforgiven*, declaring his decision to direct the picture a 'mistake' that compromised his artistic vision. As he stated in his autobiography, 'I wanted to turn it into the story of racial intolerance in a frontier town, a comment on the real nature of community "morality". The trouble was the producers disagreed. What they wanted was [...] a swashbuckler about a larger-than-life frontiersman.'[14]

In a comment that is highly ironic considering the plot revolves around an adopted child, Huston himself suggested that his agreement to direct was from the outset a flawed one, considering that he had no input into the script itself and, because of this, 'I never feel that the film is mine. At best it's an adopted child.'[15] In contrast *Soldier Blue* has been largely well received despite its ground-breakingly, explicit depictions of violence, with

---

9–23. For a general study of Ford's rendering of Native Americans see Tag Gallager, 'John Ford's Indians', *Film Comment* 29 (1993): 68–72.

12   Oshana, 'Native American Women in Westerns', 49; Friar & Friar, *The Only Good Indian*, 241.

13   Neale, 'Vanishing Americans', 16.

14   John Huston, *An Open Book* (London: Alfred A. Knopf, 1980), 283. Dan LeMay provides several examples of the ways in which the film script deviated from the book with the intention of emphasizing racism in *Alan LeMay: A Biography of the author of The Searchers* (Jefferson: McFarland and Company, 2012), 176–177. Ultimately Dan LeMay soundly criticized the film, *Alan LeMay*, 178.

15   Gerald Pratley, *The Cinema of John Huston* (Cranbury, NJ: A.S. Barnes & Co., 1977), 124.

its appeals to historical authenticity, the break out performance by Candice
Bergen, and relevance to contemporary audiences. The film was largely
conceived as an attempt to create parallels between the Sand Creek massacre of 1864 and the My Lai massacre, perpetrated by American forces in
Vietnam in 1968, and therefore perpetuated the idea that Native American
issues were simply a 'stand in' – in this instance for Vietnamese experiences.[16]

In a somewhat convoluted post-Civil War plot *The Unforgiven* features
Audrey Hepburn as Rachel, a 'foundling' adopted by the Zacharys, a white,
middle-class ranching family. Will Zachary, the father who adopted and
raised Rachel is dead, his tombstone revealing that he was killed by 'Red
Indian Devils.' He is survived by sons Ben (Burt Lanchaster), Cash (Audie
Murphy) and Andy (Doug McClure) and his widow, Matthilda (Lillian
Gish). The family works together in partnership with their neighbours,
the Rawlins, to breed and drive cattle from Texas to Wichita. Although
they discuss past and ongoing Indian threats their existence seems peaceful
until a mysterious ex-Confederate soldier, Abe Kelsey (Joseph Wiseman),
appears claiming that Rachel is in fact a Kiowa Indian. Ben refuses to
believe this is true despite seemingly irrefutable evidence: Rachel is visited
by Kiowa men, including her brother who asks for her return, and Kelsey
himself testifies before he is hung as a horse thief that he accompanied
Will Zachary on a revenge attack and witnessed his abduction of Rachel.
Eventually Matthilda confesses to having kept the secret after the Kiowa
leave parchments at their home recording Rachel's abduction. Refusing to
repudiate their relationship or return a willing Rachel to the Kiowa, Ben
loses his business with the Rawlins and racist Cash leaves home before
the Kiowa lay siege to their home intent on getting Rachel back. During
a protracted gun battle that kills Matthilda, Ben confesses his romantic
intentions towards Rachel, Cash rides to their rescue, and Rachel kills her
Kiowa brother, in so doing conclusively embracing the white family and
society that raised her. The film ends as it begins: with Rachel watching
geese flying in formation against the backdrop of blue skies.

16   Edward Buscombe, *'Injuns!' Native Americans in the Movies* (Cornwall: Reaktion
      Books, 2006), 133–134.

Soldier Blue, on the other hand, presents a white woman, Cresta Lee (Candice Bergen), whose period of captivity with the Cheyenne and marriage to their Chief, Spotted Wolf, has developed in her a sympathy and appreciation for their way of life and an antipathy towards the US military and government. The film picks up with Cresta, now retaken by white soldiers, being transported to a US cavalry camp for her impending arranged marriage to an officer. On the way the transport is attacked by Cheyenne who aim to steal the shipment of gold (not to retake Cresta). Twenty-one soldiers are killed but Cresta and sole military survivor, Honus Grant (Peter Strauss), escape and begin the journey to the camp on foot. Cresta's attitudes and outspokenness test Honus's patriotism and faith in the military but, after Honus kills attacking Indians and survives a bullet wound inflicted by a mad Indian trader, he and Cresta consummate their love affair. His wounded leg encourages Cresta to re-commence the journey alone although she knows that they will be unable to continue their affair once she makes her presence known to her betrothed. She arrives at the military camp only to be informed that no immediate aid will be sent to Honus as their resources are being devoted to an attack on the Cheyenne. Cresta, particularly horrified at the plans for an attack knowing the Cheyenne are unarmed, flees to warn them and the audience witnesses life in their camp. The remainder of the film focuses on the brutality of white conduct during what would become known as the 1864 Sand Creek massacre. Honus has made his own way back to camp and bears witness to the massacre as he searches for Cresta. Ultimately the brutality forces Honus to understand Cresta's point of view but the two lovers are separated with Honus, hysterical, chained and taken away for his objections to the battle, and Cresta wandering amongst the dead, her fate unknown.

It is important to negotiate the implications of these films being set in different time periods: *The Unforgiven* is set in post-Civil War society and produced in 1960 whilst *Soldier Blue* is set in 1864, during the Civil War, and released in 1970. These different temporal localities allow the films to use stereotypes in different ways and to communicate vastly different ideas about the racial rights movement that fundamentally threatened the place of white masculinity and broader American patriarchal solutions precisely because they call up different historical conditions and ideas. Specifically,

The Unforgiven, situated as it is in the seemingly immediate post-Civil War context, calls up the hopes for racial conciliation presented by the abolition of slavery. This embraces the general push for a more equitable society including citizenship status for Native Americans and the endorsement of an assimilationist stance as a solution to racial difference. Such a solution suggested 'the Indians must be civilized. The tribes would have no other choice but to perish so that the individual Indian might survive.'[17] The post-Civil War period more clearly relates to a 'colour-blind' approach to African Americans advocated in 1960 and implemented policies of assimilation for Native Americans, including termination, funded relocation programs to increase urban migration, and Native American movements for increased equality in terms of education, employment, and living standards.[18] In contrast, by positioning *Soldier Blue* within the Civil War setting the viewer is transported to a time of ongoing uncertainty, with conflict existing between contesting models of white masculinity and white society as well as ongoing conflict between, and segregation of, Indians and whites. In so doing, the film is clearly positioned to create a hyper-linear parallel with racial politics in 1970 when rights-based movements, including Native American 'Red Power' rights movements, increasingly sought self-determination and cultural respect, and increasingly reflected upon the Vietnam War as a signifier of the fundamental failure of the American government, and of white masculinity more generally.[19]

The primary character in both films, and the mediator between Indian and white experiences, is a woman: Rachel, a Native American-born woman unknowingly abducted as a child and raised by whites; and Cresta, a white woman who has been abducted by Cheyenne and, through marriage to a

17   Brian W. Dippie, *The Vanishing American: White Attitudes and US Indian Policy* (Middletown, CT: Wesleyan University Press, 1982), 97, 92.

18   Alison R. Bernstein, *American Indians and World War II: Toward a New Era in Indian Affairs* (Norman: University of Oklahoma Press, 1991), 158. See also Kenneth R. Philp, 'Termination: A Legacy of the Indian New Deal', *The Western Historical Quarterly* 14 (1983): 165–180.

19   Donald L. Parman, *Indians and the American West in the Twentieth Century* (Bloomington: Indiana University Press, 1994), 148–154.

Native American and betrothal to a white man, straddles the racial divide. The use of women as mediators of different experiences, regardless of any other factor, is highly significant in demonstrating the increasing fracture experienced by white hegemonic masculinity at this time. Susan Jeffords asserts that one of, if not the, primary tool used to reassert a hegemonic masculinity in post-Vietnam Vietnam War representations is the maintenance of the male collectivity between all men, even military enemies, because only men can understand the true nature of war and actively participate within it. In this way, Vietnam narratives deliberately exclude women as it is this maintenance of a strict gender binary which allows for other fracturing elements of identity, such as race, to disappear in favour of one unifying characteristic: masculinity and aspiration for its 'hard' forms.[20] For Jeffords, then, remasculinization is founded upon the rigorous maintenance of gender boundaries, which is '*the* difference on which these narratives and images depend because it is the single difference that is asserted as *not* participating in the confusion that characterizes other oppositions' [original emphasis].[21] In this period of demasculinization, however, what we see through these representations is a fracturing of the male collectivity to the point that only women, by virtue of their place outside of inter-masculine hierarchies and their heightened consciousness of gender performance as a group outside of traditional gender power bases, are capable of mediating between the experiences of opposing groups. However, both films communicate very different ideas regarding the nature of that mediation.

In *The Unforgiven* Rachel primarily functions as a facilitator between competing white interests, but also as the only significant link with a Native American world. It is her true racial identity that exposes the underlying fractures in the masculinity around her: she highlights the racism in Cash, some of the Rawlins family and Kelsey, which disrupts their previously harmonious business, familial and community relationships, clashing as it does with Ben's liberalism. She also exposes the fundamental racial tension between whites and Native Americans. In these ways Rachel facilitates an

---

20   Susan Jeffords, *The Remasculinization of America: Gender and the Vietnam* War (Bloomington: Indiana University Press, 1989), 57.
21   Jeffords, *The Remasculinization of America*, 53.

understanding of community founded in peaceful cohabitation as illusionary on a number of levels. Although the masculine bonds in this film, between brothers, business associates, friends and men (albeit warring men), are exposed as fractured along attitudes to race and racial equality, it is significant that an opportunity is offered to re-establish these masculine bonds: Mr Rawlins asks that Rachel be taken by the women, stripped naked and examined for signifiers of her Native American heritage. In making this request Rawlins exhibits the central tenets of remasculinization put forward by Jeffords: the re-establishment of masculine collectivity through the conscious maintenance of binary gender identity that separates men and women. Rawlins proposes to re-establish the collectivity between white men, and moreover, the dominance of all men over women in a broader sense, by highlighting Rachel's femininity. In doing so Rachel is positioned as property that can be traded between white and Indian men and, specifically as an Indian woman, whose racial affiliation must therefore be inherent Rawlins places her outside of white, masculine authority.

This request is rejected, however, making it impossible for such bonds to be reasserted and perpetuating the fracturing of masculinity along multiple lines of identity. Indeed, a similar incident occurs when Rachel applies soot to her face and makes to leave her white home to be with her Native American brother, despite the audience being aware of her romantic attachments to Ben. In this instance Rachel proposes to subsume her own desires to that of the broader patriarchy – to allow herself to be traded in exchange for peace among men. Ben will not allow this to take place, however, shooting an Indian bearing markers of peace, thereby setting in motion the final confrontation between warring groups. Although Ben's actions and Rachel's submission to them can be read as a stereotype – as little more than a signifier that a white man knows better than a Native American woman, and cannot see how her life can be enhanced through re-joining her original family – when read in the context of the whole film this is a difficult perspective to endorse. The film commences with Will Zachary's tombstone, signifying to the audience the ongoing nature of the white/Native American conflict which proves intractable as the film progresses. By bringing this conflict between men to a head Ben acknowledges this, and provides an avenue by which those who cannot endorse a 'colour-blind' approach to race relations, can be removed from American society. But, importantly, it is an approach that also requires compromise by white men or they too shall suffer removal (see Figure 4).

Figure 4: Rachel Zachary (Audrey Hepburn) struggling with the discovery of her Native American heritage in *The Unforgiven.*

Of course, on the one hand, a 'colour-blind' approach sends a fundamentally conservative message, as the climactic final battle frames Native Americans as those who endorse separatism and disrupt the peace of white society. Moreover, the shift to a 'colour-blind' approach is one that seems inherently a move towards Native Americans abandoning their own culture in favour of white mores. Indeed, as in her study of Native American women in Westerns, MaryAnn Oshana suggested that by killing her brother Rachel proves only that 'she is culturally white and a racist.'[22] This expectation of racial sublimation is also signalled by Cash's reaction to the other Indigenous character to feature heavily in the film, Johnny Fortune. Immediately upon meeting him, Cash notes the tendency for Native Americans to assume an Anglicized name to mask their heritage and integrate within white society. However, such a view also does not take note of the nuances within these performances that complicate attitudes towards, and performances of, race in this film. For example, although Cash is openly hostile to Native

22   Oshana, 'Native American Women in Westerns', 48.

Americans and brags that he 'can smell an Indian a mile off', he has to ask whether Johnny is Native American and, of course, has no idea that his adopted sister is not white. This is an attitude generally reflected by the fact that despite racism the community cannot actually detect racial difference; indeed they actively ascribe racial stereotypes inappropriately, stating for example that 'only an Injun would be crazy enough to steal that [Rachel's] horse' when it was, in actuality, stolen by (white) Kelsey. Matthilda also uses a racially loaded phrase, 'they all look the same to me', in reference not to a racial minority but in reference to white buffalo hunters, the very group that is typically privileged in the conventional celebratory view of the Western. Incidentally, the sameness Matthilda is referring to relates to loneliness, an emasculated state of being in the sense that it challenges America's hegemonic masculinity, which typically privileges individualism and endorses the view that 'real men' need nothing and no 'Other' for self-definition or self-fulfilment. That is, masculine men are never 'lonely' in a pejorative sense; a view that is inherently contradicted in that masculinity relies on a feminine (or feminized) other for definition.[23]

This is not to say that the characters that occupy the border between Native American and white culture do not exhibit seemingly inherent racialized characteristics: Johnny is the best horse trainer around, and is called upon to capture Kelsey because he alone can use horses to mount a successful chase. Despite being raised entirely in white society, Rachel can still ride bareback and plucks the strings of a piano rather than striking the keys. These differences are seemingly received as surface differences to those around them and, when major differences do occur between whites and Native Americans, the film is at pains to create parallels between the two groups: for example, the black magic of Native Americans is paralleled to the power of music, and the Christian Bible paralleled to the

23   Indeed 'loneliness' is the adjective used by Robert Warshow in his iconic analysis of the Western hero although he imbues it with a positive connotation: 'his loneliness is organic ... belonging to him intimately and testifying to his completeness'. Robert Warshow, 'Movie Chronicle: The Westerner', in *Film Theory and Criticism: Introductory Readings*, eds Gerald Mast, Marshall Cohen & Leo Braudy (Oxford: Oxford University Press, 1992), 454.

Native American parchment. In sum the mediation that takes place here emphasizes a discourse of sameness that suggests mutual compromise and a 'colour-blind' approach can solve racial difference; an approach which also has ironic outcomes.

More than this, though, the film frames differences in men's attitudes towards race relations as a fundamental fracture between them; as a fracture far greater than racial difference itself. Although racial differences may exist, these differences are minor in comparison to the destructive nature of conflict between all men regarding this difference. In making this assertion the film presents a fundamentally subversive message: it argues that hegemonic masculinity creates hierarchies of being that violently oppress other forms of being and that create tensions between men that shatter the illusion of a homosocial bond. These hierarchies of being actively alienate men from each other, leaving women within the role of social mediator. In making this assertion the film makes a statement about the historical past, summed up essentially by Ben: 'May the Lord keep us from evil. Red or white.' That is, the film presents something of a re-evaluation of America's Manifest Destiny and divine right by presenting conflict as mutually constructed, with wrongdoings on both sides. The film falls short of envisioning the frontier as a site of invasion and conquest but rather views it as a mutually contested zone. Indeed, in Joseph Natoli's analysis of the film, this is precisely its virtue and its capacity to challenge stereotype: it does well to illustrate 'the multiplicity of narrative worlds both individuals and cultures are already in and the drama of their collisions, as many histories as there are collisions.'[24]

The film's solution to racial conflict endorses a colour-blind approach to race relations or a discourse of sameness that aims to heal the fractures created by attitudes to racial difference. This stance presents audiences with a condemned group of 'unforgiven'. Specifically, the film suggests that those who perceive and act upon racial difference condemn society to violence, and that refusing to see such difference leads to a way forward and the re-establishment of community harmony. The 'unforgiven' who

24   Joseph Natoli, *Hauntings: Popular Film and American Culture, 1990–1992* (New York: State University of New York, 1994), 147.

must be removed because they can 'see' colour are William Zachary (a white man), who is already dead, Kelsey (a white man) is hung, Matthilda Zachary (a white woman) is shot dead, and Rachel's Native American brother who refuses to accept her loyalty to her white family and is shot by Rachel herself. Tellingly the 'unforgiven' are spread across racial lines, supporting the overall sense that fault for racial conflict lies on both sides and that, similarly, sacrifices and compromises for racial harmony should also be accommodated by both sides. By putting forward this attitude the film explores a positive hyper-linear relationship – the represented past and present are similar in the sense that racial conflict continues to divide society (and men) and seeks a solution based in past experiences of racial conflict and their apparent resolution.

The inherent contradictions between subversion and containment of patriarchal norms presented in the film through approaches to racial conflict can be summed up in Audrey Hepburn's inherent physicality. Hepburn is a white actress playing a Native American woman, following the example set by many Hollywood films that cast non-Native Americans in major Native American roles.[25] For many scholars this in itself reflects and feeds into the racism of Native American representation; indeed, as Edward Buscombe points out, such casting, especially in romantic roles whose plots centre around miscegenation (as *The Unforgiven*'s does), is essentially Hollywood's way of 'having one's cake and eating it too. The audience enjoyed the daring taboo attached to interracial sex, but was comforted by the knowledge that it was only make-believe.'[26] It is important to note that even when Native American actors are used in mainstream Hollywood roles these too attract criticism. For example, the difficulty in casting Native American actors within their own tribal groupings contributes to the perception of

---

25   See, for example, Nicolas G. Rosenthal, 'Representing Indians: Native American Actors on Hollywood's Frontier', *The Western Historical Quarterly* 36 (2005): 328–352.

26   Edward Buscombe, '*Injuns!*', 154–155. This argument is also made in relation to *Dances with Wolves* (regarding the relationship between Dunbar and Stands With Fists) in more contemporary times; see Donald Hoffman, 'Whose Home on the Range? Finding Room for Native Americans, African Americans and Latino Americans in the Western', *MELUS* 22 (1997): 4–7.

a 'Hollywood Indian' or pan-Indian identity. Often Native Americans speak a form of pigeon-English that plays into the stereotype of cultural backwardness and, when Native American languages are used, they are rarely without subtitles or voiceovers, which can be seen to mediate discourse only through white understandings.[27] More broadly, the decision of Native Americans to participate in a cultural form that has been perceived as contributing to stereotypes and misunderstandings regarding their history and peoples has largely been called into question.[28]

Added to this discourse is a very real questioning of what it means to be and represent First Nation Peoples on screen. For example, when it was revealed that famous actor Iron Eyes Cody was not Native American but Italian many Native American rights organizations defended the actor based on his record of raising awareness of Indigenous issues and called for a greater understanding of cultural and spiritual identification as a factor in group identity rather than notions of blood and heritage.[29] In this sense not only is racial representation seen as inherently troubled and troublesome but the capacity to substitute Native American actors reflects not only on the ways in which Hollywood has undermined a sense of historical veracity in favour of its own norms but, more than this, reflects on the fluidity of whiteness, which can assume different identities and become the embodiment of its own projected desires. In this case whites becoming Native Americans can be read as a desire by whites to capture aspects of their own identity that are lacking but which they have constructed in

27 Hall, 'Now you are a killer of white men', 7. Of course, this is not the case for all films portraying Native Americans – *A Man Called Horse* being a notable example of lack of subtitles. *Soldier Blue* does not use subtitles during Cresta's exchange with the Kiowa men.

28 An excellent study of Native American participation in Hollywood, which examines these themes and argues that the participation of Native American actors in early Westerns did much to enhance Indian activism and collectivism, which fed into the larger movements of the 1950s and 1960s is Rosenthal, 'Representing Indians', 328–352. For an analysis of the possibilities of a Native American cinema see Beverly R. Singer, *Wiping the War Paint off the Lens: Native American Film and Video* (Minneapolis: University of Minnesota Press, 2001).

29 Buscombe, '*Injuns!*', 161.

stereotypes of others, such as the notion of Native Americans as connected with nature, lacking the corruptions of civilization, and dignified.[30] This is a subversive perspective which suggests that casting of whites as Native Americans actually arises from a sense of white cultural inadequacy. In many ways Hepburn's performance can be seen to advocate for the film's own stance regarding colour-blind politics, suggesting that, if the central characters do not notice Rachel's colour, then the audience in turn should not question Hepburn's physical capacity to play the role. In so doing the performance embodies the issues of potential subversion and containment of white hegemonic standards surrounding the discourse of racial representation discussed here, for which the film advocates a 'colour-blind' approach both intra- and extra-diegetically.

In contrast, Cresta's role as mediator between audience understandings of white and Native American experiences in *Soldier Blue* lacks any solution to racialized conflict. Cresta, played by Candice Bergen, is racially identified as white both within and outside of the film. She makes no claims to Native American heritage or a special place within Native American culture as a result of her relationship with them within the film, yet her cultural identification is mixed. Bergen's performance presents an individual capable of traversing between racial groups, adapting to expected cultural norms and advocating that peaceful co-existence is possible, yet her view is rejected: as a woman and therefore outside of bases of power her perspective is a marginalized one in terms of its translation into definite action. *The Unforgiven* demonstrates a variety of different relationships between Native Americans and whites that are both violent and non-violent. *Soldier Blue*, in contrast, views different groups only through the experiences of Cresta unless that experience is one of violence, all of which include women. Specifically, there are only three encounters between Native American men and white men shown on-screen: the attack on white soldiers by Cheyenne, an encounter between Kiowa and Honus and Cresta, and the final massacre of Cheyenne.

These encounters illustrate important perspectives regarding racialized and gendered attitudes. Importantly, the film goes to great lengths to

30   Buscombe, *'Injuns!'*, 174.

insert women into the narrative of conflict. For example, the first conflict exposes as fallacious the stereotype of blind Indian lust for white women in the typical captivity narrative by revealing that Spotted Wolf has no interest in recovering Cresta. Nevertheless, Cresta provides an introduction to attitudes towards racialized conflict here that suggests her intimate knowledge of the supposedly exclusively male sphere of conflict. The second conflict suggests that Cresta will be raped and both she and Honus killed, and the final conflict features vivid footage of white soldiers raping and mutilating Cheyenne women. The film also alludes to the impact of wartime experiences on women; it opens with a title screen that includes the passage: 'brutal atrocities affect not only the warriors but the innocent as well [...] the women and children', and Cresta informs Honus that she has seen Native American women and children impaled on the soldier's long knives, 'stuck and dying.' By including women as an essential part of the war narrative the film does explore and expose as illusionary the attitude that men gain collectivity through their physical dominance over women via the act of rape. The vividness of these scenes and their obviously ironic nature stand in contrast to Oshana's assertion that the rape of Native American women by white men goes to subvert the ongoing sense 'that they [white men] are *entitled* to the bodies of Indian women' [original emphasis].[31] In particular the final massacre juxtaposes the images of brutality with the construction of masculinity and American identity through the final speech by Colonel Iverson, where men are congratulated on 'making another part of America a decent place to live [...] for the rest of your lives you will hold your head proud when this day is mentioned.' In doing so the film problematizes the idea of a masculinity founded in violent oppression of racial minorities and women, and questions the validity of a patriarchal society founded upon such principles. Moreover, it questions whether there ever was male collectivity in war or acts of violent oppression such as rape by illustrating the oppression of racial minorities, men who cannot partake in masculine sameness because of identity difference, and white men who refuse to construct their masculinity in such a way, in this instance Honus.

31   Oshana, 'Native American Women in Westerns', 48.

This does not mean that women are un-self-reflexive victims in these narratives, but both films portray women's autonomy in different ways. Just as Rachel is aware of the capacity for men to enact their masculinity on or through her body, first by Rawlins' request to see her body and then by her own offer to forfeit herself to Indians, Cresta is also aware of the female body as a site upon which to write masculinity. *Soldier Blue* exposes this need for masculine bodily dominance, amongst other forms of dominance, as a sign of a deeply flawed masculinity, a flaw that is reinforced through the vivid portrayals and results of women who are raped and murdered. In addition Cresta turns this masculine assumption into an act of feminine performance that meets her own needs. For example, she has an ongoing dialogue with Honus regarding his physical reaction to her close proximity at night though she poses this as his problem and manipulates his uncomfortable reaction to gain his coat for warmth. In assessing the possibility of rape by Kiowa she communicates with the men in their own language and creates the knife fight between them and Honus, thereby asserting her control over Honus's body and fighting for the right to her own. Finally, when she meets her betrothed and he refuses to aid either Honus or the Cheyenne, and expresses interest only in having sex with her, she plays on stereotypes of women's helplessness and submission to men's sexual needs in order to escape.

Cresta acts not only as the connection between all groups represented in the film but acts as the moral conscience of the film. Her experiences with both Cheyenne and whites and her seemingly greater understanding of both the predicament she and Honus are in and their capacity to survive it, lends weight to her moral imperatives throughout the film, especially when compared to the naivety of Honus. Cresta is able to predict rainfall despite Honus scoffing that the sky is clear; she advises Honus to let go of his socks as they are only an inconvenience and returning for his socks is what leads them into the knife fight with the Kiowa; she can speak fluently with the Kiowa men; she can hunt, cook and fashion clothing appropriate for their journey; she can navigate the terrain and can nurse a bullet wound. Her greater depth of practical knowledge undermines not only any claims to patriarchal dominance on the basis of women's lack of understanding of the realities of frontier life, but also undermines Honus's credibility about the realities of US military action. Honus's mourning for the lives of his fallen comrades and denial of military wrongdoing ring hollow in the face of Cresta's assertion: 'what do you expect Indians to do?' and her litany of witnessed white wrongs including landed conquest, whites instructing Indians to scalp, making tobacco pouches from Indian genitalia, and atrocities committed against women and children. Ultimately her experience has led her to a simple, but for Honus, profoundly subversive conclusion: 'This isn't my country. It's Indian country' and Indian acts of violence can be viewed only as acts of self-defence in the face of an invading force. In this vein, Indian traders who supply Native Americans with arms are not condemned by Cresta as simply fuelling conflict as they are in other films of this cycle such as *The Man from Laramie* (Anthony Mann, 1955) and *The Comancheros* (Michael Curtiz, 1961), but rather seen as supplying necessary equipment for self-defence.

Ultimately, Cresta's role as a white woman who acts as intercessor between competing interests in this film marks important, evolving ideas regarding racial representation in Westerns when compared with Rachel in *The Unforgiven*. Both roles illustrate the fracture between men; however, by 1970, a shift in racial politics had occurred to discount the colour-blind approach to race relations and emphasize cultural difference and empowerment of minority groups through an acknowledgement of difference. Although women collectively can illustrate the failings of white hegemonic masculinity and the fractures between different masculine groups, the idea of a white actress undertaking a Native American role or acting to speak for the issues of Native Americans divorced from the framework of white discourse is no longer viable. Cresta acts as a guide through different worlds and advocates an approach to understanding racial difference that sympathizes with Native Americans but she never advocates that she herself is racially aligned with this group or that she is entitled to speak on their behalf. Indeed, the final massacre wherein Honus repeatedly appeals to soldiers not to attack because there is a white woman in the camp, and the fact that Cresta ultimately escapes the fate of other Native American women, marks the fractures between women along different lines of identity, specifically racial identity. In this way Cresta, too, is forced to acknowledge a discourse of difference which works to her benefit in certain situations because she is white, but works against her in others, such as her encounter with Kiowa when she too may have been raped and murdered.

This contrast between a discourse of similarity and a discourse of difference is made explicit in the portrayal of Ben in *The Unforgiven* and Honus in *Soldier Blue*, respectively. Ben may be seen as an obvious deployment of the 'man who knows Indians' stereotype; the notion of a white man who understands the ways of Indians and identifies with some of their archetypically noble characteristics, such as environmentalism, but who is also removed from Native American experiences both through his actual race and his final engagement with white institutional structures. As Mary Katherine Hall asserts in her study of Western revisionism: 'the white hero is sometimes seen as better than Indians' for this mixture of Indian qualities and whiteness.[32] Ben's understanding of Indian practices is revealed through his interactions with them: he can read the Indian 'Bible' that reveals Rachel's true identity, understands Indian magic, and demonstrates an understanding of Indian signals regarding peace and parlay rather than violence. It is clear that Ben has engaged in violent confrontation with the Kiowa before but this is mentioned in passing, in response to the fears of Mrs Rawlins and framed as reactionary violence. Ben does engage in violence with Johnny Fortune, when Johnny removes a burr from Rachel's hair after suggestively breaking a horse in a way that paralleled the taking of a woman's virginity. This fight, and Ben's broader desire to retain Rachel within his white family rather than allowing her to rejoin her Kiowa family, is framed for the audience as motivated by Ben's repressed romantic love for Rachel. After he confronts Johnny he also asks all the men present whether anyone else sees a burr in his sister's hair, which suggests that he would react the same way regardless of the race of the man who had performed the action. Of course this is undercut by the fact that he gives Charlie Rawlins, a white man, permission to marry Rachel. Although Rachel clearly has some affection for Charlie this is communicated as platonic and Charlie is portrayed as something of the fool, but Rachel is conversely fascinated by Johnny's ability with horses and appears spell-bound as

32   Hall, 'Now you are a killer of white men', 12.

he removes the burr from her hair. She also refers to her Native American brother as 'beautiful' without any knowledge of their blood kinship. Ben's willingness to relinquish his own desires should Rachel choose another white man rather than give in to her seemingly 'natural' affiliation with Native Americans, speaks to the film's central assimilationist discourse, a discourse of which Ben is the central proponent. That is, Ben is not willing to endorse the racial separatism that would result from Rachel's engagement with a Native American either through bonds of blood or marriage – Ben can only endorse racial integration through these means. Perhaps it also reflects the converse of Edward Buscombe's assertion that the casting of a white actress in a Native American role is only a play at depicting miscegenation; the reality of a white actress depicting a love affair with a racial 'other' may have been beyond the pale in the production context, as well as in the represented past.

Ben's attitudes and knowledge, then, positions him as also a product of assimilation whereby he has accumulated the knowledge which allows him to understand and participate in Native American culture to the extent that difference can be peaceably accommodated. Where segregationist racial politics are deployed or peaceable accommodation of difference cannot be found, however, Ben sets about removing obstacles to this broader assimilation. The stereotype of the 'the man who knows Indians' in this instance cannot in itself be seen as explicitly racist and divorced from an historical context that advocates for a discourse of sameness via assimilation. While fundamentally containing subversion by advocating for the central role of white men in regulating racial policy, and for the need for minority groups to shift to meet the standards of whiteness, this portrayal does have subversive elements. It suggests that white men, too, must adjust their understandings and incorporate difference into their masculine gender performances and it does acknowledge the idea that white men have and continue to inflict their will on minority groups, to the detriment of those groups. For example, after the fight between Johnny and Ben, Johnny assumes that he is fired and requests the settlement of his pay; Ben refutes this, asking why Johnny would be fired when he'd 'done all the suffering.' This can be read as a broader metaphor that both acknowledges Native American suffering at the hands of white men but refuses to accept that such suffering might lead Native Americans to wish to withdraw entirely from white society or harbour violent instincts towards whites.

Ben's attitudes in the film are contrasted to what many have conceptualized as the 'new' stereotypes regarding racist white characters proliferating during the 'pro-Indian' cycle. Price suggests, just as the Western sought to move away from stereotypes regarding 'savage' and ignoble Indians, Hollywood invented a new set of stereotypes and resultant stereotypical relationships: 'negative stereotypes were then formed about the Indian-hating, treaty-breaking cavalry officers, merchants, and Indian agents who usually ignore the Indian-wise hero.'[33] Certainly such a stereotype of white characters is present in both films. *The Unforgiven* presents Cash, Kelsey and Mrs Rawlins as blindly hating Native Americans, with the phrases 'red hide nigger' and 'Injun lover' abounding throughout their diatribes, and various peripheral characters voice concern about Rachel's heritage in such a way as to support the idea that racism abounds throughout settler society. Moreover, *Soldier Blue* frames white racism through the lens of attempted cultural persecution by whites.

However, although both films may deploy this stereotype, they do so in different ways. In *The Unforgiven* racism exists at an individual level but it and the inherent violent oppression associated with it is not conceptualized as part of a broader landed dispossession of Native American peoples. In putting forward this idea the film essentially proposes that racism can be unlearnt by individuals, as is the case with Cash, who ultimately overcomes his racism to rescue Ben, Andy and Rachel from the Native American siege on their property. This conceptualization of white racist stereotypes endorses a discourse of sameness, then, by suggesting that through mutual co-operation and accommodation of difference racism can be overcome as it exists only between individuals. This approach reflects contextual approaches to racism during the early phases of the Civil Rights Movement, and it is important to note that the notion of stereotype as applying also to white characters can also be seen as inherently subversive to hegemonic gender performances. This is because it implies that whiteness itself is not

33   Price, 'The Stereotyping of North American Indians in Motion Pictures', 161. See also Hall, 'Now you are a killer of white men', 11.

inherent but constructed and that stereotype not only works to essentialize minority groups but also those who themselves rely on the 'Other' for self-definition. 'In this way, all people are stereotyped and essentialized within a racialized network, and the portrayal of the 'Other' reflects more on the values and assumptions on the hegemonic framework that constructs such a stereotype, than on those who are themselves stereotyped.'[34]

Although *Soldier Blue* uses stereotypes of white racist characters it may be distinguished by its conceptualization of racism at an individual level as a product of broader structural forces and ideologies of which white men are either unaware or seemingly unable to extricate themselves. Honus is portrayed as having a genuine belief in the 'civilizing' nature of the conquest of the continent, initially refusing to believe that Cresta's alternate narrative could be valid and, when he does discover this alternative for himself, he finds himself helpless, unable to effect meaningful change and finishes the film chained, both literally and metaphorically, within the very structures from which he now finds himself ideologically alienated. The genuine belief of white soldiers in the righteousness of their actions is reinforced by the final speech which affirms just that. Indeed the genuine nature of the purpose of white men can be seen in the name 'Honus', a play on the word 'honour', which makes Honus's ineffectiveness and the army's brutality all the more tragic. In this sense the film puts forward a discourse of difference but, more than this, subversively questions and exposes as illusionary the fundamental ideologies that underpin American institutions at the macro-level and their expression in hegemonic expressions of masculinity at the micro-level. *Soldier Blue* can find no solution to conflict as this is seemingly inherent within gendered structures and their individual gendered performances.

Of course this portrayal of Honus also represents a departure from *The Unforgiven*'s stereotype of Ben as 'the man who knows Indians'. It is not that Honus has no knowledge of Native Americans; rather the film represents him as someone whose lack of actual insight is compounded by

34   Hamilton & Saxby, "Draggin' the Chain', 85. See also, Karen Ross, *Black and White Media: Black Images in Popular Film and Television* (Cambridge: Polity Press, 1996), xxi.

his own sense that he acts with knowledge and the privilege he places on military protocol rather his own independent thought. His desire to travel via main roads despite Cresta's knowledge of the danger, his adherence to protocol regarding military dress regardless of the conditions, his inability to shoot the mountain goat for sustenance (albeit mediated by the fact that he hit a rabbit), and his inability to distinguish between Native American groups or different types of fires (which Cresta can do) all mark him as the inversion of 'the man who knows Indians' stereotype and goes to support a discourse of difference. Interestingly this is seen as part of a continuity that relates to the father: Honus's father was also a soldier who was killed at the Battle of Little Big Horn by the Sioux and Cresta undercuts Honus's idealizing of this connection by noting that his inabilities are perhaps hereditary and this ineffectiveness is the cause of his father's premature death. In this way the film communicates a long view of the lack of deeper understanding of white men regarding their environment and the nature of their oppressive conflict with Native Americans. This incident takes a source of positive historical continuity in Honus's personal history and reshapes it in light of Honus's new understandings into one of negative historical continuity, mimicking the function of the film itself, which reconceptualizes the previously positive hyper-linear connections between past and present. Now the actions of the past, with its connections in ideology and structure can no longer be seen in an uncomplicated and celebratory way and the ultimate father – patriarchy itself – is seen as a source of negative continuity. This perspective is supplemented by Cresta's own paternal experience: her father abandoned her in early childhood which resulted in her being placed in an orphanage. In so doing the film problematizes the idealizing of the father figure, who stands as a symbol both for hegemonic masculinity, paternalistic policy, and American government. This leitmotif is echoed in *The Unforgiven* which demythologizes William Zachary who, now deceased, is revealed to have abducted Rachel in a raid on a Native American encampment and lied about her heritage. Ultimately, though, his actions are seen as motivated by an unproblematized paternalism – Rachel's parents were now dead, William's own biological daughter has recently died and he desired to protect Rachel – and indicates the film's integrationist perspective. In this way both films use stereotypes of white men and fathers but to advocate different responses to racialized conflict.

Analysing the representation of race and the use of stereotype in *The Unforgiven* and *Soldier Blue* reveals the ways in which, rather than remain static and ahistorical, similar stereotypes can be deployed, inverted and played on over the course of a tumultuous decade to communicate different meanings. In particular these films both use the role of women, white/Native American relations, the 'man who knows Indians' and notions of encompassing white racism; however, they are used to communicate vastly different ideas about racial discours: a colour-blind approach to race in *The Unforgiven* and a discourse of difference in *Soldier Blue*. Whilst this analysis reveals different approaches to race relations depending on different historical contexts, whose messages contain both a mixture of subversive and contained meanings, at the heart of both films resides a fundamentally subversive message about white men's conceptualization of hegemonic masculinity as a privileged construct. Both films indicate that hegemonic masculinity is being re-evaluated in the wake of demands for recognition of minority rights and alternative narratives, in this case Native American rights which requires, in turn, a deep re-evaluation of American history, values and patriarchal institutions. Although *The Unforgiven* attempts to reconcile these disparate narratives of white occupation of the Americas into one coherent narrative that re-establishes hegemony, by the time of *Soldier Blue*, this attempt has disintegrated into recognition of the irreconcilable nature of these narratives and the fundamental failure of white hegemonic masculinity and its manifestation in institutional forms. An analysis of the specific historical temporalities of these films and their hyperlinear relationship with the past goes to supplement the deconstruction of hegemonic masculinity that takes place in these films.

'Since Cain slew his brother': Situating Stereotypes within Historical Contexts

The Unforgiven was released in 1960, a time when, according to Natoli, 'we're at the beginning of representing to ourselves [presumably white Americans] that in regard to Native Americans we're the ones who can't possibly be forgiven.'[35] Certainly this was a period of enormous transformation in governmental policy and public attitudes regarding Native Americans. Following World War II, assimilation of Native Americans and the relinquishing of federal responsibility for Native American affairs, termination, was the foundation for governmental policy. The participation of Native Americans in World War II both overseas and on the domestic front had led to increasing migration by Native Americans from reservations to industrial and urban centres, stimulated increased inter-racial contact and caused a fundamental re-evaluation of the rights of Native Americans including growing resentment of lower standards of living, lower educational and employment opportunities, and ongoing restrictions regarding welfare and the purchase of alcohol.[36] This led to increasing Native American activism and a sense of pan-Indian identification over shared goals, including the establishment of the National Congress of American Indians in 1944 and the American Indian Citizens League in 1947.[37] In this sense, Native Americans during this period experienced conflicting urges regarding assimilation: on the one hand, increased inter-racial contact and the experience of fighting in World War II increased white awareness of Native American issues and raised the notion that peaceful integration may be possible and perhaps even desirable. On the other: 'their wartime experiences had convinced many young Indians that they had the right to determine their own course as individuals and tribal members and not rely on whites to do it for them [...] that diverged from the "melting pot" vision whites had in mind after the war.'[38] Despite the growing rights-based discourse amongst all minority groups Native American groups also sought to distinguish themselves from the aims of the Civil Rights Movement

---

35   Natoli, *Hauntings*, 134.

36   Parman, *Indians and the American West*, 108, 115.

37   Peter Iverson, 'Building toward self-determination: Plains and Southwestern Indians in the 1940s and 1950s', *The Western Historical Quarterly* 16 (1985): 165, 168 and Bernstein, *American Indians and World War II*, 151. Parman, *Indians and the American West*, 154–157 for discussion of the formation of later 'Red Power' groups in the 1960s.

38   Bernstein, *American Indians in World War II*, 158.

by emphasizing the dual citizenship of Native Americans whose capacity to integrate within white society was curtailed by their ongoing identification with traditional tribal values, lands and customs.[39] This point is itself important to stress, as it undercuts the sense that Native Americans' function in Westerns *only* as signifiers of other minority groups, especially African Americans.

In contrast to these developments in Native American politics and cultural experience, governmental policy overwhelmingly focused on encouraging integration through termination policy. Termination is largely defined as the relinquishing of federal control over 'Indian' affairs through Concurrent Resolution 108 and Public Law 280, which shifted federal control over Indian affairs to the states and replaced Indian autonomy with the respective civil and criminal laws of those states. Between 1954 and 1962 twelve more pieces of legislation were passed that extended termination's aims.[40] This also meant that tribal assets and tribal land held in trust by federal authorities were re-administered to tribes or individuals.[41] Integrationist aims were also reflected in the institutional restructuring that took place through these reforms, such as the transfer of health services targeted at Native Americans from the Bureau of Indian Affairs and to the Department of Health, Education and Welfare in 1955, and the monetary incentives offered in some states to school districts wishing to integrate Indigenous students through enrolment, and also in incentives offered to Native Americans to migrate from reservations.[42] These developments, aimed largely at integrating Native Americans within white institutional and social frameworks, have largely been seen as a negative period in Native American rights although it did act to further galvanize Native American rights movements that would become more vocal as the 1960s and 1970s progressed.[43]

39   Bernstein, *American Indians in World War II*, 128.
40   Philp, 'Termination', 165.
41   Parman, *Indians and the American West*, 135.
42   Bernstein, *American Indians and World War II*, 168 & 164.
43   Bernstein, *American Indians and World War II*, 175.

The Unforgiven arrives in 1960 and from this context considers the impact of a post-Civil War racial environment in a hyper-linear fashion. This connection infuses the film and attempts to impart to the audience key ideas regarding race relations. Most obviously the film connects the audience's own understanding of the Civil War as a period of revolutionary freedom, with whites fighting for the civil liberties of African Americans. In this context increasing calls for Native American rights were also prevalent and, in this sense, *The Unforgiven* harkens to a long history of freedom struggles coupled with solutions for racial conflict found for minority groups by white men and their conceptualizations of the desirability of assimilation. That is, the film calls upon notions of beneficial paternalism in race relations as well as positioning the audience to see the fight for Civil Rights within a broader idea that, in seeking such rights, minority groups both engage with and seek to integrate within normative, white, patriarchal institutions. More specifically, by connecting the present of the filmic context to the post-Civil War context the film also connects contemporary policy regarding Native Americans with past policy developments. As Dippie notes, 'the Civil War did serve, however, as a clear dividing line between dominant philosophies in Indian affairs. Before 1860 segregation was still the rule; after 1865 assimilation was increasingly the order of the day.'[44] Government sought to stimulate practical assimilation through a number of means but most prominently through legislation. The Dawes Act of 1887 acted to redistribute tribal lands on an individual basis, action which, Parman asserts, was designed specifically to achieve the goals of 'destroying tribal authority, eradicating native religions, and changing Indians into farmers.'[45] The 1891 amendment which allowed for allotments to be leased and the subsequent Curtis Act, 1898, which allowed the federal government to terminate land tenure without consent, further supplemented these aims to the detriment of Native American cultural and landed sovereignty. It is also, as Wolfgang Mieder notes in his study of the development of proverbial stereotypes, a period where white social practices increasingly endorsed assimilationist perspectives. Mieder points,

44   Dippie, *The Vanishing American*, 77.
45   Parman, *Indians and the American West*, 1.

for example, to the use of proverbs such as 'the only good Indian is a dead Indian' as a method to promote the point of view that Indians should suffer not only literal death but also a cultural one: 'it promoted the belief that Indians could only be "good" persons if they became Christians and took on the civilization of their white oppressors.'[46]

Ultimately, there are multiple understandings that can be taken from the hyper-linear historical connection made between the past represented by *The Unforgiven* and the present of its filmic context. The film endorses a positive hyper-linear history through its representations of Native-American and white relations in settler society. It advocates the benefits of a colour blind approach that forces cultural compromise between both groups in order to ensure social harmony. In putting forward this view the film not only accords with then contemporary attitudes regarding Native American governmental policy and broader white attitudes regarding how to deal with the emergent 'race problem' encompassing domestic affairs, but connects these attitudes with past governmental policy and white social attitudes. In so doing the film does present subversive messages which are ultimately contained. Specifically, the film subversively creates a connection with the past that illustrates the ways in which patriarchal institutional structures and their personal manifestation in masculine gender performance have consistently come under threat by the competing demands of minority groups. In so doing the film refutes the claims of white masculinity to being static and having a natural right to dominance by explicitly illustrating the ways in which this authority has been oppressively enforced since the beginning of white occupation of the continent. Conversely, this subversive message can be seen as contained by the framing of this history as one to be replicated: past assimilation practices can be used as a foundation to explore ways in which to apply integration in the present, albeit a form of integration that requires compromise on behalf of whites. Natoli asserts that the very nature of the title, which requires the audience to assign guilt over past wrongs, positions a majority white audience to frame history as

---

46   Wolfgang Mieder, "'The Only Good Indian is a Dead Indian': History and Meaning of a Proverbial Stereotype', *The Journal of American Folklore* 106 (1993): 38–60.

a means to evaluate the past, rather than to reliably examine histories in their multiplicity. In this vein, then,

> The important thing is that we have the means to sort through conflicting representations of the past and attach ourselves to the one that moves us further along this inscribed path of what we should be, or what any culture should be moving toward [...] The issue here [...] is not whether European culture ever did wean itself away from mass extermination [...] the issue rather is whether we can settle on these 'great liberating ideas' as a means of sifting through history.[47]

For *The Unforgiven* 'what any culture should be moving toward' is a white cultural standard.

In contrast *Soldier Blue* fundamentally re-evaluates these 'great liberating ideas' and the hegemonic masculinity and patriarchal structures that underpin them through its representation of Native American and white relations and characters, and also through its negative hyper-linear connection between the represented past and the contextual present. Although typically seen as motivated by American experiences in Vietnam, and therefore as an anti-war film that criticizes American hegemonic structures, the film is more than a product of its context and undertakes a deeper reflection than that. The film constructs an explicit historical connection between past and present: it begins with an appeal to historicity in the title screen which states that 'in 5,000 years of recorded civilization mankind has written his history in blood.' It brackets this assertion with a Biblical reference to Cain and with the film's own representation which 'shows specifically and graphically the horrors of battle.' Ironically, the opening song also suggests historical veracity ('tell your story, it's a true one') whilst also refuting the claims that traditional historiography can adequately demonstrate any version of historical truth, through the statement 'I'll tell it so you can understand and I ain't gonna tell it like some history man.' In so doing the film makes complex the ways in which traditional histories (and traditional Westerns) are themselves a vehicle for and reflection of hegemonic masculinity and implies that what is being undertaken here is an alternative historical narrative that holds a claim to truth that is removed from the

47   Natoli, *Hauntings*, 143–144.

conventional narrative of white American history. This claim to historical veracity is further solidified by its location in a specific place and time, and focus around a specific historical event, as well as by its reference to extra diegetic historical events such as the Battle of Little Big Horn. This is not to suggest that the film has an actual claim to historical authenticity, but rather, by framing history as central to audience experiences of the film, *Soldier Blue* requires audiences to critically evaluate their own views of history in response to their cinematic experience.

Soldier Blue joins a growing number of films that re-evaluates the capacity of whites to speak for Native American experiences and questions the gap between the reality and ideals of American society at this time.[48] This reflects not only American experiences in Vietnam and the growing radicalization of racial ideas at the end of the Civil Rights Movement, but also reflects a growing radicalization of Native American politics. This is reflected in the greater engagement of organizations such as the American Indian Movement (AIM), Americans for Indian Opportunity, the Oglala-Sioux Civil Rights Organization, and in ongoing protests, such as 'fish ins' by Native American groups aiming to create a discussion of their rights and opportunities.[49] It also reflected the growth and economic maturation of the West as a region which simultaneously brought greater attention to the Native American policy but also provided Native Americans with greater opportunity and funding to pursue active protest, and also a federal government that consciously shifted towards self-determination and put Native American affairs back on the national agenda.[50] At all levels of society, then, the treatment of Native Americans (as well as the treatment of blacks and ongoing foreign interventionism) was highlighted as a failure reflecting the inability of American society to fulfil its promises and, indeed, questions whether America was ever founded on those ideals to begin with. It is telling that the connection used to illustrate this point is during (rather than after or before) the Civil War. The Civil War itself connects the audience with ideas of white masculinity at war with itself, as

---

48   O'Connor, *The Hollywood Indian*, 5.
49   Parman, *Indians and the American West*, 154–157.
50   Parman, *Indians and the American West*, 149–152.

questioning its ideals, and trying to establish a way forward rather than any sort of resolution to the fundamental ruptures within American society, a message that *Soldier Blue* itself portrays.

Conclusion

The portrayal of relations between Native Americans and European Americans on screen has always been fraught with controversy both in popular and academic discourses. It raises fundamental questions regarding who has the right to tell stories and deploy representations, what function stereotype serves in society, and whether any subversive statement about power relationships can ever be made by a Hollywood product, even within a cycle of Westerns known for its sympathetic portrayal of Native American issues. This chapter has argued that the representation of white/Native American relations in the pro-Western cycle does indeed use stereotypes or shared leitmotifs of both Native Americans and whites but, far from being ahistorical or static, they serve different purposes and communicate different meanings in a distinctly historical way. Using shared themes regarding the intersections of race and gender, the role of women and the nature of white masculinity *The Unforgiven* and *Soldier Blue* both reflect on this period as one in which hegemonic masculinity and the ideals that underpin it are re-evaluated and considered threatened by the competing interests of minority groups. They use these themes to different effect, however, with *The Unforgiven* reflecting its 1960 context by suggesting that perhaps white hegemonic masculinity can adapt to change and, with compromise, retain its status. The implication of this for Native Americans is an integration within white patriarchal structures, a solution that appeals to the represented historical post-Civil War past for validity. In *Soldier Blue*, however, the idea of a solution to racial difference is seen as impossible, founded as American society is on the oppressive values of hegemonic masculinity and subject to the ongoing fractures between different facets of identity. This film argues that the ideals of American society regarding equality and justice can never and have never been implemented as they are fundamentally antithetical to the patriarchal institutions that American society is founded upon and the hegemonic masculinity to which white men continue to aspire. As such the film reflects upon the demasculinization of America and American men.

Violence has an integral role in both films as a means to both enforce patriarchal standards and to illustrate the ill-effects of such standards. In analysing the role of violence in Western films, however, the gun – the primary tool by which violence occurs – is largely conceptualized as a signifier of masculine potency itself. The discussion now turns to a discussion of technology including the gun, yet far from conceptualizing the gun simply as an extension of 'the man' himself, it will be argued that guns themselves have deeper connections related to access to resources, capacity to exercise power meaningfully, and ability to adapt to changing technologies. Positioning the gun as not just part of the archetype but as an historically contingent technology with a distinct relationship to masculine gender performance illuminates the ways in which representations of gun violence can do more than supplement hegemonic masculine gender performances.

CHAPTER 5

'A pistol don't make a man': Technology and Masculine Gender Performances

The three previous chapters have examined the ways in which Westerns have represented the threats to hegemonic understandings of masculinity posed by economic shifts, and women's and Native American rights-based movements and discourses during different times. Despite the apparent differences in these representations they share a fundamental question: what has been, and is, the role of violence and violent oppression in maintaining the dominance of white male patriarchy over these groups and over other performances of non-hegemonic white masculinity? This question calls to the fore one of the most commonly identified symbols of the Western: the gun. This chapter analyses the evolving and deeply historical relationship between performances of masculinity and the use of technology in two Western films: *Colt .45* (Edwin L. Marin, 1950) and *The Wild Bunch* (Sam Peckinpah, 1969). It is important to remember that the gun sits as only one symbol of technology in Western films. Guns have usually been the central focus of studies on gender, Westerns and technology without examining the ways in which the gun is part of a broader network of technological symbols in Westerns to which men have a variety of relationships. Certainly, the railroad is in many ways a more complex representation of technology as it has generally been rendered in ambiguous ways over time; that is, many films have depicted railways as a symbol of 'civilized progress' whilst also reflecting nostalgically upon the role of railways in closing the frontier and endangering the holdings of small-time landholders and their associated small town values. This can include an open hostility to the railroad as a symbol of encroaching and emasculating 'civilized' or Eastern values. Westerns of the 1950s, however, can be distinguished by their emphasis not only on the railroad as a source of nostalgia but also as a symbol of men's fracturing along class lines. Films such as *Johnny Guitar* (Nicholas Ray, 1954), *The Man Who Shot Liberty Valance* (John Ford, 1962), and *Butch Cassidy and the Sundance Kid* (George Roy Hill, 1969) all make rich and complex renderings of the railroad in this light.

It is important to note that although this chapter focuses on technology as manifest in the form of the gun and the railroad, this is not the only form of technology present in Western films: steamships, bicycles, automobiles, and the telegraph have all been used in a variety of Westerns to demonstrate changing technologies in American history with various connotations regarding masculine gender performance. Moreover, the 'pro-Indian' Western cycle has also done much to problematize the relationship between technology, white patriarchy's ideas of 'progress' and hegemonic masculinity by presenting and sometimes privileging alternative forms of technology and different modes of gender performance. However, representations of gun and rail technology have dominated in the Western and, particularly, the use of the gun has become one of the genre's defining characteristics. Moreover, the apparent differences between military and rail technology can be seen as somewhat subsumed by their intricate links during the American Civil War: not only were both of these technological innovations spurred forward by wartime impetuses but, as William G. Thomas well illustrates in *The Iron Way*, the railroad itself became a military technology, transporting not only vital supplies of equipment and manpower but becoming organizational hubs and the focus of military operations both for and against the South.[1] The gun and railroad historically and in terms of their Western representation have many common links that make a study of the two forms particularly illuminating.

It is essential to emphasize, though, the position of the gun as one of many other pieces of technology and signifiers of consumer culture

1   William G. Thomas, *The Iron Way: Railroads, the Civil War, and the Making of Modern America* (New Haven: Yale University Press, 2011).

in Western films, a factor that has been sidelined in favour of Freudian, gendered and sometimes celebratory analyses of the relationship between men and guns. Here, *Colt .45* and *The Wild Bunch* can be considered as book-ends of the period under consideration – they each use similar themes including a questioning of what constitutes hegemonic masculinity during times of technological, economic and social change, the relationships between men, including the original inhabitants of the film's respective geographical settings, and issues of morality, communal values and action, and the capacity to justly assert authority – but they deploy these themes in different ways to communicate changing ideas regarding gender and technology. That is, these films illustrate the ways in which, in a post-World War II and Cold War production context, the gun is seen as unnatural, a tool of ambiguous meaning, and a symbol of consumer culture. This sense culminates in *The Wild Bunch*, produced during the Vietnam era, which presents a fundamentally destabilizing assessment of the gun and railroad. Here both items of technology become conceptualized as nihilistic symbols of multiple masculinities trapped in cycles of violence, class, racial and gendered warfare, and alienation from broader patriarchal structures and other men, which is structurally embedded and personally enacted. The structurally embedded nature of these cycles of violence and men's alienation means that men are often represented as incapable of fully understanding the causes and motivations of their behaviour or that of broader society and are therefore incapable of changing or extricating themselves from these social structures or patriarchal ideology

Traditional discourse has typically conceptualized the gun in the Western film not as an object, as part of man's relationship with technology or consumer culture but, rather, as a natural extension of the central male protagonist himself. In assuming this position as an extension of a man, guns have become seen as intrinsically linked to masculinity and the capacity to successfully implement one's will over another through gunplay and its associated skills. That is, to be able to successfully use guns to implement one's will has been seen as a marker of hegemonic masculine gender performance. Certainly this point has been made by an array of scholarly works on the Western. For Robert Warshow 'guns as physical objects, and the postures associated with their use, form the visual and emotional center' of Westerns.[2] For Martin Nussbaum the gun 'coupled with the fast draw, symbolises maleness, individualism and the Greek *deus-ex-machina*.'[3] Elliott West, in discussing television Westerns in the post-war period, identified that 'many heroes were intimately identified with their personal instrument of death [...] the word "gun", in fact, now applied both to firearm and a person who used it exceptionally well [...] appropriately man and weapon merged.'[4] These perspectives illustrate the extent to which effectively used technology is conceived of as interchangeable with masculine gender performance.

More recently gender studies theorists have attempted to deconstruct the relationship between weaponry and masculinity on-screen, often pointing to gun use in Western films as representative of the complexity and potential subversion of hegemonic masculinity that exists in all filmic representations. Certainly this is acknowledged in Steve Neale's analysis of the male body as spectacle, where he suggests that Western gun shootouts employ both fetishistic and voyeuristic forms of audience looking that simultaneously eroticize men's bodies and seek to minimize or repress erotic pleasure in the audience, a phenomenon found often in representations of the male.[5] This perspective has been extended by theorists such as Anne Marie Gaines and Charlotte Cornelia Herzog who suggest that the costuming of the Western hero, including the naturalizing of the gun as phallic symbol, the erotic nature of chaps that frame the groin, and the repeated strapping on and off of the gunbelt and the fetishistic elements such as spurs and whips, all feed into the perception of the Western hero as an erotic and objectified body, and therefore as positioned in a distinctly feminized and

2   Robert Warshow, 'Movie Chronicle: The Westerner', in *Film Theory and Criticism: Introductory Readings*, 4th edn, eds Gerald Mast, Marshal Cohen and Leo Braudy (Oxford: Oxford University Press, 1992), 453.

3   Martin Nussbaum, 'Sociological Symbolism in the 'Adult Western', *Social Forces* 39 (1961), 27

4   Elliott West, 'Shots in the Dark: Television and the Western Myth', *Montana: The Magazine of Western History* 38 (1988): 75.

5   Steve Neale, 'Masculinity as Spectacle: Reflections on Men in Mainstream Cinema', in *Screening the Male: Exploring Masculinities in Hollywood* Cinema, eds Steven Cohan and Ina Rae Hark (London & New York: Routledge, 1993), 18.

counter-hegemonic fashion.[6] Certainly, they argue, this is further evident in the ritualized nature of the gun battle which encourages the objectification of men's bodies until the release of tensions through 'ejaculations of fire' which culminates when the hero and his nemesis '"come" together.'[7] These perspectives though, largely focus on the intersections between filmic representation and gender theory and, because of this, position representations of men's relationships to guns in the Western as ahistorical and monolithic rather than changeable over time. Indeed, positioning representations of men and the symbolism of technology, including the gun, within the historical contexts of both the filmic past and release date in a hyper-linear fashion reveals the important ways in which representations of these relationships can and do change in accordance with the problematizing of gender norms at any given time. This can be discerned by re-uniting gender and history in the study of filmic representations over time in order to understand their historicity.

Indeed, from the 1950s, an increasing number of Western films portrayed men's relationships with technology, including the gun, not as a natural extension of men's hegemony but as complex symbols of the fracturing of masculinity in the face of modernity. In this context technology becomes another arena within which men are increasingly pitted against each other both physically and metaphorically, particularly through their class location, and are forced to adapt to changing moralities, values and skill levels in a West that is evolving and closing. Certainly this is also an observation made by Stanley Corkin, who asserts in his analysis of the ways in which 1950s Western's representations of gunplay reflect attitudes to then American foreign policy, that these films

> dwell explicitly on *whether* [original emphasis] violence is an appropriate means of resolving the various crises defined in their plots [...] these fifties films question whether a social system defined by its ability and tendency to deal with disruptive elements

6 Anne Marie Gaines and Charlotte Cornelia Herzog, 'The Fantasy of Authenticity in Western Costume', in *Back in the Saddle Again: New essays on the* Western, eds Edward Buscombe and Roberta E. Pearson (London: British Film Industry, 1998), 178–179.

7 Gaines and Herzog, 'The Fantasy of Authenticity in Western Costume', 179.

by annihilating them may be flawed; they also probe the prospect that characters will become physically and morally marred beyond repair if they engage in gunplay.[8]

Films such as *The Gunfighter* (Henry King, 1950), *Broken Arrow* (Delmer Daves, 1950), *High Noon* (Fred Zinnemann, 1952), *The Fastest Gun Alive* (Russell Rouse, 1956), *The Left-Handed Gun* (Arthur Penn, 1958) and *The Man Who Shot Liberty Valance* (John Ford, 1962) are just some of the many Westerns in this era that problematize the glorification of the gunfighter and the use of guns as a means of solving broader social issues.

In problematizing the gun it becomes an object – a piece of technology and tool – rather than a pseudo extension of the central protagonist. This does not diminish its associations with masculine gender performance but rather signals a greater questioning of how men construct and perform gender hegemony; that is, a questioning of the validity of a patriarchy founded in exclusionary access to resources and violent oppression. It may be argued that at the most fundamental level the reconceptualization and questioning of men's relationship with technology signals the broader demasculinization taking place in the 1950s and 1960s. This is because it inverts Susan Jefford's notion that remasculinization occurs when male bodies, which may otherwise be fragmented or erotic, are unified through the 'power of technological display.'[9] In this sense technology merges with and empowers male bodies, giving them purpose and repressing the erotic, as the spectacle of masculinity becomes associated with the power of technology. As men are emblematic of broader patriarchal ideology this ideology itself is also empowered becoming, like the technology itself, 'pervasive, powerful and inexhaustible.'[10] This grouping of films, however, questions whether technology does or should merge with the body and actively disentangles the relationship between technology, hegemonic masculinity and patriarchal power structures.

---

8   Stanley Corkin, *Cowboys as Cold Warriors: The Western and US History* (Philadelphia: Temple University Press, 2004), 95.
9   Susan Jeffords, *The Remasculinization of America: Gender and the Vietnam War* (Bloomington: Indiana University Press, 1989), 10.
10   Jeffords, *The Remasculinization of America*, 10.

To place these films in greater context *Colt .45* follows celebrated Mexican-American War veteran and current Colt salesmen, Steve Farrell (Randolph Scott) as he hunts down the outlaw, Jason Brett (Zachary Scott). Brett has stolen a set of his state-of-the-art Colt .45 guns, implicated him in the murder of a Sheriff and, since acquiring the guns, has established a criminal gang to rob stagecoaches. With the aid of the corrupt Sheriff Harris (Alan Hale), Brett has aspirations of taking over the town of Bonanza Creek. Aided by Native Americans, who have been falsely blamed for some of the gang's crimes, and Beth Donovan (Ruth Roman), whose husband, Paul, joined the gang and tricked her into supporting them, Farrell ultimately shoots and kills Brett, proving the film's catch-cry that, despite having access to the same technology, 'a pistol don't make a man; it's the gent behind the gun that counts.' Starring one of the iconic Western stars of this era in Randolph Scott, *Colt .45* was one of the last films made by director Edwin L. Marin, of *A Christmas Carol* (1938) fame, before his death. This film also inspired a popular television spin-off of the same name which featured a Colt salesmen/undercover government agent, and appeared from 1957 until 1960.

The second film, *The Wild Bunch*, set circa 1913 in Texas and Mexico, follows a group of ageing bandits led by Pike Bishop (William Holden) who are commissioned by a Mexican warlord, General Mapache (Emilio Fernandez) to steal a shipment of guns to support his regime. Faced with the volatility of their deal with Mapache and his brutal regime and pursued by railway-hired bounty hunters led by Pike's old friend and partner, Deke Thornton (Robert Ryan), the Bunch reflect upon the closing nature of the West, their alienation from normative structures including the American government, and the realization that they, and the form of masculinity they perform, has become displaced and their destruction is assured. Ultimately this destruction is brought about by their Mexican gang member Angel (Jaime Sánchez), who kills Mapache's mistress out of jealousy and demands a case of the stolen guns from the gang so that his village is capable of mounting a defence against Mapache. Recognizing Angel's theft and revolutionary aspirations Mapache captures and tortures him, nearly to death, before the Bunch return and attempt to buy his release. Mapache cuts Angel's throat and a final, apocalyptic, battle ensues, which kills both Mapache's men and the Bunch. The film ends with Deke Thornton and his men finally coming across the devastation as civilian survivors begin to flee. Thornton's men rob the bodies of the deceased before taking the remains of The Wild Bunch to the railway to claim their bounty. Thornton joins with Angel's Mexican rebels, which includes Sykes, an elderly member of The Wild Bunch who had not participated in the attempted rescue of Angel. The film received Academy Award nominations for best music and best writing of a screenplay based on previously unpublished material at the time of its release and has generally been conceptualized as a classic of the genre although it has been subject to ongoing controversy regarding its depiction of violence. Peckinpah used then revolutionary filmic techniques including the use of multi-angle screen shots, intercutting of normal and slow-motion speed images and the use of 'squibs' (small packets of fake blood rigged to explode at the same time an actor was supposed to be shot, making the appearance of a gunshot wound more immediate and realistic) to create increasingly graphic and impactful images of violence which, some have suggested, carries its own aesthetic value.[11]

Although apparently quite different both in temporal and geographic localities and plot lines, these films do mark an evolution of ideas surrounding the relationship of men and technology. Both films are, or have spawned, significant markers of popular culture during this period, making them worthy subjects of academic analysis in their own right. More than this, both are located in distinct times and spaces, facilitating important hyper-linear connections between the represented past and the on-screen present, which does much to illuminate changing attitudes towards technology, violence and gender performance over time. Specifically, *Colt .45*

---

11   See, for example, David A. Cook, 'Ballistic Balletics: Styles of Violent Representation in *The Wild Bunch* and After', in *Sam Peckinpah's The Wild Bunch*, ed. Stephen Prince (Cambridge: Cambridge University Press, 1999), 130–154. Greater context to this discussion of violence in *The Wild Bunch* can be found in the introductory section of Stephen Prince (ed), *Screening Violence* (New Brunswick, New Brunswick, NJ: Rutgers University Press, 2000), 1–46. Devin McKinney, '*The Wild Bunch*: Innovation and Retreat', in *Sam Peckinpah's The Wild Bunch*, ed. Stephen Prince (Cambridge: Cambridge University Press, 1999), 175–199 provides a critical analysis regarding the truly revolutionary nature of these techniques in depicting violence.

constructs a hyper-linear relationship of positive continuity between the represented past and the production context by acknowledging the anxieties surrounding the Cold War, particularly around the sense of technology as spiralling beyond control to an increasingly deadly conclusion. It then sets about soothing these contemporary anxieties by calling upon past ideas regarding changing weapons technology that divorces technology itself as a source of power; instead situating power as having its locus inside men themselves. Farrell, with his military past and ongoing concern for law and order, shows the audience that successful conflict resolution has occurred in the past, with common sense and collective morality prevailing, thereby representing a paradigm for contemporary audiences to make sense of their present.

Situated at the closing of the frontier *The Wild Bunch*, however, creates a hyper-linear relationship of negative continuity between represented past and production context. It equates the sense of nihilism and economic and social change associated with the closing of the frontier with a Vietnam War context. Rather than illustrating the capacity for positive change arising from these experiences the film points out that, detrimentally, the more things change the more they stay the same. The impression left by this film is that patriarchal codes are capable of adapting to meet changing historical circumstances, in so doing privileging different forms of hegemony, but not altering the fundamental structures of power relations that alienate men from each other and from ways of extricating themselves from modes of behaviour and structural forces that has a detrimental impact on them personally and on broader American ideology politically.

Gun Technology, Gender Performance and Hyper-Linearity

The nature and extent of gun violence on the frontier historically is extremely contested. Current historiography emphasizes that, whilst the West was by no means a peaceable and harmonious place at any time, the notion of the West as uniquely violent, or that violence and a gun culture particularly shaped American character, is fallacious.[12] As Stewart L. Udall asserts, the notion of an excessively violent frontier can be seen as part of a self-reinforcing myth stimulated by popular culture from dime novels to Western films. This myth is problematic historically, Udall suggests, because it repudiates a more accurate history of Western settlers who were focused on family and mutual co-operation, shared common aims and values, and who were lightly armed and, for these reasons, experienced relatively little violence.[13] In contrast celebrated works such as Richard Slotkin's *Regeneration through Violence: The Mythology of the American Frontier* and *Gunfighter Nation: The Myth of the Frontier in Twentieth Century America* put forward the centrality of frontier violence, or the perception of the centrality of gun culture from American settlement, to the development of American national identity into the modern era.[14] Ongoing contestation regarding the methodologies used to calculate rates of violence, particularly the use of homicide rates rather than raw numbers of homicides, as well as the different experiences of different areas, such as mining communities, continues to inflame the issue of frontier gun violence for contemporary historians.[15]

In acknowledging this, Udall also accepts that a 'sharp line can be drawn' between the pre- and post-Civil War era when 'technological developments in the aftermath of the Civil War altered and ameliorated economic and social conditions.'[16] Michael A. Bellesiles, who also rejects the notion of the frontier as especially violent, supports this, arguing that the Civil War transformed the ways in which guns were produced in and

---

12   Stewart Udall, Robert R. Dykstra, Michael A. Bellesiles, Paula Mitchell Marks, and Gregory H Nobles, 'How the West got Wild: American Media and Frontier Violence, a Roundtable', *The Western Historical Quarterly* 31 (2000): 277.

13   Stewart L. Udall, 'The 'Wild' Old West: A Different View', *Montana: The Magazine of Western History* 49 (1999): 66.

14   Richard Slotkin, *Regeneration Through Violence: The Mythology of the American Frontier, 1600–1860* (1973); Richard Slotkin, *Gunfighter Nation: The Myth of the Frontier in Twentieth Century* (New York: HarperCollins, 1992).

15   See, for example, Robert R. Dykstra, 'Quantifying the Wild West: The Problematic Statistics of Frontier Violence', *The Western Historical Quarterly* 40 (2009): 321–347.

16   Udall, 'The 'Wild' Old West', 67.

demanded by American society. Specifically, the Civil War stimulated the perception of the gun as a tool of national conflict resolution above demo- cratic means which, coupled with the mass production of arms, lowered the market price in the wake of the war, led to the creation of a national gun culture that is distinctive to the United States.[17] Technical innovations that increased the effectiveness and accuracy of rifles and handguns, the manufacturing of guns that used interchangeable cartridges, as well as the salesmanship and marketing strategies surrounding guns, also made them increasingly attractive purchases.[18] The net result of this was, by the 1870s, at the personal level, an identification of masculinity with guns; indeed, 'a gun seemed to most men a requisite for their very identity' and, at the public level, an increase in the rates of gun-related violence.[19] Certainly this is sup- ported by Clare V. McKanna's research into murder rates in three frontier towns in Nebraska, Colorado and Arizona between 1880 and 1920, all of which experienced 'high levels of lethal violence' during this period.[20] This is not to overstate the significance of innovations in technology in causing increased violence in the American West following the Civil War: alcohol, unstable and transient population numbers, the multicultural nature of the

17 Michael Bellesiles, *Arming America: The Origins of a National Gun Culture* (New York: Alfred A. Knopf, 2000), 15; 430–433. It is worth acknowledging that this book has become extremely controversial, though not for these conclusions but rather for the central argument throughout the book that from settlement to Civil War America lacked a distinctive gun culture and did not experience high rates of gun violence, and because of ongoing methodological disputes regarding how Bellesiles arrived at this conclusion. In many ways these disputes can be seen as emblematic of broader issues within the study of frontier violence. For analysis of the ongoing debate regarding this work see, for example, the author's defence of the work: Michael A. Bellesiles, 'Exploring America's Gun Culture', *The William and Mary Quarterly* 59 (2002): 241–268.

18 George M. Stantis, 'Rifles and Revolvers', in *Icons of the American West: From Cowgirls to Silicon Valley*, ed. Gordon M. Bakken (Santa Barbara: Greenwood Reference, 2008): 277–292.

19 Bellesiles, *Arming America*, 430 & 434.

20 Clare V. McKanna, Jr, 'Alcohol, Handguns, and Homicide in the American West: A Tale of Three Counties, 1880–1920', *The Western Historical Quarterly* 26 (1995): 455.

frontier towns, and the economic instability of boomtown communities were added pressures on the social cohesion of frontier towns.[21]

It is within this context that the .45 Colt gun was put into production. Colt single action revolvers gained widespread use when the company was contracted by the US Army in 1873 for a total of 8,000 guns; however, by 1891, the company had supplied 37,000 to the military.[22] During continuous manufacture between 1873 and 1940 the company sold a total of 357,859 firearms, the most popular of which was the Colt .45 model. The company achieved this success through a variety of marketing strategies and a variety of retail means including travelling salesmen, 'jobbers' acting as wholesalers, and retail stores both in America and abroad.[23] Indeed, Stantis reflects that it was the Colt revolver itself that 'served as a symbol of its era [...] [and] this six-shooter remains an iconic fixture' in American culture.[24] The film *Colt .45* explicitly reflects upon this historical past – the production, sales and centrality of the Colt to images of the frontier – in multiple ways. The film's protagonist is employed as a Colt salesman, illustrating the new forms of marketing and sales methods that acted to promote the firearm, which led to its enormous popularity. *Colt .45* opens with scenes of Farrell attempting to sell a set of guns to a small-town sheriff. In so doing he reflects upon and makes the audience aware of the technological ingenuity involved in the new forms of firearms: for the first time shooters can fire six shots without reloading, it's 'easy to load and as durable as your mother-in-law.' Farrell emphasizes to the Sheriff the way in which the guns are packaged and finished, further cementing the place of the Colt as both a consumer good that confers status to its owner and as a feat in modern technological know-how. The consistent imaging of the two guns crossed over each other adds to this conceptualization of the weapon for the audience. This is performed in an almost ritualized fashion that calls upon audience understandings of the Colt as an iconic weapon. More than this, in emphasizing the role of the gun as a part of broader consumer

21   McKanna, 'Alcohol, Handguns, and Homicide in the American West', 456.
22   Stantis, 'Rifles and Revolvers', 286.
23   Stantis, 'Rifles and Revolvers', 288.
24   Stantis, 'Rifles and Revolvers', 286.

culture and as a technological advance, the film positions the audience to perceive of the connections between technology and masculinity in ways that are both threatening to and contained within patriarchal standards of gendered behaviour (see Figure 5).

Figure 5: Randolph Scott as Steve Farrell, the travelling gun salesman, in *Colt .45*. The iconography of the crossed Colt .45s is consistent throughout the film.

The revolver in *Colt .45* is positioned as part of a broader web of men's concern for demonstrating their standing through their economic power. The film is not only centred on the gun, and the notion that through gun ownership one can advance one's own standing either through socially positive or negative action, but it also focuses heavily on money as the primary incentive for all men's actions. For example, immediately upon seeing the revolutionary guns Brett asserts that his life would have been much different if he had the capacity to acquire them: he would never have been caught in the first place. The film illustrates his capacity to use this technology as a means to accrue wealth. Beth's husband, Paul, consistently reflects upon

the economic opportunities not available to him and his perceived isolation
from capitalistic structures and methods of accumulation. Specifically, as
a miner he feels he has little chance of actually finding material success,
instead he feels somewhat taken advantage of by the towns that spring up
as a result of the mining boom, pointing out that the big profits are made in
saloons and gambling halls. He uses the previous owner of his house, who
was forced to sell at lower prices due to gambling debts, as an example to
support this perception. He explicitly informs Brett that his dreams – to
travel, to shave every day – motivate him to continue to support the gang
despite deceiving his wife knowing that she would object, and despite the
seemingly good standing of the couple in the town. Indeed, Paul not only
sees consumer items as desirable regardless of the immorality involved in
their acquisition but is unable to see anything or anyone in ways that do
not relate to their dollar value. He suggests that ultimately Beth will support him as, 'you can buy the best woman with gold', and when the nature
of his criminality is revealed and Beth refuses to support him and intends
to tell the Sheriff the truth, he shoots her, not out of anger or rejection,
but because she posed a threat to his achievement of economic success.

Moreover, even lawmen are implicated within these structures in ways
that impinge upon their capacity to perform their duty in uncorrupted ways.
Implicitly this is suggested by the fact that Farrell intends to market Colt
.45s to lawmen before other people, subverting the notion that lawmen
are naturally superior to criminals by virtue of their moral righteousness
and suggesting that they must be supported by material goods. It is also
suggested by a sheriff's assumption that Farrell assisted Brett's escape and
could only be wooed into revealing Brett's hiding place if prompted by a
five thousand dollar reward. Explicitly this is illustrated by Bonanza Creek's
Sheriff who is working with the gang for his own personal gain. Ultimately,
this film reflects on the historical development of weapons technology as
inextricably linked to the development of a consumer culture, a consumer
culture that highlights the class inequalities between white men, stimulating men's alienation from each other, from capitalist structures and from
broader social values.

This world is one in which guns become symbols of the ways white
men oppress other forms of identity, including other non-hegemonic white

masculinities. This occurs not only through the obvious use of the gun as a form of violence, but also in the gun's role as part of consumer society wherein men are able to gain status and means of power, and openly demonstrate this power, through their consumer spending and through their skills to use this new technology to its fullest potential. This conceptualization subverts traditional notions of hegemonic masculinity as it demonstrates that the power derived from hegemonic displays of masculinity does not derive from a natural state or from patriarchy's claims to a natural right to dominance. Rather it demonstrates the constructed nature of patriarchal dominance whereby those who are capable of controlling capital and mastering technological advancements gain supremacy and can use their advantages to oppress others, whose alternative forms of gender become subsumed.

Brett, Paul and the Bonanza Creek Sheriff all illustrate the resentment of masculinities that are increasingly alienated from normative social structures and behaviours and are finding their way of 'doing' masculinity increasingly obsolete in a changing world. Knowing that they cannot be reintegrated into hegemonic masculinity in mainstream ways such as through law and order and normative forms of employment each man poses a challenge to patriarchal structures, attempting to create an alternative world where their masculinity is privileged. Importantly, though, this alternative world is not so different as to fundamentally challenge the supremacy of patriarchy or the centrality of violence and economic power as a means to achieve this supremacy. This failure to understand the ways in which they are trapped within modes of behaviour by these structures ensures that these characters cannot succeed or pose a successful social alternative, and they are therefore casualties in the ongoing adaptation of patriarchy to changing conditions. In this sense whilst a positive historical continuity is imparted by the film as a whole, these specific characters are trapped within a negative continuity of historical conditions that ensures that patriarchal power remains the same, and that different forms of masculinity will continue to suffer as patriarchy adapts, from the represented past to the present of the filmic release. This theme is echoed throughout many Westerns that represent criminality as an alternative social behaviour or even privilege it nostalgically as representing a passing form of masculinity, such as *Butch Cassidy and the Sundance Kid*, discussed in the next chapter

This potential to represent a negative continuity between past and present through trapped masculine gender performances is ultimately contained through the characterization of Farrell and, to a lesser extent, through the representation of Native Americans and Farrell's relationship with them. In particular, Farrell's relationship with, and understanding of, the gun acts to reinsert the gun positively as a tool in the inevitable success of white nation building. Essentially, Farrell's portrayal acts to contain leaks in hegemonic masculinity by asserting that technology (and therefore economic mechanisms that cause or inhibit one's access to technology) does not matter but, rather, one's character, approach to life and capacity to think laterally are the most important factors in dictating success. This contradicts the message of the oppositional group; that structural factors – access to resources, in this case a gun – are central to one's survival and successful ability to impose one's own standards of gendered behaviour over others. Through Farrell's ultimate survival and success, the dominance of his viewpoint is put forward and the message sent to the audience is that fractures between men exist at and can be overcome at the individual level rather than at a deep and fundamentally destabilizing structural level, which would cause a re-evaluation of American values and broader gender performances. The opening title screen which features the statement 'a gun, like any other source of power, is a force for either good or evil, being neither in itself, but dependent upon those who possess it' echoes throughout the film, with guns seemingly divorced from broader structures or culture and positioned firmly within the realm of the individual and personal choices regarding its use.

The inherent contradiction between these two perspectives in the film, the privileging of structural forces posed by Brett, and the centrality of the personal presented by Farrell, is also presented through direct historical references. Farrell is framed from the first scene as a veteran and war hero of the Mexican War (inferring the Mexican-American War of 1846–1847). Historically, 'the Mexican War showed the value of the Colt revolver, invented a decade earlier [...] [which] quickly entered the dreams of the righteous.'[25] This reference to the Mexican War rather than to other military actions is interesting; although a variety of Colt revolvers were produced from the 1830s, the .45 calibre Colt dubbed *The Peacemaker* was not produced until 1873 and the film's attitude towards the marketing and sale of the gun clearly locates the film in a post-Civil War temporal locality. This historical positioning seems to conflate the evolution of gun technology in a way that aligns with Rosenstone's notion of invention – that is, that historical realities can be condensed or simplified in an historical film without losing historical integrity.[26] In this sense the history of gun technology is conflated to illustrate an historical continuity between past and present. The film draws parallels between seemingly positive, nation-building interventions in Mexico to protect its perceived territory and that allowed American men such as Farrell to prove themselves in battle. In so doing, it overlooks the role of this intervention in leading to the Civil War. This perception of the Mexican War can be connected hyper-linearly to a post-World War II sense of rightness of cause and as an illustration of the importance, indeed, the moral imperative, of American intervention in a Cold War context. It is difficult to imagine how a reference to the Civil War, despite its centrality to the theme of weapons development, could have created a similarly positive relationship to the present due to the inherent symbolism of white masculinity fractured and at war with itself that the Civil War conveys. Ultimately, though, the reference to the Mexican War when connected with American military technology (the gun) connotes both the structural forces – military, technological, cultural, economic and social – that have led to American interventionism abroad supported by an ideology of Manifest Destiny. By framing these broader issues within the context of an individual, Farrell, they are thereby contained, as they are moved from the political and public realm and repositioned into the personal and private. The point here is that the film focuses on the individual and the ways in which individual survival were caused by a combination

25   Eric Mottram, "'The Persuasive Lips': Men and Guns in America, the West', *Journal of American Studies* 10 (1976): 62.
26   Robert Rosenstone, *Visions of the Past: The Challenge of Film to Our Idea of History* (Cambridge: Harvard University Press, 1995), 67–68.

of American ingenuity (the gun) and the nature of the individual rather than the influence of broader, structural factors. In so doing it mirrors the film's broader privileging of individual and personal over public and structural factors.

This contradiction is also illustrated in Farrell's relationship with Native Americans in the film. Native Americans are introduced in *Colt.45* when the .45 gang pose as Native Americans to rob a stagecoach, thereby attempting to deflect attention away from themselves as the true culprits.[27] The Chief agrees to follow Farrell's plan to bring the gang to justice legally, provided Farrell can do so swiftly, and his men support Farrell in many confrontations including in the final showdown. When Beth is shot and Farrell implicated in Brett's crimes they seek refuge with the Native Americans, who refuse to turn them over to the town's posse despite the posse threatening to call in the military. On the one hand, this relationship reflects explicitly on broader structural issues: the gang posing as Native Americans play on ideas regarding frontier violence, a factor further illustrated by references to military powers over Indian affairs. Moreover, when discussing an approach to dealing with Brett, Chief Walking Bear refutes that Farrell's concepts of law and order and justice based on due process apply to him and his people, an attitude that is reinforced when the Chief refuses the posse by stating: 'law no friend to Indian. Go.' By presenting these issues the film does engage with the broader ideological, structural and social values that result in the violent oppression and marginalization of Native Americans, an oppression that is achieved in part by the very technology that is privileged by Farrell. Presenting this perspective provides support for Brett's recognition and resentment of the role of structural forces being responsible for his marginalization, a destabilizing proposition. On the other hand, a number of factors undercut the potential critique of American structures and values provided by the film. For example, the primacy given to the friendship between Farrell and the Chief; the success of Native Americans in battle using a variety of weapons including guns; the submission of Native Americans to Farrell's will; and their lack of

---

27   This is an interesting example of racial performance, and the capacity of whites to self-consciously play upon and with racialized social expectations.

acknowledgement of the revolutionary nature of Farrell's guns, all detract from the idea that access to resources and technology can have a significant impact on individual or group advancement. In addition Farrell does not recapture Brett alive, but kills him, which suggests that the law of the gun arbitrated by an individual can stand in the place of democratic law. This further complicates this relationship between the structural and the individual, by suggesting that ultimately it is Brett and Farrell's individual choices that matter, not broader structural forces that lead to criminality and pit the two against each other.

Farrell's actual relationship with the gun is a complex one that reflects the increasingly difficult relationship between man and machine in both time periods. Farrell illustrates that technology is not and should not form an essential component of his masculine identity. His capacity to successfully liaise with Native Americans and gain their assistance, his sensitivity to Beth Donovan, his ability to establish the different relationships in the town before acting, and his capacity to use restraint to lure the gang into dangerous situations which ultimately cost them their lives, rather than simply laying siege to the gang, reflect his lack of reliance on technology to establish a sense of himself in the world. Indeed, the culmination of the film sees him lay aside his guns in favour of a fair fight with Brett, although ultimately this is impossible as Brett is incapable of sticking to this code of honour and, because of this, he is seen as justifiably shot by Farrell who by this time has also won Beth's affection. Conversely, however, he is repeatedly identified by his weapon, blurring the lines between man and machine. The consistent framing of his guns, positioned triumphantly crossed, can also be seen as a form of fetishization of technology that blurs the lines between body and object.[28] This fetishizing of the object can also be seen as a way to encourage what Steve Neale identifies as fetishistic looking in the audience where the gap between the viewer and object is closed and the object is acknowledged as actively participating in the discourse. Such looking captivates the audience, discouraging them from looking at an image critically (or historically).[29] Therefore fetishistic looking and man's identification

28   Slotkin, *Gunfighter Nation*, 380.
29   Neale, 'Masculinity as Spectacle', 17.

with machine could be seen as factors connected to remasculinization if not for the negative outcomes assigned to this form of identification when it comes to subsume masculine self-identity. For example, although Farrell is often identified by his weapons, this often has negative connotations for him because it results in his being framed for Brett's crimes; in this sense there is nothing distinctive or unique about men's relationship with weapons but rather weapons can contribute to confusion regarding identity. Similarly Brett is identified by (and identifies with) his weapons and his gang is named after them. Repeated references are made regarding the interconnectedness between Brett's sense of self and technology, but these references are made in such a way as to highlight this connection as a negative one, suggesting that men cannot find a form of remasculinization through the display of technology. For example, Beth reflects that guns: 'are like a disease with you [Brett]. Something that eats from the inside'; and the sheriff who arrested him at the start of the film reflects that Brett is: 'the type who can't be a man without a pistol in his hand.'

The detangling of the relationship between men and technology is further established by the successful usation of different types of technology and strategies by other groups to achieve their aims. Beth Donovan, for example, successfully plays on gender stereotypes regarding female helplessness to convince her husband to give her a light while he is holding her captive. She uses this light to ignite gunpowder, blowing off the door and facilitating her escape. When the body of her dead husband is delivered to the Indian camp where she is recovering from a gunshot wound she uses dirt, the butt of a pistol and a knife to leave without Farrell. Subsequently, when captured and propositioned by Brett, she uses psychological warfare to play upon his insecurities, thereby giving Farrell a distinct advantage. In this action Beth illustrates that warfare can be conducted strategically without technology at all provided the individual is skilled with an understanding of the enemy. Similarly the Native Americans in this film use a variety of weapons and tactics to achieve an advantage over the gang during conflict and, indeed, a Native American woman states upon seeing the gunshot wound inflicted upon Beth, 'white man do that? White man crazy.' This statement reflects self-consciously upon the destructive trap of violence and its use in oppressing other groups. On the one hand this use of different

technologies by different groups facilitates a positive hyper-linear relationship and supports the broader message of the film that individual rather
than structural forces can be attributed to gun violence by illustrating that
even groups that are disadvantaged under white patriarchy can be successful. However, on the other hand, none of these groups are extricated from
a broader system of violence and white patriarchy and their experiences
are ultimately mediated by Farrell. Their actions can be read as an attempt
to gain some autonomy with the limited resources they have, as advanced
technology is unavailable to them.

It is necessary to acknowledge here that it could be argued that what
the audience witnesses is this film in terms of gender performance is, as
Wendy Chapman Peek asserts, a 'romance of competence.'[30] Peek suggests
that post-World War II Westerns do not privilege one set of actions as
masculine but rather privileges any type of action or gendered behaviour
provided it leads to success – that is, is 'competent'. In presenting this mixture of gender behaviours these films create 'a new ideal of masculinity that
incorporates all manner of behaviours' whilst also, paradoxically, ensuring
that 'when the hero succeeds in being masculine, he actually fails to be
masculine, for he is now of confused gender, neither truly feminine nor
truly masculine.'[31] Following this argument Farrell therefore can engage
with different social groups, technologies and modes of behaviour without
compromising hegemony as, ultimately, he is successful. I would suggest,
however, that Farrell (or any character) is never separated from the system
of violent oppression or from the privilege he receives by virtue of his masculine gender performance. This is made explicit by the fact that although
other groups (Beth, Native Americans) demonstrate a similar flexibility they
are not deemed competent enough to ultimately be successful because they
are not privileged by hegemonic structures. Therefore competence leading
to success is a position that can only be occupied by a white man regardless
of the level of personal identification he has with broader social structures.

30   Wendy Chapman Peek, 'The Romance of Competence: Rethinking Masculinity in
     the Western', *Journal of Popular Film and Television* 30 (2003): 206–219.
31   Peek, 'The Romance of Competence', 206 & 208.

Indeed, when gender and history are viewed in conjunction it could be argued that the emergent theme in this Western, which would reach fruition in later nihilistic Westerns or Westerns that privilege criminality, is the historical phenomenon Richard Maxwell Brown refers to as the 'Western Civil War of Incorporation' from 1850–1920. For Brown this term refers to the struggle to incorporate Western states into modern capitalistic structures as opposed to agrarianism and the genteel patriarch economic model.[32] Therefore, violence on the frontier is also 'the history and organization of power'; a history where violence enacted between individuals reflects the disparate interests of modern capitalism with its demand for law and order and defence of conservative business interests and those who resisted incorporation and found themselves increasingly alienated from modern capitalistic structures, including 'social bandits'.[33] With the conflicting economic and social interests presented by Western incorporation also comes conflicting ideas regarding ideal forms of masculine behaviour and patriarchal structures. The conflict between these forces and the contradictions regarding access to technology, capacity to use violence, and the implications this has on modes of gendered behaviour, can be seen embodied in Farrell, who stands firmly for incorporation through his endorsement of capitalistic structures and the value of law and order. It can also be seen in Brett and Paul Donovan, who represent resistance to incorporation through their banditry and alienation from the sources of modern capitalism. Whilst this film connects the West's incorporation to modern America in a positive way, later films such as *Butch Cassidy and the Sundance Kid* (George Roy Hill, 1969) and *Ride the High Country* (Sam Peckinpah, 1962), particularly those that privilege criminality as an honourable or understandable action in the face of changing economic conditions that have undermined traditional forms of masculinity, reflect on the values of incorporation negatively, often constructing a negative hyper-linear relationship between incorporation and modern economic and social change.

---

32   Richard Maxwell Brown, 'Western Violence: Structure, Values, Myths', *The Western Historical Quarterly* 24 (1993): 4–20.

33   Brown, 'Western Violence', 7.

This reflects not only on the historical past in terms of emergent gun culture, American ideology and the so-called 'Western Civil War of Incorporation', but connects the historical past to issues in the contemporary scene. Firstly, the increasing self-consciousness regarding the role of the gun can be seen to reflect growing concerns regarding the representation of violence in Hollywood itself. Indeed, film censor George Mirams' 1951 article 'Drop that Gun!' illuminates the issues around images of violence particularly as used in the filmic Western, providing a breakdown of different forms of violence and crime across a sample of Western and non-Western films. Mirams points to a trend for violent representation, in particular, murder via gun violence in Westerns, as linked to the changes in the Hollywood production code which placed strict limitations on representations of sexual relationships. These films favour representations of violence instead, in so doing presenting the contradiction that 'the stark act of ending life is treated as being infinitely more suitable for public consideration than any reference to the act of beginning it [...] over-emphasized violence degenerates into sadism – and most psychologists agree that there is a connection between sadism and sex.'[34] From this perspective violence and the presence of the gun is presented in Westerns to provide titillation at a time when sexual content was prohibited and, as a result, excessive violence itself became a target of censorship concern.

Whilst Mirams and Ralph Brauer both make psychological assumptions regarding the ways in which sadistic violence complements the absence of actual sexual content on screen due to stricter production codes in Hollywood in this time, more broadly both illustrate the concern about representations of violence and the impact that this has on viewers. The gun-conscious films of this era, including *Colt .45*, can be seen to reflect upon this contemporary concern regarding violent representation, but *Colt .45* draws a hyper-linear connection with the past that demonstrates the positive exercise of violence to protect law and order and to assist in

---

34 Gordon Mirams, 'Drop that Gun!' *The Quarterly of Film, Radio and Television* 6 (1951): 9–10. An identical point was discussed in Ralph Brauer with Donna Brauer, *The Horse, The Gun and the Piece of Property: Changing Images of the TV Western* (Bowling Green, OH: Bowling Green University Popular Press, 1975), 59.

nation-building. Constructing this hyper-linear connection with the past in this fashion then enacts contemporary concerns regarding violent representation but ultimately soothes them by demonstrating the foundational nature of violence in the broader American narrative and ideology.

By the late 1960s, however, *The Wild Bunch* over-emphasized and made apparently brutal the representation of violence on-screen. In undertaking this representation the film demonstrates a grittier, more realistic violence that impresses its destructive realities.[35] This film creates a negative hyper-linear relationship between past and present realities, providing a commentary on American ideology. This commentary suggests that American society is founded in violent oppression of all non-hegemonic groups and American interventionism with associated destructiveness and paternalism assumptions. In sum, both films reflect contemporary concerns about the representation and impacts of filmic violence. However, as book-ends of this period (1950 and 1969, respectively), they communicate different understandings of the past and how that past relates to these issues. For *Colt .45* violence on-screen may be problematic but it should be viewed in the framework of the positive impacts gun technology has had in founding the nation. *The Wild Bunch*, however, sees brutality on-screen as a reflection of, and dialogue with, a broader, negative and destructive culture of brutality evident in American foundations.

More than this, as Stanley Corkin suggests in his analysis of this cycle of films, the central question that these films pose regarding the use of violence reflects upon the broader foreign and domestic policy concerns of the era. Thus, Corkin asserts, the use of atomic weaponry by the USA at the conclusion of World War II 'created some sense of omnipotence, (but) it also triggered related anxieties' that were played out throughout the Cold War and were reflected in these Westerns.[36] These 'anxieties' related to the

---

35   As Mark Crispin Miller suggests, whatever the accusations Peckinpah faced regarding his representation of violence, ultimately his aims were noble rather than exploitative: 'Peckinpah wants to worry his audience … his excesses … derive from a sane, passionate, old-fashioned set of values.' As noted in 'In Defense of Sam Peckinpah', *Film Quarterly* 28 (1975): 2–3.

36   Corkin, *Cowboys as Cold Warriors*, 96.

use of technology and the balance between technological innovation and respect for humanity, fears of the effects of advanced weaponry in future warfare, increased Cold War tension in the face of Communist successes both abroad and in growing fears of Soviet and Communist infiltration of America domestically, and growing domestic unease regarding how to face these problems including conflicts with anti-nuclear and anti-war protest groups. Added to this was the impact of the Korean War, which began in 1950, the same year as both *The Gunfighter* (Henry King, 1950) and *Colt .45* were released.[37] This is, of necessity, a very brief outline of deep-rooted and complex cultural and political issues that Westerns of this era proved capable of exploring 'at a historical moment where such public criticism is becoming all but impossible politically.'[38]

This genre proved particularly capable of undertaking such an exploration because of its capacity to connect past historical moments with ongoing contemporary issues, thereby contextualizing them and empowering the audience to view these issues and themselves in an historical way. Films such as *The Gunfighter* and *The Fastest Gun Alive* (Russell Rouse, 1956), and 'pro-Indian' Westerns, reflected upon these issues in a way that saw violence, technology, and aspirations for hegemonic masculinity as intrinsically linked, negative, and illuminating and reinforcing a fundamentally contradictory American ideology.[39] However, films such as *Colt .45* self-consciously examine and critique these issues yet find that the use of gun violence, exclusionary access to resources, and the exclusionary forms of masculine identity, are not fundamentally problematic in the construction of American identity; indeed, many films of this era make this same argument, though without the same level of explicitness and are typically conceived of as unproblematic representations of pro-American and pro-patriarchal models.

---

37   Corkin, *Cowboys as Cold Warriors*, 95–98.
38   Corkin, *Cowboys as Cold Warriors*, 95.
39   It is interesting to note that Corkin identifies *The Gunfighter* as a film that criticizes American ideology and the cult of the gunfighter, yet poses no viable social alternative to this mode of behaviour and value system. This aligns very much with the characteristics of negative hyper-linearity. Corkin, *Cowboys as Cold Warriors*, 111.

Gun Technology, Masculine Gender Performance and
The Wild Bunch

As the Cold War heated up, an increasing technologization of political
rhetoric and public life, particularly under the Kennedy administration,
became evident. The sense of American government as run by the 'techno-
cratic bureaucracy' – that is a group of bureaucrats with specialist knowledge that obscures the workings of government and is seen as beyond
the understandings of ordinary citizens – acted to alienate Americans
from broader governmental and economic structures. This was heightened by Kennedy's focus on technology and mechanization as the answer
to America's industrial future.[40] Will Wright suggests that in this public
discourse technology becomes the end rather than the means by which
social goals are achieved, and political action becomes negative or static as
the broader public lacks the technological skills to engage in policy making
and managers lack incentive to stimulate radical change.[41] Kennedy's assassination acted to make most explicit the issue of America's gun culture,
with associated conspiracy theories illustrating the growing sense of an
enemy within and growing distrust of government.[42] Of course America's
celebrated space program coupled with nuclear research in an increasingly
'hot' Cold War, also acted to illustrate the duality surrounding American
attitudes towards technology in this period. However, as American forces
became bogged in the 'quagmire' of Vietnam, the ambiguity surrounding
the use of military technology and its connection to American ideology,
along with its capacity to enact hegemonic gender forms, was resolved: the
Vietnam War signalled growing disillusionment with militarism and an

---

40   Morris Dickstein, *Gates of Eden: American Culture in the Sixties* (New York: Basic
      Books, 1977), 61 and Will Wright, *Six Guns and Society: A Structural Study of the
      Western* (Los Angeles: University of California Press, 1975), 174.
41   Wright, *Six Guns and Society*, 176–177.
42   Tom Engelhardt, *The End of Victory Culture: Cold War America and the Disillusioning
      of a Generation* (New York: Basic Books, 1995), 184–186; Cook, 'Ballistic Balletics',
      151.

awareness of the gap between American ideals and realities and, through this, the flaws of a masculinity that attempted to live up to these ideals. As George E. Herring asserts, the failure of Vietnam juxtaposed to the successes of previous military actions necessitated American re-evaluation of itself as unbeatable and 'its faith that the massive application of force was the solution to military problems.'[43] This, in turn, undercut fundamental tenets of American patriarchal ideology and its enactment in hegemonic masculinity by destabilizing the connection between violent oppression of oppositional groups and gendered and landed success.

It is in this context that Sam Peckinpah's *The Wild Bunch*, with its explicit displays of violence, emerged. Certainly much has been made of Peckinpah's personal connection with the genre: Peckinpah spent summers as a youth on his grandfather's Sierra Nevada cattle ranch and its eventual sale resulted in his 'veneration for the West', his 'commitment to, and belief in, its mythic symbolism', and the melancholic tone of his conceptualization of the West.[44] *The Wild Bunch* can be viewed as a result of his personal experiences as well as the culmination of a Western oeuvre that was uniformly dark in tone, presenting men often alienated from each other and from themselves, engaged in acts of senseless brutally in a world without justice or meaning.[45] Although *The Wild Bunch* was both criticized and lauded for its depiction of violence, it is clear that Peckinpah himself saw the relationship between technology, violence and hegemonic masculinity as a meaningful and integral part of his work, stating of *The Wild Bunch*, for example: 'I hope the viciousness of the fights stays in the

43   George E. Herring, 'Preparing *Not* to Refight the Last War: The Impact of the Vietnam War on the US Military', in *After Vietnam: Legacies of a Lost War*, ed. Charles E. Neu (Baltimore: John Hopkins University Press, 2000), 58.

44   Stephen Prince, 'Introduction: Sam Peckinpah, Savage Poet of American Cinema', in *Sam Peckinpah's The Wild Bunch*, ed. Stephen Prince (Cambridge: Cambridge University Press, 1999), 20–21.

45   Although a writer and director in the TV Western Peckinpah's directorial credits include *The Deadly Companions* (1961), *Ride the High Country* (1962), *Major Dundee* (1965), and, after *The Wild Bunch*, *Pat Garrett and Billy the Kid* (1973) featuring counter cultural icon Bob Dylan.

film so people can really know how bad killing is.'[46] Clearly Peckinpah's experiences with both the mythic and real West, his concerns with representations of gender, technology and violence, and the historical forces at play, presented symbolically by the Vietnam War, all came to bear in his work and bore significant fruit in *The Wild Bunch*.

The film is set in the early 1900s and as such demonstrates, historically, ongoing advancements in weapons technology beyond the representation in *Colt .45*. Specifically the film presents the machine gun, extensive railway networks, as well as the automobile, to impress upon the audience both the later temporal locality and the juxtaposition of increased technological advancement against the greater dehumanization and demasculinization at the personal and social levels. Unlike *Colt .45* solutions to broader social problems cannot be solved between individuals but rather are structurally embedded and unsolvable by the men in the film, and the masculinities they represented, fractured as they are between different aspects of identities and their own personal interests. In this world access to technology is most clearly one avenue by which patriarchal authority is established and hegemonic masculinity is enacted and by which violence is facilitated as a method to maintain such authority. The need to maintain such control is obviously paradoxical in that it undermines claims regarding patriarchy's natural right to dominance and is acknowledged as a problematic symptom of a fundamentally flawed system in this film, particularly in the sense that the past technology and American interventionism in Mexico is connected in a negative hyper-linear relationship to then contemporary concerns regarding Vietnam and broader social problems.

Like *Colt .45* the film is structured around gun technology and uses a similar theme of gun theft, although in *The Wild Bunch* the concern of the central group is not recovering guns to be used by privileged groups but rather the wholesale sense that technology is out of control and men cannot use technology in socially advantageous ways. The film opens with the criminality of a shoot-out in a Texas town, however, the perception of an ambiguous moral divide is clear from the opening scenes where children

---

46   Sam Peckinpah from the Sam Peckinpah Collection folder no. 74, 75 as cited in Prince, 'Introduction', 25.

are shown laughing as they construct a battle between fire ants and a scor-
pion, this laughing cruelty being the central theme of the film as a whole.
Indeed, the juxtaposition of the meeting of the Temperance Union with the
senseless and arbitrary nature of violence during the robbery goes to further
impress the ambiguity of morality and the pointless nature of action where
luck rather than skill or character can have a greater consequence. This is
demonstrated, for example, when Thornton takes a shot at Pike during the
robbery but an unwitting tuba player enters the field of fire and dies in his
place.[47] Ultimately, in this film access to resources rather than an innate
sense of morality or other factors (such as Farrell's capacity to use personal
connections or his intellect) is the defining factor in whether men can
demonstrate a hegemonic masculinity. Access to resources not only defines
hegemonic masculinity but also empowers this masculinity to define the
parameters of aberrant forms of being – that is, to exclude others based on
factors such as criminality, femininity, socio-economic standing, or racial
identity. In this sense violence is not a cause but a symptom of the role of
technology and the broader capitalist system in fracturing masculinities
along multiple lines of identity.

The complete fracturing of masculinities under the weight of technology and economic conditions is evident in the film in two main ways: the
hierarchical relationship within America demonstrated by the railroads
and the relationship between Mexicans, and Mexicans and Americans
demonstrated by the Bunch and General Mapache's men. Firstly, the initial robbery in the film is part of an ongoing dispute between the railway
company and the gang who continues to rob them. Rather than criminal-
izing the gang, however, the townspeople blame the railway for not being

---

47   Fortune itself is shown to have a large role in men's lives rather than free will or per-
     sonal autonomy. This is illustrated in the flashbacks that show personal instances that
     have moulded Thornton and led to his position outside of the Bunch. For example,
     Pike was in love with a married woman and by chance her husband discovers and
     attempts to kill them. Somehow Pike survives but his lover is killed. Thornton's arrest
     and imprisonment was presaged by Thornton imploring Pike to leave the town, as
     he senses the law closing in. As Pike refuses police enter and it is simply Thornton's
     position in the room, close to the door, that leads to his arrest and allows Pike to
     flee. Their positions could easily be reversed.

able to maintain law and order in the town. Ultimately, the railway hires Thornton, an ex-Bunch member who is trying to keep a clean record after imprisonment, to lead a posse composed of civilians and military rustics to defeat the Bunch before they steal again. In a telling scene Thornton and the railway boss argue over the righteousness of hiring the bounty hunters and the quality of the men in employ, with Thornton deriding a world where morality and legality is dictated by those with access to resources and capital. Thornton asks the railwayman, for example, how it feels to 'hire your killings with the laws' arms around you? How does it feel to be so goddamn right?' The sense of capital as corrupt and controlling the arms of law and order and public opinion is reinforced through the professional ineptitude of the military contingent of the posse and the immorality of the civilian contingent who are more concerned with robbing the graves of the dead than fulfilling their contract, and both groups prove incapable of independent action without Thornton's guidance. More than this, though, it is the railway system itself that transports gun technology, which is ultimately stolen by the Bunch to support Mapache's rule in Mexico.

This film, then, acts to link capitalism, technology and violent oppression in a nihilistic way that discounts morality or hopes for meaningful discourse in favour of society controlled by faceless corporate interests.[48] These interests stimulate white patriarchal authority at a societal level, as

---

48   It is important to note that some do not conceptualize this film as wholly nihilistic; for example, as Michael Bliss suggests: '*The Wild Bunch* is in many respects a film about a lost past and a dimly perceived future that seems bereft of possibilities. Yet at the core of the film is a subtle sense of optimism that is constantly at odds with grim realities.' Michael Bliss, 'Introduction: Times Maybe, Not Them – The Enduring Value of Sam Peckinpah's Films', in *Peckinpah Today: New Essays on the Films of Sam Peckinpah*, ed. Michael Bliss (Carbondale: Southern Illinois University Press, 2012), 3. Indeed, Pike's assertion that 'when you side with a man, you stay with him. If you can't do that you're some animal. You're finished' can be construed as code of morality that refutes the notion of nihilism. I would suggest, however, that ultimately Pike realizes that in abandoning Angel he has defied what little morality he has found in the world and he goes back to retrieve Angel's corpse with the knowledge that his morality has been illusionary and he cannot effect real change: he and The Bunch are finished.

illustrated by white interventionism in Mexican affairs, and the notion of warfare as a viable means of asserting control. It also reflects attempts to attain hegemonic masculinity at the micro-level, which traps men into modes of behaviour and forces obedience to broader social structures. In this world the railway becomes emblematic of the corrupting power of capitalism, where those that control economic systems and technology are capable of asserting their will over others, an attitude that reaches its climax in violence. These interests are also capable of setting standards of masculinity that meet economic needs regardless of the desirability of the requisite gender performance for individuals and other aspects of society. Historically, this representation acts to illustrate 'capitalism's destruction of the society it supposedly sustains, the perfect evocation of Vietnam-era, destroy-the-village-in-order-to-save-it ideology.'[49] This attitude towards technology and capitalism is also reinforced by the visual representations of railroads and trains throughout the film: they appear black and dirty, cutting into and through the natural landscape obviously and harshly.

The focus on structural factors acting to alienate or even pit men against each other is further extended by the representation of Mexican warfare. Specifically the relationship between Mapache, representative of the dominant group, and Angel, representative of the rebellion, enact the same relationship as the capitalist structures within an American context. Mapache has access to resources and capital and is therefore capable of dictating modes of behaviour, and of emasculating and killing Angel, who does not have access to power or meet his standards. Unlike Brett, Angel's failure does not stem from a lack of righteousness or morality but precisely because he indicates Brett's point: the individual cannot make a difference in the face of broader social structures and individuals who have resources and capital to support them. Indeed, in this film the concept that people have a dollar value, put forward by Paul but rejected in *Colt .45*, is explicit in *The Wild Bunch*, and nothing is removed from the capitalist system. The Bunch and posse are both mercenary groups and Thornton is motivated

49   Christopher Sharrett, 'Peckinpah the Radical: The Politics of the Cold War', in *Sam Peckinpah's The Wild Bunch*, ed. Stephen Prince (Cambridge: Cambridge University Press, 1999), 95.

by his own personal interests. The film abounds with prostitutes and it is Angel witnessing his love interest sitting on Mapache's lap, and shooting her dead, that exposes his true attitude to Mapache. Pike also solicits sex and it is the realization that the prostitute's baby is laying on the floor, and witnessing the interaction between mother and child, that prompts him to return for Angel. This acts as a reminder of life and the pricelessness of humanity in an otherwise soulless and death-filled world. Although Pike may find humanistic motivation, no character proves capable of finding a way out of, or an alternative to, the patriarchal capitalism that binds them. Angel intends to use Mapache's technology against him to violent ends, women are used and traded as commodities, and destructive violence is shown as the only resolution to conflict though it ultimately solves little.[50]

The relationship between the Bunch and Mexican peoples represents historical connections between past American interventionism and the values that enabled it, and the impact this had on ongoing foreign policy decisions leading to Vietnam. The Bunch's first substantial encounter with Mexicans as a people is when they hole up in Angel's village following the opening robbery and shootout. These scenes are presaged with Pike's acknowledgement that 'those days [the days of the gun] are closing fast.' Although a troubling time for Angel, who discovers his father is dead and his girlfriend gone, for the white members it is a time of reprieve from the sense of a closing frontier. This idealized time that sees some members playing with young women prompts the village elder to reflect that: 'we all dream of being children again [...] maybe the worst of us most of all.'[51] The impression created here, that by going to Mexico the Bunch can

---

50   It is necessary to note that the depiction of women in this film has also been con-
      ceptualized as signalling nothing other than misogyny and sexism. See, for example,
      Joan Mellen, *Big Bad Wolves Masculinity in the American Film* (London: Elm Tree
      Books, 1978), 18 & 248.

51   Children are used throughout *The Wild Bunch*, typically as signifiers of a lost and
      idealized state that never actually existed. Although the elder may reflect on an ideal-
      ized childhood state the reality is children who knowingly torture a scorpion. A child
      is also shown being held by a woman strapped with ammunition belts. Childhood
      is not seen as an idealized or protected state except in retrospect with the distance
      of time. In this way childhood is used as a symbol of the state of revisionist history

reclaim a new frontier and prolong their capacity to perform their version of masculinity, echoes American attitudes during this time and in other Westerns, particularly *Butch Cassidy and the Sundance Kid*. This closely relates to Kennedy's rhetoric surrounding the 'New Frontier' in the early 1960s and the ideological assumption that it was America's responsibility to intervene in foreign affairs and transplant its institutions abroad, particularly in South-East Asia which faced the encroachment of Communist forces.[52] Such interventionism acted not only to transplant democracy but, also, benefited America by fortifying its ideology and its manifestation in hegemonic masculinity, as it is through these 'frontier' experiences that they are tested and renewed.[53]

Peckinpah then goes about thoroughly disputing the validity of this ideological assumption, historically, through the relationship between the Bunch and Mapache's men. Any semblance of altruistic motivations or understandings is dismissed as the mercenary group acts to economically exploit the instability of the region. They sell their access to resources to facilitate Mapache's oppression of oppositional groups through superior American military technologies. The Bunch show no concern for the ways that they alter the political landscape by empowering one group at the expense of organic native rebellion, nor do they express moral concerns regarding their actions despite being made aware of revolutionary impetuses by Angel. This is to the Bunch's detriment, as the group they are empowering ultimately uses their technology against them, ensuring their deaths. In presenting this Peckinpah calls upon a history of failed American interventionism in South America to express a negative continuity with American

---

itself, with the past conceptualized in an idealized way that does not reflect historical realities. Children are used throughout many Westerns, typically shown modelling the gunfights they have witnessed, thereby demonstrating the social ways in which standards of hegemonic masculinity are inculcated socially. Examples of this include *Winchester '73* (Anthony Mann, 1950) and *The Gunfighter* (Henry King, 1950).

52 Slotkin, *Gunfighter Nation*, 489.

53 This attitude has been a common thread throughout American discourse – examples used here should illustrate this historical continuity. David Fromkin and James Chace, 'What Are the Lessons of Vietnam?' in *The Vietnam Reader*, ed. Walter Capps (London: Routledge, 1991), 95 examines the claims of interventionism as moral duty.

motivations, actions and outcomes in Vietnam. The final apocalyptic violence of the film, where a machine gun is used to mow down all men, can
be seen as an historical symbol, emblematic of 'modern technologies of
violence [...] partly responsible for systematic savageries like the Vietnam
War' (see Figure 6).[54]

Figure 6: The death of Mapache (Emilio Fernandez) in the final apocalyptic massacre
in *The Wild Bunch*. The vivid demonstration of violence through film techniques
such as slow motion and inter-cutting, and the use of new technology such as
squibs, were revolutionary.

It is important to note that this structural emphasis, rather than the
personal, and the representation of American interventionism in Mexico
as destructive, stands in direct contrast to the representations put forward
in *Colt .45*. This contrast is important in highlighting the ways in which
these films bookend important historical events within the period itself,
and the ways in which those events cause the re-evaluation of the past and
its significance in American life. In particular, the Vietnam War, minority
rights-based movements, and the increasing mechanization of industry had
acted to destabilize traditional notions of American ideology and highlight
its flaws in such a way that, by 1969, a positive hyper-linear relationship with

54   Prince, 'Introduction', 21.

the past that de-emphasized America's structural and ideological failings such as that presented by *Colt .45* was no longer possible.

Conclusion

Colt .45 and *The Wild Bunch*, set in different temporal localities and bookending the period of demasculinization considered here, demonstrate that the gun does not function simply as an ahistorical symbol that is intrinsically linked to men's potency but instead that understandings of the gun can and do change over time. These films use similar themes such as the importance of personal choices versus structural forces, the role and validity of enforcing gendered behaviours and value systems through violence, and the significance of capitalist structures in facilitating and empowering distinct groups, but they deploy them in different and historically contingent ways. *Colt .45* creates a positive hyper-linear connection between the represented past and the present by illustrating a past where the Colt .45 was integral to successful American interventionism in Mexico, demonstrated emergent consumer culture, and facilitated the emergence of strong individuals. In constructing this hyper-linear relationship the film acted to acknowledge and soothe contemporary anxieties regarding the role of technology in Cold War society. By 1969, however, the Vietnam War became emblematic of the deep fissures in American society caused by a fundamentally flawed patriarchal, capitalist system and, because of this, self-conscious examinations of the role of gun technology could no longer assume a celebratory tone.[55] *The Wild Bunch* reflects this mood by constructing a negative hyper-linear relationship between represented

---

55   This argument in many ways extends Christopher Sharrett's assertions that the railway as emblem of technology in *The Wild Bunch* denotes 'everything hypocritical and morally reprehensible abut capitalism ... [and] capitalism's destruction of the society it supposedly sustains, the perfect evocation of Vietnam-era, destroy-the-village-in-order-to-save it ideology.' Sharrett, 'Peckinpah the Radical', 95.

past and present where the advancements in technology at the turn of the century are shown to contribute to, and illuminate, the fissure in American standards of hegemonic masculinity and destructive American interventionism abroad. This is connected to attitudes regarding the Vietnam War, and therefore a long history of failed American interventionism motivated by patriarchal interests and enacted by those aspiring to what might be seen as futile hegemonic masculine standards. Indeed, *The Wild Bunch* is one of many of the 'south of the border' Westerns of this period, which tap into historical ideas surrounding American interventionism and connects them to contemporary ideas surrounding interventionism in South East Asia. Certainly this is the case with *Butch Cassidy and the Sundance Kid* (George Roy Hill, 1969), the focus of the following chapter.

This perspective does not discount the number of Western films that either explicitly or overtly supports an American gun culture, the resolution of conflict through violent means, and a masculinity that endorses violence as a legitimate means of maintaining an exclusive identity. However, these supportive films and their depictions of gun technology are not entering an archetypal space divorced from the history they represent or the historical context in which they are made. Indeed they intimately engage in creating historical understandings through their depiction of men's interactions with both guns and the multitude of other forms of technology Westerns depict such as railroads, telegraph, automobile and steamships. Certainly, an analysis of *Colt .45* and *The Wild Bunch*, which explicitly examines and renders complex the depiction of gun technology and its relationship to masculinity, capitalism and violence as a method of social control, does much to illustrate the deeply historical nature of these films.

CHAPTER 6

'Who are those guys?': Understanding American Intervention in the 'South of the Border' Western

This volume has explored the ways in which changing economic, social and technological conditions, and particularly rights-based movements, from 1950 to 1970, have contributed to a perceived 'demasculinization' of American men and a fundamental questioning of the desirability of hegemonic standards of gendered behaviour at the structural and individual levels. Indeed, it can be argued that Western films of this period both illustrate the fracturing of men's identities in this context and assist audiences to understand and historicize this fracturing by allowing them to view past periods of crisis following the American Civil War. In doing so these films construct a relationship between past and present that can have positive, negative or discontinuous implications for the ways they view their own time. In many ways the Vietnam War came to embody the various fissures of American society during this period. With contestations regarding war and war technology, American interventionism, accusations of race and class discrimination in conscription, difficulties reintegrating veterans into society, and the re-evaluation of American ideals and the exclusionary forms of identity it stimulated, the Vietnam War acts as both event and signifier of the broader domestic issues plaguing American society at this time.[1] Indeed, it is ultimately the Vietnam War that facilitated

---

1   See, for example, Vietnam as abstract subject for Tom Engelhardt, *The End of Victory Culture: Cold War America and the Disillusioning of a Generation* (New York: Basic Books, 1995), 198. Vietnam as metaphor is seen as obscuring the structural nature of American domestic issues in Brain Balogh, 'From Metaphor to Quagmire: The Domestic Legacy of the Vietnam War', in *After Vietnam: Legacies of a Lost* War, ed. Charles E. Neu (Baltimore: John Hopkins University Press, 2000), 43.

the vocalization of demasculinization; the so-called 'Vietnam Syndrome', which afflicted the American nation, was marked, according to President Nixon, by distinctly feminine characteristics: compromise, negotiation, collectivism, and emotionality.[2] It is interesting, however, that despite the historical impacts of the Vietnam War, direct representations of it in film did not occur until well after the conclusion of the War, with the exception of the John Wayne propaganda effort *The Green Berets* (John Wayne, 1965).[3]

However, whilst the setting itself may not be the Vietnamese jungle as in *The Green Berets*, Vietnam as an issue was most certainly represented in Western films. These films used the West as a site of original interventionism in American affairs and connect this past with contemporary issues surrounding Vietnam. As such they question the morality of American foreign policy over time, even to the extent that the American past can be seen as founded in interventionist, even imperial, impulses. This is evident in the increasingly sympathetic portrayals of Native Americans, which expose the myth of an American nation founded on 'free' land, but also in the emergence of 'South of the Border' Westerns that examine American intervention in South America. As Noel Carroll asserts, professional Westerns set south of the United States, typically in Mexico, present certain key characteristics including that: they are composed of groups, rather than individuals; the group is military or professional in nature; the group is motivated by mercenary interests or professional pride; and the group embodies, and allows to be examined, enduring American values such as freedom and the validity of intervention.[4] Films such as *Vera Cruz* (Robert Aldrich, 1954), *The Magnificent Seven* (John Sturges, 1960), *The Wild Bunch* (Sam Peckinpah, 1969), *The Professionals* (Richard Brooks, 1966), and *Butch Cassidy and the Sundance Kid* (George Roy Hill,

2   Susan Jeffords, *The Remasculinization of America: Gender and the Vietnam War* (Bloomington: Indiana University Press, 1989), 43.

3   John H. Lenihan, *Showdown: Confronting Modern America in the Western Film* (Chicago: University of Illinois Press, 1980), 25.

4   Noel Carroll, 'The Professional Western: South of the Border', in *Back in the Saddle Again: New essays on the Western*, eds Edward Buscombe and Roberta E. Pearson (London: British Film Industry, 1998), 47–60.

1969), all present elements of these themes and critique to varying degrees the validity of American interventionism in South America, and in turn, American interventionism in Vietnam.[5] In many ways it is significant that Westerns were the chosen vehicle in popular culture to critique American interventionism; they not only provided an historical prism through which to evaluate American ideology in practice, but also an historical arena for viewers to contextualize and make sense of their own present. A vehicle such as this speaks to a rich American history in a deep and meaningful way precisely because of their explicit historical cues.

Vietnam as both distinct issue and rallying point for broader domestic unrest will be examined here in relation to the 1969 George Roy Hill film *Butch Cassidy and the Sundance Kid*. The film follows the two titled bandits, played by Paul Newman and Robert Redford respectively, as they, and their Hole in the Wall gang, plan and execute the double robbery of the Union Pacific Flyer. This sets in motion a pursuit by a 'super posse' hired by the railroads. Butch and Sundance initially seek respite in the frontier, then attempt to enlist in the Spanish-American War before fleeing to Bolivia, accompanied by Sundance's school teacher girlfriend, Etta Place (Katharine Ross). The outlaw pair attempts to turn 'straight' there but ultimately resume their criminal activities, which prompts Etta to leave and draws the attention of Pinkerton detectives and Bolivian forces. The film concludes with the iconic freeze frame of Butch and Sundance, guns drawn, emerging to face the certain death of the surrounding, innumerable, Bolivian army. There was some controversy regarding *Butch Cassidy and the Sundance Kid* when it was released, as it was originally entitled 'The Wild Bunch' and hit cinemas in the same year as Sam Peckinpah's *The Wild Bunch*. It also uses similar themes of criminal gangs outpaced by technology and seeking their fortune in South America.[6] However, the script for *Butch* actually pre-dates *The Wild Bunch* and, in contrast to

5   Other Westerns set either partly or entirely in Mexico are numerous; for an overview of the subgenre see Noel Carroll, 'The Professional Western', 46–62.

6   David A. Cook, 'Ballistic Balletics: Styles of Violent Representation in *The Wild Bunch* and After', in *Sam Peckinpah's The Wild Bunch*, ed. Stephen Prince (Cambridge: Cambridge University Press, 1999), 147.

Peckinpah's dark tones and excessive violence, Hill illustrates in this film the power of humour and a likeable cast of characters in creating a similar sense of nihilism and in illustrating the failure of hegemonic masculinity and American patriarchal institutions to stimulate meaningful lives and communities. Of course, *Butch Cassidy* is also set apart by the fact that it is based on 'real' people and events (see Figure 7).

Figure 7: The iconic finale of *Butch Cassidy and the Sundance Kid*, with the title characters played by Paul Newman and Robert Redford, captured freeze-framed, guns drawn against certain death.

Regardless of the connections between the two films *Butch Cassidy and the Sundance Kid* is worthy of analysis for a multitude of additional reasons. The film was enormously successful both in critical and commercial terms: it won four Academy Awards and, by 1973, had become the highest grossing Western film ever made and the thirteenth highest grossing film of all time.[7] Moreover, the film has interesting historical intersections both in terms of the major players involved in its production and in terms of its representations. In production terms, director George

---

7   Box office taking noted by Will Wright, *Six Guns and Society: A Structural Study of the Western* (Los Angeles: University of California Press, 1975), 95. The film won Oscars for Best Cinematography, Best Music – Original Score, Best Music – Original Song and Best Original Screenplay. It was also nominated in the categories of Best Director, Best Picture, and Best Sound.

Roy Hill was a Marine pilot who served in World War II and Korea and therefore had practical knowledge of American interventionism and the South East Asian region.[8] Hill's oeuvre also reflects a preoccupation with matters of representation, temporality and identity as illustrated in films such as *Slaughterhouse-5* (1972), *The Great Waldo Pepper* (1975) and, less explicitly, in *Thoroughly Modern Millie* (1967), *Hawaii* (1966), and *Period of Adjustment* (1962). Clearly Hill was well positioned to examine contemporary issues such as Vietnam by constructing a relationship between these issues and the historical past. Paul Newman was already an established actor at this time, with a reputation for diverse, occasionally subversive roles including in Western films *The Left Handed Gun* (Arthur Penn, 1958), *Hud* (Martin Ritt, 1963) and *Hombre* (Martin Ritt, 1966). He, along with other method actors, came to be considered 'symbols of rebellion' and clearly Newman brought his credibility and liberal politics to bear in his portrayal of Butch Cassidy.[9] Moreover, in terms of historical representation, the film is based on real people and events and uses specific historical cues, whilst also actively playing with the notion of historicity through a variety of techniques, including transitioning between colour schemas, inserting characters in staged historical scenes and through the ironic title screen: 'most of what follows is true.' Despite these factors *Butch Cassidy and the Sundance Kid* has largely been sidelined in academic analysis in favour of works that appear more explicitly counter-cultural. Indeed, when *Butch Cassidy* has been examined in academic contexts, the critics have tended to range from seeing it as 'poorly directed and tiredly directing old stereotypes' to the 'gentlest critique' of the cycle of negative Westerns.[10]

8   William Goldman, *Adventures in the Screen Trade: A Personal View of Hollywood and Screen Writing* (London: Macdonald & Co., 1983), 206.

9   Nora Sayre, *Running Time: Films of the Cold War* (New York: Dial Press, 1978), 28. Newman's liberalism and conflict with Nixon are discussed in Tom Engelhardt, *The End of Victory Culture*, 251.

10   Joan Mellen, *Big Bad Wolves: Masculinity in the American Film* (London: Elm Tree Books, 1978), 285 and Richard Slotkin, *Gunfighter Nation: The Myth of the Frontier in Twentieth Century* (New York: HarperCollins, 1992), 591.

The film itself can be divided into two distinct components: the American setting, where the gang execute the robbery and attempt to evade the posse; and the Bolivian setting, where Butch and Sundance meet their doom. This division of the film mirrors the issue of Vietnam War as iconoclasm of broader domestic issues and as actual event: when in the domestic setting Butch and Sundance experience fractures in their masculinity and are increasingly alienated from both their peers and broader social structures due to changing economic, technological, and gendered norms. These issues become manifest when the pair seek to find refuge and expression within the seeming technological and cultural backwardness of the Bolivian frontier. However, rather than regaining a form of hegemony, their experiences act only to further impress their alienation and increasing irrelevance in a modernizing world. The film, then, uses the experiences of a 'real' Butch and Sundance, set in a distinct historical period with its associated challenges, to create a negative hyper-linear connection to the then present. This connection emphasizes the continued problems experienced by men at a personal level when they aspire to hegemonic masculinities that are inevitably changeable and unachievable. At a broader level this negative continuity illustrates the social problems that arise from enforcing these standards and, further, the destructive consequences of a patriarchy that privileges interventionism as a way of proving and maintaining a national identity. The fractures presented in *Butch Cassidy* at the domestic level of society, their further solidification through their experiences in Bolivia, and the ways in which the film actively plays on notions of filmic representation of history will be examined here, demonstrating the ways in which this negative hyper-linear connection between past and present was established.

'A Little Short of Brotherly Love' on the Home Front

Butch Cassidy and the Sundance Kid explicitly examines the relationship of men with each other, women, technology and broader social structures in the first part of the film. This underlying, interconnected thematic structure illustrates men's demasculinization at the turn of the century, which was in turn connected to the contemporary issues discussed here. It presages the complete breakdown of identity occasioned by Butch and Sundance's interventionism in South America. As the narrative unfolds it also presented American experiences metaphorically, from the threats to hegemonic standards of masculinity and their manifestation in patriarchal institutions posed by a variety of interest groups, to the ultimate breakdown of identity caused when American military failures in Vietnam became apparent. The different pressure points related to men's questioning of their identity in the domestic context will be examined.

Firstly, this film has been dismissed as a serious critique of the period because of the perception that it privileges inter-male friendships while marginalizing women; in this sense 'masculinity was treated as possible only through the exclusion of women from their lives.'[11] As has been suggested in relation to *High Noon*, in Chapter Four, this view tends to underplay the vital role of Etta in the film as a woman of deeper understanding of the structural forces at work in the lives of men and as an actor who signals the fractures in men's identities occasioned by women's movements in both the represented past and the present of filmic release. We are introduced to Etta when Sundance breaks into her house. She enters, is held at gunpoint and ordered to undress. The audience is positioned to believe Sundance has gone 'hunting' for a woman and we are witnessing the prelude to a rape, this is revealed as farce though when she chastises him: she hates it when he's late. In so doing, the film plays on typical conventions regarding men's dominance and sense of entitlement to women's bodies, and of feminine resistance and inevitable, willing capitulation to men's needs, and subverts them. In this scene, and throughout the film, Etta proves capable of playing on gender conventions to achieve her goals – she plays the role of respectable schoolmarm and sexual innocent – but reveals herself to be fully aware of Sundance's criminality, becomes complicit in it, and is in an ongoing sexual relationship with him. It is Etta who provides the bandits refuge, her superior education that is demonstrated when she attempts to tutor them

---

11   Mellen, *Big Bad Wolves*, 248.

in Spanish and, by the time of their Bolivian adventure, she is willing to physically wait for the pair as they commit their crimes. Intuitively, though, Etta understands that Butch and Sundance refuse to alter their course or do battle with the structural forces that have placed them on the path to destruction, and that she cannot do this for them. She understands that because of this intractability they must inevitably die. However, she refuses to witness this inevitability so, exercising her autonomy, she leaves them in Bolivia. This contrasts with Butch and Sundance's lack of understanding: their inability to adapt to the changing economic conditions in America, the cultural requirements of Bolivia, and, until the film's final freeze-frame capturing their last moment of life, they are in denial regarding the consequences these failures will have.

Three other women feature in the film: two, the saloon owner, Fanny, and the prostitute, Agnes, have relatively minor roles that lack impact. The other is the unnamed female passenger on the Union Pacific Flyer who is robbed by the Hole in the Wall gang. She is the only passenger who openly objects and, in doing so, she places the actions of the gang in the social context of female empowerment, railing: 'I'm not afraid of anything. I'm a grandmother and a female and I've got my rights. You can bull all the others but you can't bull me. I've fought whiskey and I've fought gambling and I can certainly fight you.' The woman places the actions against her by Butch and Sundance within a framework of growing women's rights, both through first wave feminism and the temperance movement. More than this, she is suggesting that simply through her status as a woman, and also through her power within the domestic sphere signalled by her role as a grandmother, that she has innate power, while the men's roles are fraudulent. Ultimately though, this woman has little actual impact upon the actions being undertaken, reflecting the broader inability of women to alter the course of men who do not see their destructive relationships with patriarchy. Following her appeal Butch and Sundance pretend to take her hostage, with Butch imitating her voice, in order to get the railwayman, Woodcock, to open the doors for them. In so doing, the film plays upon typical conventions regarding chivalry as an essential characteristic of a protagonist and demonstrates an awareness in the characters of both gender conventions and the malleability of them.

This is not to suggest that the film presents a wholly pro-feminine perspective in an unproblematic way. Certainly the pseudo-rape scene, where the camera is positioned from Sundance's perspective, objectifying Etta's body with her face and individual identity entirely obscured by shadows, puts forward a disconcerting sense of masculine power and dominance that cannot be entirely diminished by the fact that it is not actually a rape scene. Men are the main characters and occupy the majority of the screen time and the plot. Ultimately, all women here are powerless to effect meaningful change within a system of masculine competition and destructiveness and either choose to withdraw from this system like Etta (or Amy in *High Noon*) or engage in, and rage against, it like the Temperance Woman (or Helen in *High Noon*). It is to suggest, however, that the film presents women within a broader network of patriarchal structures, as self-consciously aware of the impact of gender and gender performance in their lives, and develop distinct attitudes towards both these structures and their manifestation in gendered behaviours. Moreover, this awareness is represented in a distinctly historical way: Etta's role as a school teacher, one of the few 'respectable' occupations open to women hoping to achieve independence, and references to the Temperance Movement, women's rights and feminism, all act to locate the film within the context of first wave feminism. The diversity of women's roles and representations – a school teacher, prostitute, saloon owner, and grandmother – demonstrates the diversity of women's roles and power bases. In this way the gendered dislocation experienced by the masculinities in the film can be viewed within the prism of broader gender upheaval caused by feminist movements and women's growing calls for empowerment in its many forms. This is connected, hyper-linearly, to the production context where women's rights movements, sexual liberation, second wave feminism, and women's increasing participation in the work force and tertiary education, all acted to destabilize traditional gender binaries and caused a fundamental re-evaluation of the power bases of white, hegemonic masculinity.

The increasing alienation of men is also demonstrated through their relationships with technology, which is represented in the film in the forms of rail, bicycle, dynamite and gun. Like *The Wild Bunch* the railroad is a technological symbol that forces men to confront class differences. It is the railroad men who hire the Superposse and, just as Thornton rails against the inequalities and immoralities presented by the same situation, Butch too sees the problems with this, problems he expresses in deliberate class terms: 'A set-up like that [hiring the Superposse] costs more than we ever took – Probably inherited every penny you [railway owner] got! Those inherited guys – what the hell do they know?' Woodcock, the railway employee and stereotypical 'Organization Man', himself acknowledges that the price of acceptance into a socially mobile class system is the sublimation of his personal identity, values and freedoms.[12] He expresses this in his admiration for the daring of the gang whilst also asserting that: 'Butch, you know if it were my money, there is nobody I would rather have steal it than you. But, you see, I am still in the employment of E.H. Harriman, of Union Pacific Railroad.' The corrupting effect of this is evident when the sheriff attempts to raise a civilian posse to pursue the gang. Despite the fact that the gang has effectively preyed on the town through bank robberies and by stimulating prostitution, alcohol consumption and gambling the civilians remained unmoved; their interest is only aroused by the salesperson who gives them a pitch for bicycles, a technology also symbolic of consumer capitalism.

Despite this resentment of the negative impacts that those who control capital and resources have on their lives Butch and Sundance cannot extricate themselves from this system, nor do they appear to desire such a separation. Butch and Sundance quickly spend the money they gain through criminality and comment about Butch's inability to manage money responsibly. Moreover, when the trio first arrive in Bolivia, despite Sundance and Etta's obvious displeasure with the rural, 'uncivilized' landscape, Butch highlights the positive, framed solely in economic terms:

Butch: You know, it could be worse. You get a lot more for your money in Bolivia, I checked on it.

Sundance: What could they have here that you could possibly want to buy?

---

12   'Organization Man' is used in this context to refer to the title of William H. Whyte's 1956 novel, *The Organization Man*. Along with Stan Wilson's *The Man in the Grey Flannel Suit* (1955) become symbols of men's alienation from their labour and a masculine identity derived from work occasioned by mechanization, industrial hierarchies and the increasingly global economy.

Indeed, Butch and Sundance express no affiliation for the natural landscape and oppose technology not on the grounds that it disrupts the rejuvenating power of nature and their capacity to derive a masculine identity from it but, rather, from their limited access to it and its power for social mobility. This fact is illustrated explicitly when Butch, who has purchased a bicycle and engages playfully with Etta using it, disposes of it before their journey to Bolivia, yelling 'the future's yours you lousy bicycle!' Indeed, the technology that they do have access to generally demonstrates their incompetence: the gang uses excessive amounts of dynamite in their robbery of the Flyer causing an explosion that could have injured the men and scatters the paper money they are attempting to steal to the wind. Butch has never used a gun to commit a murder until they are attacked in the Bolivian context and the nature of an identity derived from ability to use a gun successfully is called into question. The duo's desire to be integrated within systems of social mobility provided by technology is also demonstrated by the fact that Butch and Sundance relish the technological backwardness of Bolivia. Here a lack of technological sophistication means lessened bank security and they are therefore able to exercise their own will and their criminality. However, although this provides a brief respite, they ultimately fail here too because they do not understand or value alternate Bolivian culture.

The referencing of new technologies such as the bicycle and the expansion of the railroad situates the film clearly within a context of changing technologies and economic systems at the turn of the century. As illustrated in discussions of *The Naked Spur, Colt .45* and *The Wild Bunch*, Westerns of this period are capable of constructing deep hyper-linear relationships between the past and present that examine the role that changing economic conditions and forms of technology have in destabilizing hegemonic forms of gender identities. *Butch Cassidy and the Sundance Kid* contributes to this discourse by suggesting that a re-evaluation of masculine standards is inevitable due to the changing skill-sets required in an industrializing society whose frontier is rapidly closing. Just as in the aforementioned examples this film connects this sense of alienation from changing structures to a production context in the 1960s where men are seen as 'depersonalized cogs in the corporate machine [who have therefore] also lost their sense of themselves as men.'[13] In this way, the film contributes to the growing number in the genre that, by the end of the 1960s, sees a negative continuity between the past and present around a locus of capitalism. In particular these films see one reason for society's disillusionment in the capitalistic system where competition and exclusive access to resources are privileged values, yet these values act only to stimulate hierarchical forms of gender identity. This, in turn, pits individuals against each other in destructive, often violent ways, to the detriment of many.

More than this, though, the film connects historiographical ideas surrounding the rejuvenating power of the frontier on American institutions and men's masculinity in the past to attitudes surrounding these ideas in the 1960s. Frederick Jackson Turner's conceptualizations, emerging themselves at the turn of the century – at the closing of the frontier – saw a unique American type of masculinity emerge from the frontier experience, a type that not only related to the individual but applied to unique American social systems and political institutions.[14] However, with the closing of the American frontier came a growing melancholy regarding the passing of frontier masculinity and a lack of opportunity to prove and continually improve American men through its hardships.[15] It is interesting then that Butch and Sundance retreat to a new frontier, one that they assume they can exploit because of its lack of technology and will allow them to assume a form of hegemonic gender performance. The pair is incapable of understanding that despite the lack of technological innovation Bolivian society functions in a fundamentally different way and reclamation of hegemony is an impossibility. Specifically, Butch and Sundance stand on the outside of Bolivian society, incapable of speaking the language and demonstrating

13   Michael S. Kimmel, *Manhood in America: A Cultural History*, 2nd edn (Oxford: Oxford University Press, 2006), 158.

14   Frederick Jackson Turner, 'Social Forces in American History [annual address as the president of the American Historical Association at Indianapolis, December 28, 1910]', in *The Frontier in American History*, ed. Frederick Jackson Turner (Malabar, Florida: Robert E. Krieger Publishing, [1920] 1985), 213–214.

15   Frederick Jackson Turner, 'The Significance of the Frontier in American History', in *The Frontier in American History*, ed. Frederick Jackson Turner (Malabar, FL: Robert E. Krieger Publishing, [1920] 1985), 37.

little understanding for the Bolivian way of life and, ultimately, they come undone because of local knowledge and forms of communication: the brand on their horses is recognized and reported through individuals before coming to rest with authority who acts to eliminate them. In many ways this echoes American experiences in Vietnam where protestations regarding the moral imperative to intervene were re-conceptualized as racially and culturally arrogant, and where American forces were undone by guerrilla networks that they were incapable of understanding or combating despite their access to far superior military technology.[16] Despite Kennedy's calls to the new frontier, which called upon deep reservoirs of American understanding regarding the nature of the frontier experience, Vietnam was exposed as a frontier that did nothing to test and rejuvenate the masculinity of the men who went there or the society that sent them but rather illustrated its failings and caused a fundamental re-evaluation of an American past founded in landed oppression of Indigenous peoples and perpetuated through violent interventionism.[17]

Of course, not all Western films of this era portrayed American interventionism in a negative light or constructed a hyper-linear relationship of negative historical continuity surrounding past and present issues. *The Magnificent Seven* (John Sturges, 1960) stands as the most obvious example of positive continuity in this period. Displaying Noel Carroll's characteristics of the 'professional' Western subgenre mentioned earlier, the film features a team of seven men hired by a small Mexican village to defend them against the criminal gang that robs and terrifies them. Each man possesses a unique skill and motivation for participating in the defence of

16 See, for example, Senator J. William Fulbright's denouncement to Congress of America's 'arrogance of power' in its Vietnam War policies in 1966 as cited in *Major Problems in American Foreign Relations* (Concise edition), eds Dennis Merrill and Thomas G. Paterson (New York: Houghton Mifflin Company, 2006), 424–425; and the discussion of military technology and attitudes to the application of extreme force in George E. Herring, 'Preparing *Not* to Refight the Last War: The Impact of the Vietnam War on the US Military', in *After Vietnam: Legacies of a Lost* War, ed. Charlies Neu (Baltimore: John Hopkins University Press, 2000), 58.

17 See Richard Slotkin, *Gunfighter Nation*, 489–490, and Tom Engelhardt, *The End of Victory Culture*, 165, for Kennedy's use of the frontier terminology.

the town yet, despite this, the team comes to respect each other and the town they have been hired to defend, despite the ambivalence of many to their presence. When gang leader Calvera and his men return and find the town occupied a shootout commences in which the bandits are successful. They offer the Magnificent Seven the opportunity to leave the town and return to America but the Seven ultimately refuse to flee; they return to the town and successfully defend it. Four of the Seven die in the effort, one decides to stay in the town for love and two ride off for destinations unknown. The historical metaphor of the film is generally acknowledged; as Slotkin asserts the film 'applies the race-war symbolism of the West to a 'Mexico' story that is an allegory and a prophecy of the course of counter-insurgency in Vietnam.'[18] The plot structure alone suggests a relationship of positive continuity although further techniques aid in this perception. It is important to note, too, that it is significant that the film was released in 1960, before the destabilizing of American identity through this war and domestic unrest became apparent. The fact that the Seven is composed of a man who identifies partly as Mexican (although he is named O'Reilly), and that they endorse the value of a Mexican village, goes to support Jefford's point that Vietnam War narratives reinforce gender differences as a way to sideline the significant and potentially destabilizing differences between men, particularly along racial lines.[19] Indeed, women are almost wholly absent from the text, reinstating gender binary through their absence, except as village women and wives who require the protection of men from men. More than sideline difference, the two central characters in the film Chris Adams (Yul Brenner) and Vin Tanner (Steve McQueen) actively rebel against the notion of racial discrimination by protesting against the ill treatment of a Native American corpse that American townspeople refuse to bury respectfully.

The Magnificent Seven simultaneously casts men, and by proxy the nation that prompts them into action, as martyrs for people who do not necessarily understand the magnitude of their sacrifice whilst also demonstrating that their sacrifice is noble and worthwhile because the town

18   Slotkin, *Gunfighter Nation*, 461.
19   Susan Jeffords, *The Remasulinization of America*, 53.

embodies values worth saving. The town is incapable of saving itself, however, and must rely on outside aid, thereby providing a moral imperative that justifies interventionism. This is portrayed most nobly by Bernardo O'Reilly (Charles Bronson) who befriends young boys in the village. Ultimately O'Reilly dies for the village and its values but not before imploring the boys not to consider their fathers cowards:

> You think I am brave because I carry a gun; well, your fathers are much braver because they carry responsibility [...] And this responsibility is like a big rock that weighs a ton. It bends and it twists them until finally it buries them under the ground. And there's nobody says they have to do this. They do it because they love you, and because they want to. I have never had this kind of courage [...] That's why I've never started anything like that.

However, evident in this speech are both patriarchal norms that justify interventionism and a subtle subversion of them: whilst O'Reilly feels justified in judging cultural 'others' and informing the children of what they should find brave he too sits outside of normative social institutions such as marriage, family and gainful employment. Indeed, all of the Seven sit outside of these structures and their deaths can be read as inevitable in the sense that they are socially aberrant and do not wholly fit within standards of masculine behaviour. This can be seen to reflect historical contexts, in both the past and present, in which society struggles to reintegrate War veterans into domestic structures, where men are attempting to find meaning in increasingly mercenary labour, and where men are faced with seemingly contradictory messages regarding the ideal form of masculinity. In particular, these mixed messages refer to the desirability of freedom and individualism versus a responsibility to community and family.[20] Even films that are patently positive arrive at this point through the negotiation of social factors that are threatening to hegemonic standards of masculinity.

At the heart of the capacity for the professional Western subgenre to present narratives that are subversive towards patriarchal standards

---

20 Bernd Elzer, "'At Last My Hero': Alternative Masculinities in the 1950s Hollywood Melodrama', in *Rebels Without a Cause? Renegotiating the American 1950s*, eds Gerd Hurm and Ann Marie Fallon (Bern: Peter Lang, 2007), 157–159.

is to what extent they actually do privilege inter-male contact. The most fundamental way in which demasculinization is demonstrated is through the relationship between men – in *Butch Cassidy and the Sundance Kid*, between members of The Hole in the Wall Gang, between the Gang and oppositional forces including the posse, and between Butch and Sundance. Generally *Butch Cassidy* is conceptualized as an iconic 'buddy flick' where the relationship between the central protagonists and other male groups acts as an example of the 'homosocial bond.'[21] Eve Sedgewick's conceptualization of the homosocial bond suggests that men's positive relationships with each other are given social privilege as these networks act as a support structure for broader patriarchal dominance.[22] It could be suggested, however, that rather than homosociality, the film demonstrates multiple, competing, masculine interests all of which suffer in some way under the system of patriarchal dominance. Indeed, even in films that construct a relationship of positive hyper-linearity this can be the case; *The Magnificent Seven* does privilege male groups but these groups often have little in common and are forced into competition with each other. However, the fracturing between and within masculine groups is explicit in *Butch Cassidy and the Sundance Kid*.

There are several masculine groupings in the film which have little in common and demonstrate men's competition and suffering under patriarchy. The Hole in the Wall gang are social outcasts due to their criminality but, more than this, are shown as constantly in competition with each other and largely incompetent. This is demonstrated immediately upon being introduced to the gang, when Harvey Logan (Ted Cassidy) challenges Butch for leadership of the gang. Butch responds by paying lip service to patriarchal notions of a 'fair fight' but ultimately confuses Logan and unchivalrously kicks him in the groin. This exchange sets a subversive tone which demonstrates that masculine groups do not exist in 'natural' harmonious ways; rather these groups are regulated through a violence that

21   As cited in Cynthia Fuchs, 'The Buddy Politic', in *Screening the Male: Exploring Masculinities in Hollywood Cinema*, ed. Steven Cohan & Ina Rae Hark (London & New York: Routledge, 1993), 194–195.

22   Cynthia Fuchs, 'The Buddy Politic', 194–210.

relates little to justice, quality leadership or superior skills. Indeed, the super posse, much like the gang itself, is composed of men motivated by mercenary interests. For the most part, then, they are portrayed as mechanized: they are represented as shadowy figures, without a true identity or relationships with each other, divorced from their function in pursuing the gang. Only two members are identifiable, and they are made so by elements that are inauthentic or complicate their sense of themselves in the world: lawman Joe Lefors is made visible by his white straw hat, both unfashionable and impractical in the chase context, and Lord Baltimore, a Native American tracker who adopted an English name, in so doing denying his heritage and the mythic source of his superior ability. These themes of personal relationships obscured by mercenary interests are echoed in the other male groups: the Bolivian bandits who mirror the Hole in the Wall gang; Bolivian law enforcement; and, in the relationship between railway bosses and those in their employ, all of which are dictated by monetary and self-interests.

The point here is that simply presenting Butch and Sundance, or any one group, as out-dated modes of being is fallacious: patriarchy is structured in such a way that all male groups (and individuals) are perpetually forced into destructive competition with each other.[23] Although individuals may have agency their capacity for real change to either behaviour or to the system that structures it is limited by the nature of homosocial competition, as well as access to resources and other factors. Whilst a 'patriarchal equilibrium' may exist that adapts to changing historical conditions in such a way that maintains men's high status collectively, the effect of changing conditions is to pit men against each other with various effects on different types of masculinities and on different individual gender performances.[24] The result of this perpetual competition between men and male groups is an illusionary homosocial bond, where men may join forces to increase

23   This contests this notion that many nihilistic Westerns simply presents an older masculinity 'with their backs to the wall' as presented by Christopher Sharrett, 'Peckinpah the Radical: The Politics of The Wild Bunch', in *Sam Peckinpah's 'The Wild Bunch'* ed. Stephen Prince (Cambridge: Cambridge University Press, 1999), 83.

24   Judith M. Bennett, *History Matters: Patriarchy and the Challenge of Feminism* (Manchester: Manchester University Press, 2006), 77–81.

their potential to accrue power but their relationships with each other lack authenticity and do little to create a deeper meaning in men's lives.[25]

In this way the film reflects upon the sense of men's displacement occasioned by industrialization and mechanization of workplaces, where those men lacking the skills to adapt to change are marginalized and traditional sources of men's power – their labour and physicality – are sidelined in favour of marketplace values.[26] It also illustrates that the frontier no longer provides a viable space for men to reclaim these traditional forms of masculinity or to escape from the broader fracturing elements of modernizing society. This corresponds to men's alienation from increasingly corporatized capitalistic structures that obscures a capacity to derive a meaningful identity following World War II. Also, just as the safety valve of the frontier was removed at the turn of the century, 1960s youth culture expressed a longing for ways to communicate a sense of authentic self in a society which was increasingly alienated from government, fearful of the impacts of corporate America on personal identity, and anxious about the War in Vietnam and the possibility of conscription.[27] As Robin Bates asserts, he was able to identify strongly with the characters in the film precisely because 'while I enjoyed thumbing my nose at authority, deep down I realized where the power really lay. It was only a matter of time, I knew, before the posse got me.'[28] Importantly, then, *Butch Cassidy* presents for

---

25   Such relationships are also demonstrated prominently in *The Wild Bunch*, where not only are the Bunch forced into violent conflict with other groups and with broader society but are also in competition with each other. For example, when the leader Pike injures his leg it at first appears that he may be unable to continue, which prompts not sympathy or bonding between men who seek to aid him, but rather murderous intent.

26   See, for example, Michael S. Kimmel, *The History of Men: Essays on the History of American and British Masculinities* (New York: State University of New York, 2005), 38.

27   Joan Mellen identifies similar factors behind the identification of young American men with Clint Eastwood's 'Man With No Name' character (although she draws different conclusions from this), *Big Bad Wolves*, 267–268.

28   Robin Bates, 'Connecting to Film History Through Writing', *Cinema Journal* 39 (2000): 85.

the audience a past whose issues they can intimately identify with, by its reflection on the ways in which patriarchal, capitalist structures are inherently geared towards men's competition and exclusionary forms of identity which culminates in violent excess or the sublimation of individuality in favour of social mobility.

Even the seemingly model homosocial relationship between Butch and Sundance demonstrates demasculinization and the alienation of men from each other. Individually, the sense of masculine inadequacy is reflected at the fundamental level of the character's names. 'Butch', in reality a nickname granted Cassidy deriving from his 'straight' profession, butchery, is clearly at odds with Newman's portrayal which presents Butch as sentimental, romantic and irreverent.[29] Sundance's moniker 'Kid' is conclusively deconstructed by Joan Mellen, who suggests that ultimately the prevalence of this derivative in Westerns is 'at once a code and a testament to the hero's toughness and fear of age as he yearns to be forever seventeen, eager and potent. Only unconsciously does it carry the infantile nature of the grown man's frantic need to escape self-doubt with a six-gun or at the gambling table.'[30]

'Lord Baltimore' the adopted affectation of the Native American tracker also demonstrates the power of naming, as does the railroad employee, Woodcock. Woodcock is repeatedly robbed by the gang and develops an odd appreciation and fear of them, functioning as both their victim who is injured in the explosion the gang use to open a safe, yet he is also alienated from the economic forces of the railroad and admires the gang for their rebellion against these normative elements. His name reflects the duality of his nature and his ultimate failure to achieve his own, independent gender performance: Woodcock connotes a hard yet impotent masculinity and is a reference to the North American game bird. Just like a game bird Woodcock too is prey to larger, more powerful forces in the form of the gang on the one hand, and economic structures that keep him trapped in a job for which he feels distaste on the other. Both Butch and Sundance, along with Lord Baltimore and the disempowered railroad

---

29   A discussion of the 'real' Butch's name is presented in Anne Meadows, *Digging Up Butch and Sundance* (Lincoln: University of Press, 2003), 22.

30   Joan Mellen, *Big Bad Wolves*, 255.

worker Woodcock, demonstrate men's outward adherence to patriarchal standards whilst, at the same time, subversion and failure to live up to these standards. Importantly Butch, Sundance and Lord Baltimore are all aliases, connoting men's attempts to construct a version of masculinity that they feel is unattainable simply by being themselves.

The behaviour of Butch and Sundance, with a leaning towards the comedic capacity for explicit verbal communication and a light-hearted approach to life, has largely been conceptualized as evidence that the film cannot function as a proper critique of American experiences in the represented past or the contemporary social scene. This is, as Jane Tompkins conceptualized, because men's silence in Westerns is essential to their construction of masculine identity in two major ways: firstly, men's silence highlights that verbal communication is 'weak and misleading' as opposed to action, and those men who are most capable of using language are usually made so because they possess, or benefit from, power discrepancies.[31] Secondly, men's silence – or, when they do choose words, their capacity to communicate succinctly, meaningfully and sparingly – is usually defined in relation to the 'inadequacy of female verbalisation.'[32] Indeed, this argument is extended by Steve Neale, who analyses the psychoanalytic nature of language acquisition and suggests that there is a perceived connection between verbalization and castration in men.[33] Butch openly uses verbal communication and Sundance ironically notes the dominant perceptions of men's communication by stating that he is 'naturally blabby I guess.' Ultimately, rather than the comedic elements of the film being seen as naturally pro-social they can also be seen, conversely, as a gender critique that undermines patriarchy's claims to natural dominance through 'its

31   Jane Tompkins, *West of Everything: The Inner Life of Westerns* (New York: Oxford University Press, 1992), 49, 51. This is a point supported by Mellen, *Big Bad Wolves*, 269.

32   Tompkins, *West of Everything*, 59.

33   Steve Neale, 'Masculinity as Spectacle: Reflections of Men in Mainstream Cinema', in *Screening the Male: Reflections of Men in Mainstream Cinema*, eds Steven Cohan and Ina Rae Hark (London: Routledge, 1993), 12–13.

rejection of the frivolous, superficial, ephemeral and trivial.'[34] Even if we are to accept that a homosocial bond exists between Butch and Sundance, it does not necessarily follow that such a bond is necessarily supportive of patriarchal structures as it functions in a way that is contrary to hegemonic standards of masculinity.

Therefore, at an individual level and in terms of their functioning in society, Butch and Sundance complicate notions of a homosocial bond. This is also evident when considering their relationship with each other: throughout the film the audience is positioned to detect the differences between the two men that allows them to function together in a destructive way, without ever truly knowing each other or understanding their pathology. Butch is the 'brains' of the outfit, displaying a proclivity for verbal communication, pacifism, capitalism and entrepreneurialism, and a romantic nature. In contrast Sundance is 'the gun', favouring violence, even destructiveness, as a valid form of problem solving, non-verbal communication and pragmatism in his gender performance. At first these differences are seen as complementary characteristics that allow the pair to function well together; indeed, Sundance even laughingly acknowledges this difference, telling Butch to 'keeping thinking [...] that's what you're good at.' However, it is revealed that, far from a 'bro-mance', Butch and Sundance lack fundamental knowledge of each other: it is revealed that Butch is unaware that Sundance grew up in Atlanta and that he cannot swim and, likewise, Sundance is unaware that Butch has never murdered before and neither is aware of the other's real name. Both seem to deny the obvious love triangle that exists with Etta, a fact that Etta attempts to address by asking Butch whether he ever wonders if things would have turned out differently if she had met him first, rather than Sundance. Ultimately, this mutual ignorance of the other is not significant until put under the stress of the Bolivian frontier. When their lack of knowledge is exposed self-serving illusion is stripped away to reveal the true nature of their relationship, a

---

34   Martin Pumphrey, 'Why do Cowboys Wear Hats in the Bath? Style Politics for the Older Man', in *The Movie Book of the Western*, eds Ian Cameron and Douglas Pye (London: Studio Vista, 1996), 61.

relationship that can be seen as symbolic of American ideology and justifications for American interventionism.

American Men Dying Bloody in Bolivia

When in Bolivia Butch and Sundance attempt to turn 'straight' by working
as payroll guards for a mining company, however, the pair find themselves
held up by Bolivian bandits. It is this murderous confrontation, Butch's first
active participation in a murder, which forces them to understand their
true natures and the destructiveness of their relationship. The gravity of
this scene in stimulating this self-reflection is demonstrated by Hill's use
of slow motion and cross-cutting between falling victims and Butch and
Sundance to emphasize the impact of violence on them and their identities. The fundamental re-evaluation it occasions is explicitly reflected in
the script, although it does not appear in the final cut of the film. Here
Sundance turns to Butch and states: 'What are we doing here? [...] You got
to tell me – I got to know – what are we doing? – I'm not sure anymore –
are we outlaws – you're smart Butch so you tell me.'[35] In this confrontation
Butch, by physically killing for the first time, must acknowledge that he
cannot justify his life of crime through his well-meaning charm or his vague
egalitarianism but rather must come to terms with the fact that his pacifism
is illusionary; as leader of The Hole in the Wall gang he is responsible for
the socially deleterious effects of crime and violence on society and individuals. These effects are caused by little more than economic exploitation
rather than any real social rebellion or as an alternative to existing social and
economic structures. Throughout the attack Sundance assumes a leadership
position, speaking on their behalf and only using Butch in the capacity of
a translator. This suggests that he can no longer shift responsibility for his
own homicidal nature and its destructiveness onto Butch but must see

---

35   William Goldman, *Butch Cassidy and the Sundance Kid* [screenplay] (London: Corgi
      Books, 1969), 144.

it as an integral part of his own nature. This scene, as culmination of the pathology we have already witnessed in their relationship throughout the film and using the mirror of other bandits, forces the protagonists to see themselves as they truly are and understand the ways they have used each other to maintain an illusionary identity.

The understanding of the true nature of their gender performance, however, stands for far more: their micro-level behaviour comes to embody the discrepancies in American ideology at the macro-level. Just as their own confrontation with Bolivian bandits in South America stimulates an understanding of their true natures, the Vietnam War became the iconic event which represented the gap between American myth and reality. The Vietnam War – after ongoing Cold War pressure and domestic unrest, stimulated by the African American Civil Rights movement, other minority rights movements, second wave feminism and changing gender norms stimulated by this, and by post-World War II reintegration of war veterans, as well as industrial and technological change – served as a definitive fissure in American promise versus reality. Specifically, the American perception of 'Manifest Destiny' that justifies exceptionalism and sees interventionism as an American responsibility dictated by divine purpose and natural superiority, along with the notion that to transplant American institutions and test American manhood through ongoing frontier experiences, was of benefit to the nation. These ideas collided painfully with increasing public questioning of these assumptions. This questioning emphasized economic, racist and imperialistic motivations rather than altruism as a reason for America's ongoing interference abroad.[36] These discrepancies in American ideology versus reality strongly align with the discrepancies between Butch and Sundance's personal myths and the reality of their aspirations for hegemony. Like the culture of their origin Butch and Sundance have functioned to obscure the reality of their actions. In creating such a connection the film illuminates the link between personal gender performance and

---

36   Mark Cronlund Anderson, *Cowboy Imperialism and the Hollywood Film* (New York: Peter Lang, 2007) provides an interesting analysis of the intersections of American ideology and interventionism as represented in film.

the way in which this performance cyclically feeds into, maintains, and is
maintained by broader patriarchal social structures.

   Butch Cassidy and the Sundance Kid does more than symbolically
represent the contemporary issue of Vietnam via the past and the lives
of Butch and Sundance and their Bolivian experiences, rather, American
interventionism is referred to explicitly through direct references to the
Spanish-American War. This occurs in the film in two major instances:
the first is presented when Butch and Sundance are invited to the farewell
party of a local saloon's piano player before he leaves for war. Sundance
queries what war they are talking about and Butch responds with the slogan
'Remember the *Maine*?', Sundance sarcastically responds, 'How could I
forget?' When they enter the saloon 'Remember the *Maine*' is clearly visible on a banner in the background. The second specific reference is made
when Butch and Sundance are fleeing the Superposse; they seek to enlist
in the Spanish-American War as a method of escape yet they are rejected
by the law officer, Sheriff Bledsloe. Although clearly friendly with the
pair Bledsloe informs them that the government will not pardon them a
lifetime of criminality simply by joining the military. He insists that they
bind and gag him as evidence that he is not corrupt, illustrating the arti-
ficiality of moral distinctions between law and order and lawlessness, and
expresses anger that they would burden him with this request. Indeed, in
Bledsloe's eyes, they should have simply let themselves be killed long ago
and he implores Butch and Sundance to realize that they are 'nothing but
two-bit outlaws on the dodge. It's over. Don't you get that? Your time is
over and you're going to die bloody. And all you can do is choose where.'

   The Spanish-American War is explicitly and self-consciously evoked,
bringing to the fore the issue of interventionism in American history and
creating parallels between this interventionism and the audience's own
experiences of American foreign policy in South East Asia. In so doing a
hyper-linear connection is made with the past that encourages the audience to view the roots of their disillusionment with American action in
Vietnam in light of a long history of American landed aggression with its
associated destructive, even imperial consequences. In this way American
failure in Vietnam is not seen as an anomaly or isolated event but rather
as an inevitable result of both an ideology that conceptualizes a duty to

intervene in foreign relations whilst also being motivated by mercenary interests or cultural insensitivity and a history of enacting such impulses. Indeed, Sundance's ironic question 'what war?' speaks, potentially, to multiple historical ideas. On the one hand it could be argued that this question acknowledges the bellicose nature of American society and ironically comments that war participation is so extensive that the actual wars themselves can be referred to interchangeably. It could also refer to the idea that Sundance genuinely is not aware of American foreign policy and speaks to a lack of critical appreciation by Americans of their government and the historical past.

Although the Spanish-American War is conceptualized as an American success there are several key factors that make it particularly relevant to a 1960s context. The first is the degree of domestic unrest that characterized discourse on the War and delayed US intervention. The Cuban revolt broke out in February 1895, however, domestic opposition to interventionism in the area delayed American involvement until 1898. Piero Gleijeses points to multiple reasons for this delayed interventionism related to the domestic context: specifically increasing anti-war protests suggested that war would come at a heavy price both in money and men without promise of material reward. For a country 'mired in a severe economic, social and political crisis', including economic and technological shifts and recovery from economic depression, war with Spain over Cuba was a politically risky manoeuvre made more dire by the fact that there was no clear way to achieve victory.[37] Specifically, there was no obvious way to colonize it and, as a republic, it, along with Haiti, posed a threat to regional stability.[38] Moreover, Cuba had a racially diverse population composed predominantly of black, Indian and Spanish citizens: not only did America question its capacity to control such a population but there were also growing questions surrounding the influence of such a rebellion on domestic race relations. This was particularly significant in the context of increasing racial instability between white and African American citizens arising from the

---

37   Piero Gleijeses, '1898: The Opposition to the Spanish-American War', *Journal of Latin American Studies* 35 (2003): 686.

38   Gleijeses, '1898', 704.

realization that promises of greater racial equity made as a result of the Civil War would not be fulfilled.[39]

The domestic unrest in America from the outbreak of the Cuban revolt until forces were finally committed in 1898 clearly parallels the domestic unrest before entry in full force in Vietnam. The Civil Rights Movement highlighted the increasing fissures in American society along racial lines, and caused a fundamental re-evaluation of the realities of American ideology founded in racially exclusionary forms of identity. Native Americans joined this chorus and members of both groups questioned the validity of investing money into a foreign war instead of improving socio-economic conditions for minority groups.[40] Of course it is important to acknowledge that reactions to the commitment of troops to Vietnam is not monolithic, rather the issue of Vietnam was extremely divisive.[41] These racial fissures were further exacerbated by the fact that, demographically, those men who were poor, uneducated and black were over-represented in American military personnel in Vietnam; personnel who were subsequently neglected upon returning home.[42]

Just as there was no clear definition of success leading up to the Spanish-American War, the question of what American forces hoped to achieve in Vietnam plagued the war effort. Indeed, as John Fromkin and James Chace assert, polls of United States Army Generals demonstrate that seventy per cent 'believed that it was not clear what America hoped to achieve in the Indochina war', and many considered that although America was

---

39 William Loren Katz, *The Black West*, 3rd edn (Seattle: Open Hand Publishing, 1987), 167.

40 Simon Hall, *Peace and Freedom: The Civil Rights and Antiwar Movements of the 1960s* (Philadelphia: University of Pennsylvania Press, 2005), 1.

41 See, for example, Hall, *Peace and Freedom*, for a breakdown of the historical linkages between the Civil Rights and Antiwar Movements and Scott Sigmund Gartner and Gary M. Segura, 'Race, Casualties, and Opinion in the Vietnam War', *The Journal of Politics* 62 (2000): 115–146 for an interesting breakdown of the intersections between race and opinion relevant to the conflict.

42 Marilyn B. Young, 'The War's Tragic Legacy', in *Major Problems in the History of the Vietnam War* (2nd edn), ed. Robert J. McMahon (Lexington, Massachusetts: DC Heath Company, 1995), 640–642.

not attempting to colonize Vietnam 'that is exactly what a great many Americans thought that we were doing.'[43] The exploitative side of American interventionism not only related to landed acquisition but also to economic interventionism, specifically 'concern about raw materials and markets' in the region and the role of Japan and China.[44] This also related to America's place in the world in opposition to Soviet Communist expansion and to old world powers, specifically France, which had continued involvement in Vietnam until a ceasefire agreement was formulated in 1954. Just as the prospect of the Spanish-American War highlighted the fissures in American society around race-based rights, economic and technological change, distribution of resources, military aims, and America's place in the world, the prospect of participation in Vietnam, as well as the actual engagement itself, tapped into similar and ongoing areas of domestic turmoil.

Ultimately, though, the sinking of the *Maine* acted as an iconoclastic event, crystallizing a shift in US attitudes towards the Spanish-American War. As Gleijeses asserts, while the *Maine* provided the impetus, President McKinley was forced to commit American forces because of 'the growing awareness that Spain was alone, fear that continuing uncertainty would depress business, suspicion that Spain might indeed be responsible for the *Maine*, and the pressure of public opinion.'[45] Interestingly, this creates an explicit historical parallel to the 1960s: it was the sinking of the *USS Maddox* in the Gulf of Tonkin on 30 July 1964 that justified Kennedy's entrance into Vietnam with full force.[46] Indeed, the Cuban revolt that sparked the Spanish-American War connects to ongoing issues of Cuban nationalism and the failed attempts at containment enacted by successive American presidents, most obviously in the Bay of Pigs disaster overseen

43   David Fromkin and James Chace, 'What are the Lessons of Vietnam', in *The Vietnam Reader*, ed. Walter Capps (London & New York: Routledge, 1991), 91.

44   William Appleman Williams, 'The City on a Hill on an errand into the Wilderness', in *Vietnam Reconsidered: Lessons from a Lost War*, ed. Harrison E. Salisbury (New York: Harper & Row, 1984), 13.

45   Gleijeses, '1898', 708.

46   Maurice Isserman & Michael Kazin, *America Divided: The Civil War of the 1960s* (Oxford: Oxford University Press, 2000), 113–114.

by President Kennedy in 1961.[47] In this way Cuba itself speaks as a symbol of active resistance to US ideology and its values, as well as to a history of failed American interventionism that highlights its destructive impacts on both parties, as well as a tendency for cultural arrogance and exploitation of developing nations. *Butch Cassidy and the Sundance Kid* creates metaphorical and explicit historical references to past American interventionism in South America through the relationship between Butch and Sundance, through references to the Spanish-American War, and by demonstrating conditions on the home front during this period. These references connect to contemporary issues in American society at the time of the filmic release, in particular domestic unrest and disillusionment with American interventionism abroad as a reflection of flawed ideology.

It is important at this point to address concerns regarding directorial intent regarding communication of historical issues. Whilst audience reception is both difficult to assess and beyond the scope of this work it is significant that almost all of the Westerns viewed here make explicit, specific historical references. From specific guns, to modes of transportation, to events and personages, and, less tangibly, social issues and phenomena, Western films do not exist in an ahistorical, archetypal space but, rather, a deeply historical one. The historical space used by Westerns is significant in that it allows audiences to view and reflect upon the past to make sense of their present. In almost postmodern fashion *Butch Cassidy and the Sundance Kid* engages with the role of Westerns in expressing historical ideas both in its visual techniques and textual cues in such a way that directorial intent to make such a connection appears inevitable.

This sense of film as 'playing' with history is imparted immediately: the film opens with the title screen 'most of what follows is true' followed by a black-and-white silent film of the Hole in the Wall Gang to the sound of an old projector turning over. In so doing Hill plays upon audience assumptions regarding a 'true story' – that the director inherently aims

---

47   See, for example, Thomas G. Paterson, 'Spinning Out of Control: Kennedy's War Against Cuba and the Missile Crisis', in *Major Problems in American Foreign Relations*, eds Dennis Merrill & Thomas G. Paterson (New York: Houghton Mifflin Company, 2006), 398–409.

at historical authenticity – by suggesting that he is actively constructing a version of history. It could be argued that what Hill is acknowledging here, by stating that 'most' of his film is 'true', is Rosenstone's identification of the centrality of invention in the historical film. Rosenstone suggests that an integral component of the historical film is 'invention', referring to the capacity to conflate historical information into ways that conform to visual and narrative conventions whilst still communicating a version or essence of historical truth. Thus 'we must recognize that film will always include images that are at once invented and true; true in that they symbolize, condense, or summarize larger amounts of data; true in that they impart an overall meaning of the past that can be verified, documented or reasonably argued.'[48] This 'invention' is performed to construct a hyper-linear relationship between represented past and the context of the filmic release, a relationship and function that is demonstrated by Hill's self-conscious use of signals of temporality to make the audience aware of the constructed nature of historical texts.

The active construction of history and the power of authorial manipulation are subsequently demonstrated throughout the film. For example, the film presents several colour shifts: it opens in black and white before turning to colour and finishing with the final freeze-frame photograph finale. These shifts play on the audience ideas that by entering the cinema they have transgressed their own temporality – which sees the past in anti-quated black and white – to have become fully immersed in the 'colour' of the past. Similarly, the two distinct segments of the film, the US context and the Bolivian context, are divided by a montage of sepia coloured stills. These stills portray historical scenes with Butch, Sundance and Etta transposed into them. In doing this Hill uses the typical conventions of the historical film but in ironic, unexpected ways. These techniques work as a reminder to the audience that what they are seeing is a construction of the past; a construction that is made to create parallels to the audience's own

---

48   Robert A. Rosenstone, *Visions of the Past: The Challenge of Film to Our Idea of History* (Cambridge: Harvard University Press, 1995), 71.

understandings of their history, and to encourage their critical examination of the material presented. This contradicts Marnie Hughes-Warrington's assessment that hyper-reality, the abundant use of signals of reality, to the point of excess, removes films from that reality and from true historical memory.[49]

The most obvious example of active intent in the construction of historical reality was actually intended by scriptwriter William Goldman but did not make the final cut of the film. Goldman intended for a silent film of Butch and Sundance to be watched by the pair in Bolivia, after Etta's departure. The prematurely titled 'The Hole-In-The-Wall Gang Are All Dead Now But Once They Ruled the West', expressed in English for the benefit of the cinematic audience rather than in Spanish for the Bolivian audience, provided Butch and Sundance with the opportunity to critique representations of themselves and comment upon the historicity of the visual image.[50] Clearly Goldman intended through this sequence to break down the barriers between audience and image, intra- and extra-diegetic, representation and reality, past and present. Although this film explicitly addresses the ways in which history is constructed on film, highlighting the constructed nature of historical links between past and presented, represented material and the audience, it would be naive to suggest that any auteur, particularly those enamoured with the genre, would delve into an historically rich genre but pay little heed to how that history functions and how it relates to the current experiences of a viewing audience. As Rosenstone asserts, history on film can productively inform our understandings when we consider the point of the historical film is 'to point to past events, or to converse about history, or to show why history should be meaningful to people in the present.'[51]

49   Marnie Hughes-Warrington, *History Goes to the Movies: Studying History on Film* (London & New York: Routledge, 2007), 102.
50   William Goldman, *Butch Cassidy and the Sundance Kid* [Screenplay], 159–164.
51   Rosenstone, *Visions of the Past*, 63.

Conclusion

Butch Cassidy and the Sundance Kid provides insight into the ways in which contemporary concerns regarding US interventionism were contextualized by the Western film genre. This film does this by portraying events at the turn of the century including the lives of Butch and Sundance as metaphor for American ideology, references to the Spanish-American War, and the domestic unrest of the period stimulated by economic, technological, social, and gender transformations to create a negative hyper-linear link to the present of 1969. The representation of these issues acts to link to concerns regarding American intervention abroad, particularly in Vietnam and Cuba, and a fundamental re-evaluation of American ideology occasioned by wholesale shifts in American society. Such a hyper-linear relationship acts to illuminate the notion that contemporary issues are not unique but rather a legacy of a detrimental patriarchal ideology and its manifestation in individual masculine gender performances. This ideology and resultant gender performances privilege competition and violence as a valid means of maintaining social control and regulating exclusionary forms of identity. Such an attitude finds manifestation in aggressive interventionist foreign policy throughout US history, from an idealizing of the frontier, which caused *inter alia* the landed oppression of Native Americans, through to intervention in Vietnam.

    Butch Cassidy also demonstrates the multiple elements within American domestic spaces that act to have fracturing impacts on notions of hegemonic masculine gender performances, and indeed the desirability of these performances. The film examines the pressures of women's movements and economic and technological shifts as fissures that complicate men's understanding of desired gender forms, let alone their capacity to perform them successfully, in both the represented past and the present of filmic release. Moreover, the capacity for men to develop meaningful relationships with each other, to both support each other and form a power base for patriarchal institutions is questioned. Indeed, although men may be able to band together if motivated by self-interest the notion that this leads to deep understandings of each other or relationships that stimulate well-being is thoroughly dispelled here. By examining such a social setting the film is doing two things. Firstly, it is demonstrating the historical links between the domestic unrest at the turn of the century with that of the 1960s contexts. Such unrest both cyclically fed into, and is fed by, changing understandings of masculinity. In this sense shifting ideas about patriarchy displaced some traditional forms of gendered being (in this case embodied by Butch and Sundance) who were replaced by other masculinities who better fit new social values. This domestic unrest would culminate in American intervention in 'new' frontiers both in the represented past and in the present of the filmic release.

Secondly, by demonstrating the variety of fractures evident in white, masculine gender performances, the film demonstrates the complexity with which the intersections between gender and history are handled by the genre. Although Western films have been examined with a focus on the representation of one thematic element in masculinity and how it has illustrated changing ideas of gender as related to history – an approach that is necessary for purposes of clarity and scope – this film illustrates the ways in which most Westerns combine different aspects of a variety of thematic elements, rendering complex understandings of gender and history, in the process. *Butch Cassidy and the Sundance Kid* examines themes of women's empowerment, technology, economic structures and interventionism, for example, whilst *The Unforgiven*, examined here for its portrayal of relations between Native Americans and European Americans, also demonstrates the role of women and family, and technology, in post-Civil War society.

Ultimately, Westerns of the 1950s and 1960s take a multi-thematic approach that aims to explore the nature of men's gender selves in times of historical change. Men's gender is often rendered complex by changing social conditions; social conditions that are represented in such a way as to speak to both the represented past and the present of filmic release. Such a hyper-linear historical connection assists audiences in understanding the origins of their own social issues, founded as they are in an American patriarchal ideology and frontier experiences. This connection can highlight positive, negative or discontinuous aspects of the relationship between past and present.

CHAPTER 7

'As unmarked as their place in history': Black Westerns, an Alternative History of Masculinities?

This chapter explores the representations of black experiences on the frontier as portrayed in the 1972 film *Buck and the Preacher*, the directorial debut of Sidney Poitier. The film follows the migration of African Americans from the South following the end of the Civil War as they search for land and freedom in the West. However, racist Southerners, hired by 'persons unknown', violently harass their wagon trains in an attempt to thwart their efforts and have them return 'home' to conditions of bondage. When the migrants are robbed by the Southerners it appears they will be unable to pay for their passage overland; it is then up to freedom-fighting, wagon-master Buck (Sidney Poitier), and his new-found, con-man friend, Preacher (Harry Belafonte), to resurrect their hopes. The pair sets about negotiating the wagon-train's path with Native Americans, recovering the money through whatever means necessary, and ensuring their people's safety. With the assistance of Buck's lover, Ruth (Ruby Dee), Buck and the Preacher shoot some of the bounty-hunters in an attempt to regain their people's money but, finding it already spent, they rob a bank. Pursued for their crimes, a posse targets both them and the wagon train, before a final showdown leaves Buck and Preacher, assisted by their Native American guides, victorious. The film ends with the wagon train making its way into the green pastures of the West, and Buck, Preacher and Ruth riding out, facing the camera, for destinations unknown.

This film sits on the outer edge of the period of production under consideration here: indeed this is an important reason for its inclusion, as it functions to demonstrate the demasculinizing of white, hegemonic masculinity under the weight of the fracturing elements of the 1950s and 1960s but, one could argue, it also subtly taps into concepts of remasculinization,

as defined by Susan Jeffords, which would take place in the 1980s.[1] Jeffords
discusses in her text *The Remasculinization of America* the ways in which
patriarchal instability and renegotiation of gender norms in the 1950s, 1960s
and 1970s gave way ultimately to 'somewhat different but no less forceful
relations of dominance' via patriarchy.[2] She suggests, then, via a study of
popular representations of the Vietnam War that American patriarchy was
'remasculinized' by 'reaffirming masculinity and thereby the relations of
dominance it embodies, [and therefore] other relations of dominance are
reinforced as well and the system of patriarchy as a whole is supported.'[3]
This discussion of *Buck and the Preacher* seeks to critically analyse to what
extent this representation poses a departure from traditional portrayals of
the Western and hegemonic masculinity and to what extent it engages in
a negotiation with patriarchal powers to establish, as Jeffords suggests, a
'somewhat different but no less forceful' form of patriarchal dominance.
The self-conscious use of history as a form of cultural recovery, the capacity
of film to play with stereotypes, genre conventions and an emergent black
cinema movement, and relationships between depictions of racial 'others',
are all prominent ways in which the film both demonstrates demasculinization but which can also connect to issues of remasculinization. The
representation of African American history, the relationship between this
representation and hyper-linear history, and the nature of stereotype, will
form the foundation of this discussion.

It is commonly accepted that the Western film genre has provided
no space for black history. As Jenny Barrett acknowledges, the tenets of
Turnerian history upon which the genre is based – the evolution of an
ideal white masculine form and its associated manifestation in patriarchal
institutions – seemingly precludes the possibility for alternative, minority
voices and their diverse, often counter-hegemonic perspectives.[4] When

---

1   Susan Jeffords, *The Remasculinization of America: Gender and the Vietnam War*
     (Bloomington: Indiana University Press, 1989).
2   Jeffords, *The Remasculinization of America*, xii.
3   Jeffords, *The Remasculinization of America*, xiii.
4   Jenny Barrett, 'Bucking the Trend: Poitier on the Frontier', *European Journal of
     American Culture* 30 (2011): 5–6.

Western film scholars do acknowledge the representation of black history it is usually in the form of metaphor, where Native American issues in the past come to 'stand in' for then contemporary racial issues surrounding African Americans prompted by the Civil Rights Movement. In representing one racial minority as a substitute for another, some scholars argue, the potentially subversive political messages sent by these films are neutralized.[5] This attitude regarding the absence of black voices in Western films throughout the early to mid-1900s has been echoed in academic literature of the same period, which, despite a small number of black autobiographies, was overwhelmingly dominated by analysis of white, male experiences in the frontier.[6] However, stimulated by the Civil Rights Movement, Philip Durham and Everett L. Jones's landmark *The Negro Cowboys* (1965), and William Leckie's *The Buffalo Soldiers* (1967) marked a significant shift towards scholarly work that emphasized the diversity of frontier experiences and acted to reinsert black voices into the frontier in an important act of cultural recovery.[7] This shift has been further emphasized by the work of New Western historians, which focuses on African American experiences on the frontier in terms of domestic arrangements, violence, interactions with white settlers and Native Americans, and as military personnel, and also seeks to analyse the role of Western states in negotiating calls for racial

5   For an overview of the debate regarding Native American representation and links to 1950s and 1960s African American rights movements see Steve Neale, 'Vanishing Americans: Racial and Ethnic Issues in the Interpretation and Context of Post-war 'Pro-Indian' Westerns', in *Back in the Saddle Again: New Essays on the Western*, eds Edward Buscombe and Roberta E. Pearson (London: British Film Industry, 1998): 8–28.

6   See Stephen Knadler, *Remapping Citizenship and the Nation in African-American Literature* (Hoboken, NJ: Routledge, 2009): 118–142, for an analysis of the early autobiographies of black cowboys and the ways in which they demonstrated a negotiated form of identity.

7   Philip Durham and Everett L. Jones, *The Negro Cowboys* (New York: Cornwall Press, 1965) [see also Philip Durham, 'The Negro Cowboy', *American Quarterly* 7 (1955): 291–301], and William H. Leckie, *The Buffalo Soldiers: A Narrative of the Negro Cavalry in the West* (Norman: University of Oklahoma Press, 1967).

equality, particularly after the Civil War.[8] This lack of formal historical interrogation into the role of black Americans in the West until the mid to late twentieth century has been conceptualized as a contributing factor in the ongoing lack of representations of ethnic diversity in Westerns. It is interesting then that, despite a rise in historical research, scholars have not noted a corresponding rise in the number and quality of filmic representations for black peoples in Western films.

It is not strictly true, however, that the Western has airbrushed blacks from Western history. Julia Leyda, for example, does well to illustrate the emergent 'black-audience' Western subgenre of the 1930s. Although of generally low production values relative to mainstream Hollywood productions, these Westerns provided black actors with an opportunity to play leading roles and allowed black audiences to view a variety of racial representations on screen within the viewing context of a predominantly black audience. It also, according to Leyda, caused a renegotiation of the themes of 'ownership, entitlement and citizenship' fundamental to the Western genre.[9] Certainly, since then, a small though not insignificant subgenre of black Westerns, or Westerns that present black characters that are named and central to the main storyline, has emerged. Indeed, this assertion is supported by Laurence Goldstein who suggests that the development of such a subgenre was an inevitability in the 1960s 'when the Vietnam war

---

8   There are a number of books on African American military participation in the West, see, for example, Michael Lee Lanning, *The African-American Soldier: From Crispus Attucks to Colin Powell* (Secaucus, NJ: Carol Publishing, 1997) and Ron Field *Buffalo Soldiers, 1866–91* (Oxford: Osprey Publishing, 2004). Other relevant histories include: Quintard Taylor, *In Search of the Racial Frontier: African Americans in the American West, 1528–1990* (New York: W.W. Norton, 1998), John W. Ravage, *Black Pioneers: Images of the Black Experience on the North American Frontier* (Salt Lake City: University of Utah Press, 1997), James F. Brooks (ed.), *Confounding the Colour Line: The (American) Indian-Black Experience in North America* (Lincoln: University of Nebraska Press, 2002) and, of course, the ongoing works of William Loren Katz in a variety of works including *The Black West*, 3rd edn (Seattle: Open Hand Publishing, 1987).

9   Julia Leyda, 'Black-Audience Westerns and the Politics of Cultural Identification in the 1930s', *Cinema Journal* 42 (2002): 46–70, 50.

and the Civil Rights Movement initiated a revision of national mythology among the generation raised on Westerns.'[10] Such films include: *Rio Conchos* (Gordon Douglas, 1964), *Duel at Diablo* (Ralph Nelson, 1966), *The Professionals* (Richard Brooks, 1966), *Scalphunters* (Sydney Pollack, 1968), *100 Rifles* (Tom Gries, 1969), *El Condor* (Jon Guillerman, 1970), *Soul Soldier* (1970, John Cardos), *The Man and Boy* (E.W. Swackhamer, 1971), *Big Jake* (George Sherman, 1971), *The Cowboys* (Mark Rydell, 1971), *The Legend of Nigger Charlie* (Martin Goldman, 1972), *Buck and the Preacher* (Sidney Poitier, 1972), *Charley-One-Eye* (Don Chaffey, 1973), and Sammy Davis Jnr's roles in rat-pack, tele-movies and TV westerns.[11] This is not to suggest that the Western genre reflects a diversity of racial and ethnic backgrounds or perspectives: clearly it does not. It is also not to suggest that when black Americans are presented in Western films these representations are naturally positive: Vashti (Butterfly McQueen), the simple-minded maid in *Duel in the Sun* (King Vidor, 1946), Pompey (Woody Strode) the loyal help-mate in *The Man Who Shot Liberty Valance* (John Ford, 1962), and the many unnamed and unacknowledged African American extras, usually occupying service positions in Western films, attest to the problematic of racial

10 Laurence Goldstein, "Mama How Come Black Men Don't Get to Be Heroes?': Black Poets and the Movies: Invitation to a Gunfighter', *The Iowa Review* 23 (1993): 113. Indeed, Laurence suggests in this passage that such national revisionism prompted a culture where 'hating John Wayne became something of a national pastime' during this period.

11 Sammy Davis, Jr appeared in *Sergeants 3* (John Sturges, 1962) and *Little Moon and Judd McGraw* (Bernard Girard, 1975), the TV movie *The Trackers* (Earl Bellamy, 1971), and had guest appearances in the television series *Lawman, Zane Grey Theatre, Frontier Circus, The Rifleman* and *The Wild Wild West*. Black infiltration of the television Western was actively called for in this period: in 1964 Jim Brown was cast as a TV cowboy in *Rawhide*, a popular television series, as a result of pressure from NAACP. See Daniel J. Leab, *From Sambo to Superspade: The Black Experience in Motion Pictures* (London: Secker & Warburg, 1975), 237. It is worth noting that Mario Van Peebles, son of iconic Blaxploitation filmmaker Marvin Van Peebles, paid homage to the black Western and the role of blacks in the West with the 1993 Western *Posse*. Morgan Freeman's turn as side-kick to Clint Eastwood and husband to a Native American woman in the revisionist Western, *The Unforgiven* (Clint Eastwood, 1992) also drew attention to blacks in the West in the more contemporary era.

representations in Western films.[12] It is to suggest, though, that the image of the Western as wholly uncomplicated by matters of race except when dealing with Native American issues, or that black issues are only represented via metaphor, is also untrue. Indeed, increasingly as racial issues came to widespread prominence in American society, this subgenre of films acted to both recover and explore the experiences of black Americans in frontier society and present and problematize the stereotypes of African American representation applied by a white Hollywood structure at this time.

It is clear that *Buck and the Preacher* is a significant case study of the black Western. It is produced by and features two of the central black stars of the 1950s and 1960s in Poitier and Belafonte, who each have distinct identities in relation both to representation and rights-based movements, respectively, in this period. As such *Buck and the Preacher* is both intrinsically political and proves capable of commenting upon issues of stereotype in representation. Moreover, the central role both men play in the production, and Poitier plays in direction, provides a connection between the racial message films of the 1950s and the, by this time, emergent Blaxploitation genre of film; a movement which raised important questions regarding the capacity and right of white studios and creative forces to tell black stories. Although this film was conceptualized by, produced by, and

---

12   Examples of the black representation in this fashion include: *Dodge City* (Michael
      Curtiz, 1939), where blacks are presented as train porters (one is named); *Fort Worth*
      (Edwin L. Marin, 1951), which presents an unnamed housekeeper and a named porter;
      Bend of the River (Anthony Mann, 1952), which presents Tilly, a play on the 'earth
      mother', Adam, a dim-witted steam-boat assistant and another unnamed African
      American; *North to Alaska* (Henry Hathaway, 1960), which presents an anonymous
      coachman; *4 For Texas* (Robert Aldrich, 1963), which I would particularly highlight
      for the volume of African American actors used as extras and placed in service occu-
      pations; *Major Dundee* (Sam Peckinpah, 1964), which particularly presents a black
      military presence; *Hang 'Em High* (Ted Post, 1968), which depicts William, a black
      jailer and three anonymous black guards; and, *Will Penny* (Tom Gries, 1968), which
      shows an anonymous black cowboy. A black cowboy, Sparks, is also depicted in the
      landmark *The Ox-Bow Incident* (William A. Wellman, 1943), although his role is
      in the film is slight. It is central to note, however, that these representations are still
      historical despite their conceptualization as stereotypical, minor and/or ahistorical.

starred black actors, unlike other Blaxploitation efforts it also had large cross-over and mainstream appeal without compromising its appeal to a black audience. Indeed, Donald Bogle acknowledged this appeal to black spectators, stating that 'black audiences openly screamed in joy and *Buck and the Preacher* emerged as a solid hit.'[13] Indeed, this cross-over appeal even managed to satisfy some of those critics of black cinema who claimed these films were often detrimental to liberation movements due to their portrayal of women and a violent, revolutionary black masculinity; 'Huey Newton, a significant activist in the Black Panther Party condemned most of the "black" films of the early 1970s as being counter-revolutionary but singled out *Buck and the Preacher* (1972) and *Sweetback* [*Sweet Sweetback's Baadasssss Song*] as brave exceptions.'[14] The point here, then, is that *Buck and the Preacher* occupies an important place in then-contemporary struggles against white control of black images and it is part of an African American response to this control that attempts to renegotiate representation and undertake a cultural recovery of what blackness means and how it can be meaningfully transmitted via film. In so doing this film, and others of its ilk, presents a challenge to a white patriarchal culture that constructs its own identity upon the often negative imagery of 'others' and perpetuates social inequality founded in negative stereotypes of these racialized others.[15]

Also significant, though, is the intersection between racial history, generic conventions, and notions of identity presented by *Buck and the Preacher*. This film is positioned clearly from the outset as a retrieval of neglected historical voices and as a celebration of the survival and endurance of black communities. As such it presents a fundamental challenge to the notion of the West as the domain of white, hegemonic masculinity whose actions are right and just in the context of inevitable expansionism. This presents a challenge not only to the scholarly neglect of actual historical

13   Donald Bogle, *Toms, Coons, Mulattoes, Mammies, and Bucks: An Interpretive History of Blacks in American Films*, 3rd edn (New York: Continuum, 1996), 250.

14   Karen Ross, *Black and White Media: Black Images in Popular Film and Television* (Cambridge: Polity Press, 1996), 19.

15   Jan Nederveen Pieterse, *White on Black: Images of Africa and Blacks in Western Popular Culture* (New Haven & London: Yale University Press, 1992), 9, 234.

black experiences in the West during this period but poses important questions regarding the generic conventions of western representation and the capacity to subvert them through racial representation. These questions relate specifically to whether the generic conventions of the Western allow for the meaningful incorporation of social and racial issues and a diversity of perspectives or, rather, whether generic conventions constrain the possibility for such a discourse due to audience expectations regarding the nature of the text. Whatever the answers to these questions *Buck and the Preacher* participated in this contested terrain and, at the same time, encompassed hyper-lineated historical continuities and discontinuities between the represented past and the present of the filmic release.

Importantly, the film does self-consciously construct historical continuities between past and present: it suggests that African Americans have suffered broken promises regarding equality in the post-Civil War period yet have survived to establish communities and identities despite, and separate from, exclusionary white racial policy. It equates this to a post-Civil Rights Movement context where blacks had also achieved legalistic victories but continued to face the challenges of economic and social equality, and attempted to negotiate ways of being in a society that continued to examine fundamental issues of racism. However, it is ultimately in demonstrating a challenge to scholarly and generic conventions that this film functions as an example of discontinuity. This discontinuity exists in the sense that a portrayal of the historical past that privileges African American perspectives can only be made as a result of gains by Civil Rights and Black Power Movements that have sought to reclaim the black image. The film challenges a mixed-audience's ideas of the West as a white space, and of settlement and pioneering spirit, community and morality, as exclusively white experiences of the frontier which formulated a unique white masculine identity and democratic institutions. Indeed, by inserting a black counter-narrative into this foundation myth, *Buck and the Preacher* not only suggests that these characteristics apply to 'others' who have been alienated from this identity but, also, questions the extent to which these characteristics fall within the purview of white, masculine experiences of the frontier at all.

The hyper-linear relationship here is almost paradoxical: the film illustrates continuity in black experiences for the purpose of demonstrating the absence of these experiences from traditional historical and popular conceptualizations of the West. By advocating the insertion of these experiences into the traditional narrative of American origins and a diversification of national identity, this film essentially advocates a discontinuity from representations of the West as a white masculine space and as whiteness as the ancestor of, and key to accessing, a valid national identity. This historical discontinuity can be seen as the culmination of two decades of fracturing pressures upon white hegemonic masculine forms until, ultimately, it has become an entirely invalid form of gender identity and the West can be reconceptualized as a space for a diverse array of previously silenced minority voices. This is not to suggest that the film exists as a complete alternative to the 'traditional' Western; for example, its capacity to pose true alternatives to the characteristics of hegemony, and to extricate itself from the foundations of racial hierarchies upon which stereotypes rest, leaves room for the reassertion of hegemonic masculine values albeit with some revision.

'They're gonna give us nothin'": Constructing Black History in *Buck and the Preacher*

Sidney Poitier, upon reflecting on the contribution that *Buck and the Preacher* made to black representation, located its significance as expressly in historical and cultural recovery. As he asserts in his autobiography, *This Life*:

> We [he and Belafonte] wanted black people to see the film and be proud of themselves, be proud of their history. However dishonest, unpleasant, and inhuman had been the depiction of that history by those white men who had written most of the history books that tell us about ourselves, we wanted this film to say: Hey, look, here were those of us, and not just a few, who were people of great courage, of great stamina, of great personality, of great conviction. People who should be a powerful influence on our sense of ourselves.[16]

16   Sidney Poitier, *This Life* (London: Coronet Books, 1980), 385.

Poitier suggested that although the film is structured in accord with fictional narrative devices, its content, including the relationship between Native Americans and African Americans, 'was projected in the way it actually existed.'[17] Certainly the film uses explicit techniques along with a narrative structure based around the Western migration of African Americans from the South following emancipation, to tap into audiences' understandings of the historical past. This both creates parallels between black audiences' contemporary experiences and creates a discontinuity with white perceptions of the American West as a space of celebratory white hegemony.

The film opens to rolling text, setting up the historical context for the viewer by stating that the time is post-Civil War 'and by law the slaves were freed' but, experiencing ongoing racism in the South, emancipated blacks sought the aid of wagon-masters to journey West. Attacked by 'night riders and bounty hunters' intent on returning them to bondage, this text impresses the danger of the journey for all participants and the centrality of bravery amongst the journeyers and the wagon-masters to black survival. The celebratory tone of the historical representation and its place as an act of historical and cultural recovery is clear: 'This picture is dedicated to those men, women and children who lie in graves as unmarked as their place in history.' The film opens in sepia tones before bleeding into colour, and then returns to sepia tones at the film's conclusion, a technical device that alludes to the sense of the film as conveying a deeper sense of historical inter-play (a technique that is elaborated upon in the discussion of *Butch Cassidy and the Sundance Kid*). Specific historical references throughout the film, such as posse members in Southern Confederate uniforms, Ruth's reference to the failed promise of 'forty acres and a mule' and Native American allusion to the Indian Wars and black soldiers' participation in these military actions, all solidify the represented historical context, encouraging a critical examination of the past for links to the present.

Certainly *Buck and the Preacher* depicts an actual historical phenomenon: the migration of African Americans to Western states following the

---

17   Poitier, *This Life*, 386. This commentary on the relationship between blacks and
      Native Americans was supported by Harry M. Benshoff, 'Blaxploitation Horror
      Films: Generic Reappropriation or Reinscription?' *Cinema Journal* 39 (2000): 34.

Civil War. As William Katz asserts, the sense that 'black rights had again been handed over to former slave masters for safe-keeping' prompted black committees to organize the 'Exodus of 1879.'[18] Although the film depicts migration beyond Kansas to an unnamed state, statistical evidence points to 26,000 black settlers arriving in Kansas from the South between 1870 and 1880, illuminating the extent of the exodus.[19] Indeed, the extensive nature of this migration did prompt retaliatory action: Democrats conducted an investigation, suspecting Republicans of purposefully shifting black people into states where they would be able to vote against them. Moreover, 'the white South reacted with fear and panic at the thought of losing their cheap labour supply', and, as a result, attempted to hinder overland and river routes of migration.[20] On the one hand, the immediate results of the overland migration, at least in the context of Kansas were not successful: the number of migrants placed an enormous strain on relief agencies which could not cope, and migrants faced local prejudice, harsh conditions and multiple crop failures.[21] On the other hand, the experiences of black migrants by necessity caused the formation of strong communities and the establishment of local ministerial and African American leagues; organizations that would develop into prominent forces in the fight for African American Civil Rights and that would aid in the development of activism in these communities.[22]

However, it is important to point out that although this migration marks a significant influx of black Americans into Western regions, African Americans have always been present in frontier society, occupying a variety of roles and migrating both before and after the Civil War. This migration occurred for a variety of reasons including: escape from slave conditions, forced migration as slaves accompanying wagon trains, the cheap and ready

---

18   Katz, *The Black West*, 167 & 170.
19   Bruce A Glasrud and Charles A. Braithwaite, *African Americans on the Great Plains: An Anthology* (Lincoln: Bison Books, 2009), 7.
20   Katz, *The Black West*, 170.
21   Katz, *The Black West*, 175, Glasrud & Braithwaite, *African Americans on the Great Plains*, 7.
22   Glasrud & Braithwaite, *African Americans on the Great Plains*, 8.

availability of land, the perception of greater employment opportunities and equality in a frontier society, and the opportunity to establish autonomous black communities.[23] Certainly, before the Civil War, the frontier provided black Americans with extremes of social experiences: some acted as slave soldiers, members of black militias or as fighters in the Revolutionary War, whilst others found ready integration with Native American groups.[24] The charge of historiographical naivety applied to other films of racial historical recovery can be fairly applied to *Buck and the Preacher* when examined in the strictest sense of realism.[25] The experiences of black Americans on the frontier were by no means uniform or necessarily harmonious, within black communities. As Robert Haywood asserts, although black cowboys made up a substantial component of all trail-hands, experienced significantly better conditions than their Southern counter-parts, and the economic power of black citizens dampened rampant racism in frontier towns, this did not make the west a race-less or safe space for African Americans.[26] Rather, 'discrimination was an ever-present condition of daily life', which occasionally manifest in instances of violence and public backlash against the presence of blacks on the frontier.[27] Moreover, the portrayal of African American communities united and harmonious does not necessarily align to evidence that, as Clare McKanna asserts in relation to Omaha, demonstrates

23   Glasrud & Braithwaite, *African Americans on the Great Plains*, 5–6.

24   Katz, *The Black West*, 36–42.

25   Donald Hoffman, 'Whose Home on the Range? Finding Room for Native Americans, African Americans, and Latino Americans in the Revisionist Western', *MELUS* 22 (1997): 49. Hoffman is pointing specifically to the black Western *Posse* (Mario Van Peebles, 1993).

26   Robert C. Haywood, "'No Less A Man': Blacks in Cow Town Dodge City, 1876–1886', *The Western Historical Quarterly* 19 (1988): 161–182. Writing in 2009 Glasrud and Braithwaite estimate the proportion of African American ranch hands as forty per-cent: Glasrud and Braithwaite, *African Americans on the Great Plains*, 6.

27   Haywood, "No Less A Man', 181. Certainly works such as Dykstra and Hahn's analysis of the resistance to black suffrage in northern states demonstrates the difficulties faced by African Americans throughout the nation, not simply in southern states; Robert R. Dykstra & Harlan Hahn, 'Northern Voters and Negro Suffrage: The Case of Iowa, 1868', *The Public Opinion Quarterly* 32 (1968): 202–215.

far higher rates of lethal violence amongst African Americans relative to whites.[28] The reason for these higher rates of violence can be attributed to the experience of a culture of violence in the South, higher rates of handgun ownership for the purpose of self-defence, and a tendency to react quickly to provocation within the broader context of racial discrimination.[29] Ultimately, a representation that privileges the West as an Edenic solution to Southern (or Northern) racism, a perspective that is seen in uniformly positivistic terms by harmonious black communities, does not reflect the diversity of African American experiences or attitudes towards racism in American ideology and structures.

There are important subtleties in the portrayals of blackness represented by Poitier, Belafonte and Dee though, which go towards presenting diverse experiences and reactions to racism in the historical context of frontier life. Specifically, Poitier presents a version of hard black masculinity that advocates for freedom and autonomy for black communities distinct to, though not entirely divorced from, white America. As Buck he has a personal history of military service in the army, a factor that alienates him from a true alliance with Native Americans who reject his appeal that 'we are all brothers [...] his enemies are our enemies' with the statement 'you black people fought with the enemy against our people.' Buck both actively rebels against structures of white racism, represented by the racist posses, whom he kills, and by the racist prostitute Esther, whom he hits, holds hostage and robs at different times. But Buck refuses to flee to Canada, as Ruth proposes, or reject American society wholly as incapable of incorporating black citizens. This is echoed by the wagon train whose members would rather 'die in the snow' than return to Southern racism but can foresee a future free of persecution in the West. In this sense Buck reflects both a post-Reconstruction perception amongst blacks that inclusion could be achieved through 'bourgeois respectability, economic self-sufficiency, and/or military service [...] [and] a successful assimilation of middle-class

28 Clare V. McKanna, 'Alcohol, Handguns, and Homicide in the American West: A Tale of Three Counties, 1880–1920', *The Western Historical Quarterly* 26 (1995): 474.
29 McKanna, 'Alcohol, Handguns, and Homicide', 479.

norms, especially those that equated national citizenship with economic agency or manliness.'[30]

The portrayal of the black community certainly adheres to this model: the community is self-sufficient and upholds a forthright morality regarding both its survival and caring for others. In particular, the stereotype of rampant black sexuality is refuted by demonstrating twice the rejection of sexual acts in favour of community morality: when a husband is seen touching his wife she slaps away his hand when their baby starts to cry and he lies back down comically, and a young woman attempts to sneak away from camp to rendezvous with an eager young man. As she stands her mother, who had appeared asleep, grabs the hem of her dress. Again the tone is comic as the young lady resumes her position and the boy sneaks away disappointed. Similarly, Buck is shown in a committed relationship with Ruth, and they desire family and peaceable settlement; the question is whether a white society will permit this form of integration. The portrayal of community de-emphasizes any notion of racial difference but rather endorses a sense of black integration within normative ideas of morality and respectability, domesticity and economic capacity that aligns with post-Reconstruction ideas of racial assimilation. Moreover, Buck's role in perpetuating the racial oppression of others through his military service and his initial judgement of Preacher, a lower-class black man, goes to support the notion of aspiration to national, white standards of citizenship.

This portrayal of Buck also demonstrates Knadler's notion of 'accommodated citizenship' as an historical conceptualization of self-identity amongst black Americans in the post-Reconstruction period.[31] Knadler's notion of a dual sense of 'accommodated citizenship', conceptualized in relation to black men's reconciliation of their frontier experiences with their racial identity, suggests that black men moulded their self-perception to both fit 'a dominant racial uplift ideology [...] yet, on the other hand, their stories reveal a more "accommodating" citizenship, one that allows sufficient space for other kinds of competing and even contradictory identifications.'[32]

---

30   Knadler, *Remapping Citizenship*, 119.
31   Knadler, *Remapping Citizenship*, 120.
32   Knadler, *Remapping Citizenship*, 120.

Whilst Buck can enact white policy through his military engagement against Native American forces, he simultaneously sees mirrored in their struggle a broader racial struggle in American society of which black people are a part. He identifies with their struggle and learns the customs of this group in order to aid his own people in resistance to racist structures and groups as he sees them. While Buck has an accommodated citizenship within broader white society (not least in the sense that he is not a complete separatist) he also accommodates contradictory identifications with other minority groups that oppose white power structures.

It is highly significant to note that this notion of racial solidarity across minority groups founded in shared oppression by whites is rendered complex in the film. Although Buck appeals to such solidarity despite his own background, and Indian Braves ultimately intervene to save the lives of Buck and the Preacher, the notion of shared suffering is thoroughly refuted by the Native American chief, who refuses to share buffalo beyond what is necessary for the survival of the wagon train, arm them or fight for them in any way. He, through a translator, asserts in a history of his people's suffering that 'tomorrow we will be like ghosts, like the spirits that come in dreams with no earth to walk on. But we will fight [...] we need our guns, bullets and powder for our own fight.' Certainly this distinction between racial experiences is both a testament to the film's self-consciousness in portraying some diversity of perspectives as well as supplementing the actual historical perspective that 'the Indian and Negro "problems", even for those who defined them as such, were never really analogous.'[33] In this instance Brian Dippie refers both to white attitudes regarding a sense that Native Americans could never assimilate or sublimate their racialized selves in service to white America; an attitude that was supported in relation to African Americans. It also represents a lack of parity in the public policy promises regarding the plight of Indigenous peoples following the Civil War compared to black people in this period.[34]

33   Brian W. Dippie, *The Vanishing American: White Attitudes and US Indian Policy* (Middletown, CT: Wesleyan University Press, 1982), 81.
34   Dippie, *The Vanishing American*, 77–92.

Ultimately, the characterization of Buck demonstrates the complex representations of history and identity in the Western. Buck's relationship with actual historical phenomena such as African American military service in the Indian Wars, his engagement as a wagon-master during the black 'Exodus' from the South, and his complex relationship with Native Americans, all testify to the West as a space that is racially diverse and complex and individuals within it that have overlapping and changeable identities. The multi-faceted nature of his relationships with various groups, which represent vastly divergent ideological impetuses, also demonstrates the notion of 'accommodated citizenship' put forward by Knadler as a model to aid understandings of the complex identities forged by blacks through their experiences on the frontier. Moreover, the diversity of Buck's experiences demonstrates a refutation of black representation as stereotypical, one-dimensional and ahistorical; rather Buck models a black experience that is realistic in its complexity. It also demonstrates a masculinity that is both 'hard' in its capacity for violence yet with a meaningful capacity to engage in personal relationships and meet harmonious community standards.

An attitude of accommodated citizenship is also demonstrated in Belafonte's Preacher. Preacher grew up as the slave of a travelling white preacher. One day, the Preacher sent him out for whiskey and, during his absence, sold his mother. In a rage Preacher killed the man, took his possessions and assumed his identity. By taking his slave-master's identity Preacher can be seen as the ultimate accommodated citizen in that he takes the cues of whiteness and uses them for his personal gain. He does not identify with the broader black community, at least initially, he possesses no knowledge of Native Americans and spends the film looking for ways East and a quick dollar. He represents a drifter's attitude that privileges personal entrepreneurialism and survivalism over collectivist politics. He is therefore clearly entrenched within white power structures; however, he proves capable of subverting white expectations of race in ways that demonstrate his alienation from national citizenship. Specifically, he literally adopts the guise of a white man, and using his Bible and his understanding of Christianity, is capable of adhering to white, stereotypical expectations of what blackness should be, in so doing working those expectations to his advantage. For example, he plays the part of the kowtowed preacher to gain the trust of the

Southern bounty hunters and learn of the bounty upon Buck's head, and he uses this trust to give Buck the element of surprise during his ambush of them. Indeed, this capacity to use white expectations of black citizenship and subvert them for his own ends is symbolized obviously by his relationship with his Bible: after spending much of the first half of the film clinging to his Bible and expressing his complete faith in the 'good book', it is revealed his true faith lies in the 'cannon' of a gun he keeps in the Bible's hollowed out interior.[35] In this way Preacher both understands and demonstrates both meanings of the term 'accommodated citizenship' and also illustrates the diversities of black attitudes to racist ideologies.

Ruby Dee's Ruth represents the complete separatist response to racism, arguing in her monologue that migration to Canada is the only solution for blacks, as racism is so rampant that 'it's like a poison has soaked into the ground. They're gonna give us nothin'. No forty acres. No mule. And not freedom either.' For Ruth there is no space for even an accommodated version of national citizenship; space to express an authentic sense of self including expressions of racial identity can only be found outside of the US system. Despite this separatist stance Ruth sublimates her personal identity for the sake of Buck's vision of race relations. This position directly endangers her physical welfare, as the white posse attempt to use her connection with Buck to have him recaptured. It also requires her to shelter both Buck and Preacher and provide them with food and encouragement both in her home and on the trail. Although, taken together, the trio present a range of responses to racist conditions, the oppression of Ruth's approach certainly raises important and problematic issues regarding attitudes towards women's roles in racial rights movements and the perceived capacity for women to make decisions separate from men regarding their own self-determination. It is important to note that the ambiguity in the ending does provide space for a reading that suggests that Ruth's approach may be favoured by Buck and Preacher. Indeed, for Donald Bogle, the problem of Ruth's characterization as a wife whose views are secondary to her

35   This is not the first Western film of this era to use a Bible for this purpose: *Cat Ballou* (Elliot Silverstein, 1965) also had this feature.

husband's needs is no problem at all; such criticism 'seemed a bit beside the point here. The important thing was that she played her role so well.'[36]

In historical and in gendered terms the problem with this portrayal is the fact that her desire to flee America is not contextualized within her personal history as a black woman, a problem that echoes throughout the film. For example, the particular experiences of black women as gendered subjects, whose experiences are further complicated by their racial status is sidelined; indeed, none of the women within the wagon-train are developed as characters with authentic motives. Further, it is a young, black woman who is charged with carrying the wagon-train's money and her murder by whites sets in motion the final confrontation, thereby positioning women as objects within the domain of men. Placing women in this light, as lacking a particular history as gendered selves, as submissive to the needs of the group above self-identity, and as objects to be avenged (or used for emotional or physical support) is problematic in terms of the role of this film in challenging hegemonic masculinity. While Buck and the Preacher might oppose a patriarchy that oppresses on the arbitrary basis of race, the film does not necessarily go so far as to destabilize the nature of gender binaries that underpin patriarchy.

Buck and the Preacher develops links between this historical past, and the divergent approaches black communities and individuals have taken in approaching American racism, to the production context using inter- and extra-diegetic cues. Technically, the use of a blues/jazz soundtrack, which opens the film, acts to impress upon the audience immediately a link with ongoing developments in black culture and position the film as partaking in the historical recovery of black culture. It creates a hyper-linear link that connects the past with part of an ongoing project to recover and celebrate black culture. Julia Leyda points to a similar phenomenon occurring in black westerns of the 1930s, which used anachronisms such as contemporary music, fashions and references to the Harlem renaissance in such a way that conflated time and established a sense of the past and present as linked and integral to establishing a unique African American identity.[37]

36   Bogle, *Toms, Coons, Mulattoes, Mammies, and Bucks*, 199.
37   Leyda, 'Black-Audience Westerns', 62.

It is clear that the diversity of approaches to race and racism portrayed in the filmic past, and the ways in which these characters negotiate their dual identities as black Americans, are designed in such a way as to mirror the contemporary experiences of blacks in an emergent post-Civil Rights Movement age.

The film displays a diversity of racial experiences and approaches to racial discrimination that parallels an increasingly diverse post-Civil Rights racial discourse. *Buck and the Preacher* reflects a context that points to the limitations of the legalistic achievements of the Civil Rights Movement, comparing these to the legalistic achievements of the post-Civil War society by, for example, the reference to 'by law the slaves were freed' and to the short-lived entitlement to forty acres and a mule. Rather, the film reflects a production context that has moved beyond legalistic remedies to racial oppression and has instead protested and resisted structural, economic and cultural ways in which racial inequality is enforced and encoded within American society. Such thinking was dominant in Black Power Movements; however, it is important to note the meaning of 'black power' itself is a contested site. Black power may range from the reclamation of black images and the reinsertion of black voices into broader historical narratives to the establishment of separate black cultural institutions; it ranges from endorsing self-defence to validating armed resistance, and it ranges from endorsing black collectivism, nationalism, separatism or a re-engagement with Africa. As William Van Horne asserts in his history of black power as paradigm for black empowerment, the concept of black power is characterized by a 'truly remarkable conceptual elasticity' that remains open to any and all methods of achieving black autonomy.[38] Such a diversity of perspectives, approaches and personal experiences are reflected in the characterizations of African Americans in *Buck and the Preacher* and relates to a similar search for ways to undertake meaningful social change in a post-Civil War environment.

The parallels and discontinuities expressed here can only be fully realized within the lens of emergent black film-making in this period and

---

38   Winston A. Van Horne, 'The Concept of Black Power: Its Continued Relevance', *Journal of Black Studies* 37 (2007): 370.

the off-screen personas of Poitier and Belafonte, perspectives which are examined. Ultimately, the contrast in approaches between Buck and the Preacher stand for different experiences regarding, and solutions to, racism in American society. They also point to competing ways to perform black masculinities with varying effects. These experiences construct hyper-linear parallels about the historical experiences of blacks between both temporal realities but also an important discontinuity: increasingly blacks were in a position to represent their own histories and ways of being. As Jenny Barrett commented: 'the film undoubtedly benefits from the achievements of the Civil Rights Movement [...] [as it] paved the way for a public discourse on African American experiences throughout history', thereby making a discussion of black representation over time integral to understanding the historical constructions of black masculinity, and its potential departure from white hegemonic standards of masculinity, in this film.[39]

'I've got my reputation to think about': Production Context, Stereotype and a Resurgent Masculinity in *Buck and the Preacher*

To understand the historical significance of *Buck and the Preacher* it must be placed within the broader context of African American representation and stereotype, and the careers of the two central leads, who also function significantly in the production process. This film does not sit divorced from racial stereotype because of its place as a film featuring and produced by blacks but, rather, plays with and historicizes stereotype, a process that occurs in all films. The film addresses stereotype through the naming of the central characters, the relationship between them, and the relationship between Buck and the Preacher, their community and the Southern bounty hunters. The audience's understandings of stereotype are also actively informed by

39   Barrett, 'Bucking the Trend', 13.

their understandings of Poitier and Belafonte, whose existing oeuvres and political participation in Civil Rights discourses shaped public understandings of race, representation and politics in the period.

Before addressing the nature of stereotype in *Buck and the Preacher* it is important to conceptualize this film within the context of an emergent 'black cinema' movement. The term 'black cinema' itself is highly contested, with arguments regarding the degree of black input that is necessary for a film to be classified as 'black', whether such film-making is possible within a context of the dominance of white control of film-making capital and resources, and, indeed, whether such film-making is even desirable as it sees racial representation as strictly falling within the domain of one racial group rather than as a broader societal issue that encompasses all people.[40] There can be no doubt, however, that white citizens had (and have) extensive control over the conceptualization, production, and distribution of black images; studios, technical and craft unions and cinemas were (and remain) predominantly staffed by whites in the 1960s. This problem was recognized by the 1969 Equal Opportunity and Employment Commission inquiry, which concluded that there was 'clear evidence of a pattern or practice of discrimination' in the film industry. Its ultimate solution, as Eithne Quinn asserts, lacked teeth through an absence of binding obligations; rather it implemented a goal of twenty percent minority employment to be obtained via a two year voluntary agreement with industry groups.[41] Moreover, the increasing depiction and participation of blacks in communicating their own representation has been largely attributed not to pressures from rights-based organizations but, rather, to the desire to capture a growing black

40   See, for example, Thomas Cripps, *Black Film as Genre* (Indiana: Indiana University Press, 1978) and, also, Phyllis R. Klotman, 'About Black Film ...' *Black American Literature Forum* 12 (1978): 123–127 for a brief overview of literature related to black film in this period.

41   Eithne Quinn, "Tryin' to Get Over': *Super Fly*, Black Politics, and Post-Civil Rights Film Enterprise', *Cinema Journal* 49 (2010): 88. The exclusion of blacks from Hollywood structures is noted also by William Lyne, 'No Accident: From Black Power to Black Box Office', *African American Review* 34 (2000): 45.

film audience and to meet the demands of a lucrative white youth audience who were sympathetic to seeing black experiences on screen.[42]

The so-called 'Blaxploitation' genre of films – films typically composed of a black cast, with very low production values and targeting a black audience – exemplified these broader concerns and divided African American opinion. For many filmgoers the Blaxploitation genre provided the opportunity to witness black rebellion against white power structures, often demonstrated through the vigorous black masculinity of the central protagonist as well as depicting blacks within previously exclusionary genres and roles.[43] Others, however, saw such films as counter-revolutionary in the sense that, like previous images, they presented a one-dimensional image of blackness, they were typically apolitical and ignored the structural causes of inequality, they modelled a destructive and socially aberrant form of blackness for young men and were largely misogynistic.[44] On the one hand the ability to open a discourse regarding racialized images and to attempt to reclaim them can be seen as a complete breakdown of the notion of a hegemonic white masculinity whose attributes are aspirational and are manifest in broader patriarchal institutions. On the other hand, the commodification of these new representations by white, capitalist interests and, as a result, the failure of these representations to engage in a politicized and meaningful dialogue regarding the nature of social inequality, presented a 'patriarchal equilibrium'.[45] This equilibrium allowed for the temporary

42   Mark A. Reid, 'The Black Action Film: The End of the Patiently Enduring Black Hero', *Film History* 2 (1988): 29. Reid points out that, in relation to youth culture, a *Variety* survey found that 74% of filmgoers were aged under the thirty in 1969–1971. See also, Jacqueline Bobo, "The Subject is Money': Reconsidering the Black Film Audience as a Theoretical Paradigm', *Black American Literature Forum* 25 (1991): 421–432.

43   See, for example, the argument provided by Harry M. Benshoff, 'Blaxploitation Horror Films', 31–50. For a complex examination of the intersections between capitalism, Blaxploitation and Hollywood commodification of image see William Lyne, 'No Accident: From Black Power to Black Box Office', *African American Review* 34 (2000): 39–59.

44   Reid, 'The Black Action Film', 29.

45   Judith M. Bennett, *History Matters: Patriarchy and the Challenge of Feminism* (Manchester: Manchester University Press, 2006), 77–81.

illusion of a questioning of white masculinity and an alternative form of masculinity to emerge that lacked the exclusionary quality of earlier forms in order to allow for the remasculinization of the male image and its associated institutions in 1980s filmic representations.

The script for *Buck and the Preacher* was found by Harry Belafonte, who opened one of the first black production companies in 1957.[46] It was then passed to Sidney Poitier, who acted as co-producer and replaced the film's original white, director Joseph Sargent. It also used a high number of black extras. Despite this black input the film cannot be classed as a Blaxploitation effort; indeed, Belafonte ended his two year estrangement from Poitier because he recognized that whilst the film expressed, in his opinion, vitally important messages regarding African American history, he did not have the resources or connections to have the film made and was willing to give up the rights to the script in order for it to find the funding necessary to come to fruition and be of high production quality.[47] The film was funded largely by Columbia Pictures and Poitier acknowledged the power they had over the final product, indicating, for example, the high possibility of filming being shut down completely when he and Belafonte decided to sack Sargent.[48] Moreover, neither Poitier nor Belafonte were associated with Blaxploitation: Poitier had a long and well-established association with assimilationist racial message films and Belafonte was 'disgusted' with the genre, considering it to be counter-productive to the black rights movements and anti-women.[49]

In comparison to the nihilistic and often brutal portrayals of black masculinity in Blaxploitation efforts of this period, *Buck and the Preacher* presents a different and socially constructive form of masculinity, and this was explicitly acknowledged by Poitier who stated that 'we wanted Black

---

46 Stephen J. Ross, *Hollywood Left and Right: How Movie Stars Shaped American Politics* (Oxford: Oxford university Press, 2011), 202.

47 Poitier, *This Life*, 378. Incidentally, the estrangement between Poitier and Belafonte occurred regarding Poitier's objection to Belafonte's desire to hold a public rally to coincide with Dr King's funeral service, 375–376.

48 Poitier, *This Life*, 382–385.

49 Ross, *Hollywood Left and Right*, 224.

audiences to see that the heroes of that period were others than the "bad niggers," and the malcontents.'[50] Nevertheless, the production context of *Buck and the Preacher* does demonstrate the balance between white capitalist control of black images and the attempts by black filmmakers, producers and performers to present counter representations in ways that demonstrate both a discontinuity with the past (in terms of their ability to function as a form of cultural recovery) whilst still working within the demands of white power structure. This is also demonstrated through the film's engagement with issues of stereotype in black representation.

Addressing stereotype takes place in the movie at the most fundamental level: that of names. The naming of Sidney Poitier's character 'Buck' relates to one of the fundamental stereotypes of black representations as identified in Donald Bogle's leading work *Toms, Coons, Mulattoes, Mammies, and Bucks*. As Bogle asserts, the stereotypical representation of the 'black buck' was a black masculinity characterized by 'big, baadddd niggers, oversexed and savage, violent and frenzied as they lust for white flesh. No greater sin hath any black man.'[51] Poitier's portrayal of Buck both renders complex and subverts this idea of the black buck stereotype. Firstly, the filmic Buck only adheres to the stereotypical representation of a buck in the eyes of whites: to the Southern bounty hunters he is a 'baadddd nigger' because of his ability to thwart their efforts to force blacks to return to the South and, ultimately, to exercise his will against them through violent confrontation. His violent lashing out is directed only at white representatives of racism: the Southern bounty hunters whom he kills; the racist white prostitute whom he hits and robs; and the banks, symbolic of inequitable access to resources, from whom he steals the money to support the wagon train's journey. This goes towards subverting stereotypes of the 'buck' in the sense that, although Buck may behave violently, this violence is not senseless or meaningless but rather a direct reaction to the violence committed by whites against him and his spirit. This film demonstrates Buck's motivations and, importantly, the uncertainty and effects of his actions on him. Indeed, the sense of this as a racialized battle for control of the

---

50   As cited in Ross, *Hollywood Left and Right*, 223.
51   Bogle, *Toms, Coons, Mulattoes, Mammies, and Bucks*, 13.

wagon-train's destiny is demonstrated by Buck when he sits, sullenly con-templating how to assist his people, before announcing that 'I don't know which way to turn no more; I think they've beaten me.' The film does not play the character of Buck as a one-dimensional man out for revenge or using his sexuality rampantly for personal gain as is the case in the iconic *Sweet Sweetback's Baadasssss Song* (Melvin Van Peebles, 1971), but, rather, shows Buck as capable of respect and tenderness in his relationship with Ruth, as bound by a deep sense of moral conviction regarding his purpose, and as an intelligent contributor to the lives of those in the black and Native American communities (and perhaps it is for these reasons most of all that he is classed a 'baadddd nigger' by white men).

By using the name 'Buck' and characterizing Buck in such a way the film draws upon a long history of stereotypical representations of black men. Poitier's portrayal exposes the racist underpinnings of a stereotype that conceptualizes black violence which is divorced from a broader soci-etal context of encompassing racialized violence. It also problematizes a stereotype of the black buck as a one dimensional figure in American culture, but rather presents Buck as capable of multiple behaviours and approaches depending upon the context. In many ways what we see in this portrayal is a challenge to white ideas of a hegemonic masculinity, 'bucking the system' in several important ways. Firstly, it destabilizes the foundation of a white hegemony defined specifically by its relationship to essentialized 'others' and, particularly, through a sense of racial superiority. By envisioning Buck as a stereotypical 'buck' only in the eyes of whites, the film exposes the way in which whiteness casts racialized others in ste-reotypical terms to underwrite a sense of its own identity regardless of the truthfulness of such stereotypical terms or the impacts of these terms. Moreover, by exposing the multifaceted nature of Buck's character the film refuses to partake in the denial of individuality and complexity upon which racist assumptions rest.[52]

It must be noted, however, that the subversive effects of Poitier's portrayal are influenced significantly by the fact that his filmic oeuvre

---

52   See, for example, Jan Nederveen Pieterse, *Black On White*, 11 & 233.

throughout the 1950s and 1960s had led to him being labelled a stereotype: as 'Super Sid' or the 'Ebony Saint'.[53] Films such as *The Defiant Ones* (Stanley Kramer, 1958), *Lilies of the Field* (Ralph Nelson, 1963), *A Patch of Blue* (Guy Green, 1965), and *Guess Who's Coming to Dinner?* (Stanley Kramer, 1967) all articulated a seemingly assimilationist approach to race relations, one that stressed a colour-blind approach to racial difference and repeatedly saw Poitier portrayed as 'a friendly, desexualized black man that was little more than a nonthreatening confidant to virginal white women.'[54] Indeed, this was well acknowledged at the time, with Harry Belafonte publically stating that he refused many of Poitier's most famous roles including *Lilies of the Field*, for which Poitier won the Best Actor Academy Award, the first black actor to do so, on the grounds that they portrayed blacks in racially offensive ways and as lacking history or culture.[55] Poitier himself was self-conscious about the perception that he had compromised his personal politics and racial heritage by choosing such parts, a factor that came into play when he chose to become involved in the production of *Buck and The Preacher*.[56] There are several factors that are important to consider here: the first is to what extent Poitier's portrayal of Buck can be seen as constrained by audience's pre-conceived expectations of him. In this sense, an audience and studio system can allow for potentially destabilizing images of black men as they are contained by Poitier's personal affiliation with non-radical politics and previous roles in assimilationist pictures that aimed to soothe the anxiety of white audiences facing significant ideological and structural challenges on racial grounds. The other aspect of this is the extent to which Poitier's portrayal can actually be considered a departure from the traditional genre conventions of the Western film: as Harry Benshoff argues

---

53   This is a commonly acknowledged aspect of his filmic identity: see, for example, Bogle's reference to 'SuperSidney' in *Toms, Coons, Mulattoes, Mammies, and Bucks*, 183.

54   Matthew H. Hughey, 'Cinethetic Racism: White Redemption and Black Stereotypes in 'Magical Negro' Films', *Social Problems* 56 (2009): 545.

55   Henry Louis Gates, Jr, *Thirteen Ways of Looking at a Black Man* (New York: Random House, 1997), 169–170.

56   Poitier, *This Life*, 388–389. This is also noted in Bogle, *Toms, Coons, Mulattoes, Mammies, and Bucks*, 250.

in his analysis of the Blaxploitation adaptations of horror film, many see
the appropriation of these conventions as doing little more than reversing
traditional racial hierarchies rather than challenging them and such an
elevation of a minority group intrinsically subscribes to, rather than challenges, a racist ideology.[57] Genre films tend to be seen primarily as vehicles
for entertainment rather than serious commentary on deep-seated social
issues and, as such, the extent to which Poitier plays a black man rather
than simply another cowboy is questionable.[58] Indeed, both of these factors can be seen as containing the potentially radical departure this film
has in constructing an alternative history and an alternative masculinity
that challenges white hegemony.

Similarly, Preacher can be seen as both a radical departure from traditional conceptualizations of black masculinity and also as subversiveness
contained. On the one hand, Preacher demonstrates a new form of black
stereotype which came to prominence around the Blaxploitation era, a
stereotype of 'black entrepreneurial individualism.'[59] Such a stereotype codi-
fied ideas surrounding the Black Power Movement into the representation
of an assertive, urban, hustling black masculinity that privileged values of
individualism and consumer capitalism as a means to personal advancement.
Preacher demonstrates these values through his desire to return East, his
ability to 'play' on white group expectations for personal gain and through
his ambiguous affiliation with Buck, which begins in hostility regarding
Buck's theft of his horse. Although Preacher may ultimately participate in
Buck's plans he does not express an ideological affiliation with them and
maintains an individual identity. Indeed, he only participates in the final
shoot out because he cannot conceive of a way to turn around and go back
East. As Eithne Quinn asserts in relation to the film *Super Fly* (Gordon
Parks, Jr, 1972) such a display can be highly problematic in that it under-
mines a sense of communal purpose or black nationalist movement.[60] It

---

57   Harry M. Benshoff, 'Blaxploitation Horror Films', 33 & 42.
58   Benshoff, 'Blaxploitation Horror Films', 33.
59   Quinn, "Tryin' to Get Over', 102. Quinn makes this assertion in relation to the film
      Super Fly (Gordon Parks, Jr, 1972).
60   Quinn, "Tryin' to Get Over', 101–102.

may also be argued that such a perspective allows for the reassertion of traditional hegemonic standards of masculinity by privileging capitalist structures. This is because capitalism can be construed as a driver of social inequality and also because, by privileging capitalist structures, attention is deflected away from meaningful ways in which to engage with rights-based discourse. In many ways, though, such a stereotype is historicized in this period: it presents a post-Civil Rights discourse that illuminates the failure of the movement to secure expectations of social and economic uplift, particularly for urban and working poor blacks.[61] For Laurence Goldstein, however, such a focus on individualism, which can also be seen reflected in the diversity of experiences that divide Buck and Preacher, is a necessary step in the refutation of stereotype and a more meaningful engagement with black history. As Goldstein asserts, black arts movements of this period including film emphasized:

> how personal needs, not political agendas, deserve attention if meaningful reform is ever to occur in the lives of people of color. Such films open a moral space for the redefinition of black society as a congregation of individuals, not types [...] [they] hoped that some new mythology based on black history and culture could be constructed to compete with an oppressive and evasive white mythology signified by the western.[62]

The complexity of representation is evident in the portrayal of Preacher, which complicates the issue of group politics and the possibility for meaningful change through the self-conscious use of stereotype.

This perspective must also take into account, on the other and more subversive side of the issue, the tongue-in-cheek nature of Belafonte's portrayal. This portrayal, complete with stained teeth, exaggerated preaching accent, and great physicality, turned on its head Belafonte's previous reliance on his sex appeal and, instead, he played comically on the notion of the hustling stereotype.[63] The comedic aspects of this performance can

---

61   Quinn, "Tryin' to Get Over", 100–101.
62   Goldstein, "Mama How Come Black Men Don't Get to Be Heroes", 129.
63   Donald Bogle referred to Belafonte's performance as 'a wonderfully developed and stylized performance [...] no longer was he simply Mr Beautiful Black America;

in many ways be seen as a reflection of Harriet Margolis's conceptualization of self-directed stereotype, by which she refers to 'the deployment of stereotypes by people being stereotyped in order to undermine those stereotypes by exposing their ridiculous underpinnings – [which therefore] involve an element of satire.'[64] Preacher can be seen not simply as a stereotypical portrayal but as an exaggerated stereotype, where its over-the-top nature plays on and with audience expectations of urban blackness as represented in other Blaxploitation films. Indeed, the sense of this characterization as a self-conscious gender performance is illustrated precisely by its being stripped away: the seriousness with which Preacher confronts the bodies of murdered blacks, his revelations regarding his own past, and his awe of Buck's capacity to liaise with Native Americans all reveal him as a deeper and more complex character who is located within a specific historical and cultural framework. In this way his characterization can be seen within the text as a self-conscious deployment of stereotype to play on racist white expectations of blackness and, outside of the text, as a self-directed stereotype that problematizes, humorously, the issues associated with black self-perception and use of urban, hustler stereotypes. In both instances Preacher provides insight into the ways in which even stereotypical representations can be used to meet the needs of an individual through self-aware performativity, as well as the ways in which stereotypes function in historically contingent ways. Such a performance, then, undercuts a white hegemonic masculinity whose claims to legitimacy rest upon essentialized images of self and other (see Figure 8).

The portrayals of whiteness and the interactions between competing groups in this film further illustrate the often contradictory messages and impetuses of *Buck and the Preacher*. Specifically, white men within this group are largely portrayed as caricatures of Southern racist brutality – they

---

now Harry Belafonte had discovered himself, at forty-four, a rough-and-ready, gutsy quality that had vitality and delighted audiences', *Toms, Coons, Mulattoes, Mammies, and Bucks*, 191.

64   Harriet Margolis, 'Stereotypical Strategies: Black Film Aesthetics, Spectator Positioning, and Self-Directed Stereotypes in 'Hollywood Shuffle' and 'I'm Gonna Git You Sucka', *Cinema Journal* 38 (1999): 53.

Figure 8: Harry Belafonte plays against his sex symbol
typecasting as the hustling 'Preacher' in *Buck and the Preacher*.

are uniformed Confederates, dirty, violent, and seemingly stupid. Whilst
these characters can be seen, subversively, as a symptom of white anxiety
regarding potential African American freedoms and political gains and
their lack of individuality a reflection on the dehumanizing nature of the
posse, this subversiveness is contained by the essentialized racial network
within which they appear. These characters lack any function other than as
signifiers and therefore reflect the binding nature of stereotype wherein all
people of all races are consumed by one-dimensional representation within
stereotyped racialized spaces.[65] As Pieterse asserts, this is a problem for two
reasons: firstly, by racially stereotyping any person, even if the intention
is to elevate previously marginalized groups, that media endorses the very
essentialism that provides the foundation for racism.[66] Similarly, secondly,
this portrayal creates an inversion of racial hierarchies, which privileges
the experiences of minority groups, who sit above sympathetic whites and
Southern racists, rather than setting about dispelling the notion of racial

65   Karen Ross, *Black and White Media*, xxi.
66   Pieterse, *White on Black*, 232–232.

hierarchies at all.[67] Whilst it can be argued that white Southern resistance to black migration to Western states after the Civil War was an actuality, the portrayal of southern whites need not engage in a one-dimensional portrayal of their motivations or experiences; indeed, by not presenting an all-encompassing challenge to racial stereotypes in all their forms it can be argued that this film is limited in its overall challenge to white hegemony.

In addition to this, the only positive portrayals of white masculinity occur when Westerners, lacking the Southern accent and therefore presumably from the North or Northwest, voice opposition to white resistance. This takes place in the film when a Sheriff informs the bounty hunters that 'those folks (African Americans) are free to come and go as they like: that's the law', and forbids killing. When the posse objects to this, arguing they are simply preserving a way of life, he refutes any investment in this. When Buck and the Preacher do commit a crime (a bank robbery) and the Sheriff must pursue them, he forbids the posse from persecuting the wagon train. It is this action that leads to him being murdered by a posse member, precipitating the final shoot-out. The only other presence is that of Western farmers whose employment of the wagon-train as agrarian labourers originally funded their overland journey. Ultimately, such a portrayal emphasizes the legalistic nature of the Civil Rights gains, pointing out that while blacks may have legal protections from discrimination, such protection does not necessarily correlate with shifting societal attitudes or racist actions. This important reflection has a strong relationship with a post-Civil Rights Black Power Movement that emphasized social inequalities and the structural nature of disadvantage and racial discrimination, although the strong emphasis on regionalism does much to sideline these concerns. Such representation creates a dichotomy of 'good' and 'bad' whites and 'pro-' and 'anti-black' areas, in so doing shifting much of the blame for discrimination onto individuals, or onto particular regions, rather than envisioning it as an encompassing American issue to which Northern, Southern and Westerns states have contributed. A privileging of Northern/Western perspectives is certainly interesting in the context of an increasing focus on the North as

---

67   Pieterse, *White on Black*, 225–226.

a site of racial contestation from the mid-late 1960s, particularly under the influence of Black Power Movements. Ultimately it can be conceptualized that in this context it was more palatable for white Northern liberals who financed *Buck and the Preacher* to continue a demonization of the white South and marginalize their own racial issues; a factor that reflects upon the problems associated with representation in 'black cinema'.[68]

The sense of engagement with ideas of racial hierarchy is also reinforced by the portrayal of Native American characters in *Buck and the Preacher*. Julia Leyda suggests that black westerns in the 1930s avoided the representation of Native Americans or Mexicans, as doing so would have entrenched these films within the 'maze of racial power relations' and complicated the nature of spectatorship for black audiences.[69] *Buck and the Preacher* makes a significant contribution by entering this maze: in so doing the film demonstrates the historical reality that the West was occupied by a variety of racial identities, who interacted with each other and white power structures in a variety of ways. This is related, hyper-linearly, to a context wherein different minority groups have protested their treatment in contemporary America in different ways, highlighting a diversity of interests, approaches and issues regarding racial equality in the twentieth century. On the other hand, though, the film engages in typical hegemonic notions of racial hierarchy by endorsing the view of Native American peoples as suffering an inevitable demise: indeed the statement that they will eventually be 'ghosts' despite their strategies of resistance and cultural preservation explicitly endorses a fatalistic determinism regarding Native American experiences. More than this, the portrayal of Native American characters is almost otherworldly; they appear when Buck needs them, lend aid even against their better judgement and act as guides through parts of the journey. Their presence occupies the space of spirit guide and, though the audience is made aware of their own struggles, their interests and

68   This conclusion is also supported by the author's work on the 1967 film *In the Heat of the Night* (Norman Jewison, 1967) as discussed in Emma Hamilton and Troy Saxby, "Draggin' the Chain: Linking Civil Rights and African American Representation in *The Defiant Ones* and *In the Heat of the Night*', *Black Camera* 3 (2011): 75–95.
69   Leyda, 'Black-Audience Westerns', 61.

diversity of experience is marginalized in favour of functioning to support the black experience. Certainly, though, the concept of Native Americans as a 'vanishing' race whose capacity for assimilation or integration into white society was limited does reflect on some historical schools of racial thought in the post-Civil War period.[70] This reflects upon the difficulties of racial representation, where *Buck and the Preacher* attempts to mean-ingfully engage with a diversity of racial experiences and attitudes in the historical West, subversively destabilizing previous conceptualizations of the West as a site of heroic white pioneering and instead demonstrating it as a site of multiple, contested identities and ways of being. Conversely, it can be argued by presenting Native Americans as foils to the experiences of others and as subject to historical inevitability the film does engage in a racialized discourse that privileges and places in hierarchy some racial experiences over others and therefore it does not radically depart from traditional white, hegemonic conceptualizations of race.

Similarly, it is difficult to suggest that the film wholly deconstructs a white hegemonic masculinity and its manifestation in patriarchal institu-tions when considering the role of both black and white women in the film. Black women, shown in the wagon train community and given greater depth through the characterization of Ruth, are seen here only as wives and mothers. Even Ruth, who seemingly sits outside of these roles as a woman who lives alone and endorses black separatism through escape from America, subsumes her needs and ideology to Buck's. Indeed, it would appear that her desire to be wife to Buck and mother to his future children is greater than her convictions. For the rest of the film she is portrayed as entirely domesticated: she cooks for Buck and Preacher, provides them with emotional support and assists, though does not actively partake in, their criminal activities. This is not to suggest that power cannot be found in these roles. The women in the black community and Esther, the white prostitute, clearly find power through their sexuality and their ability to grant or deny men's access to their bodies. This power, though, is often exposed as illusionary: men use violence to kill a black woman and rob her

70   Dippie, *The Vanishing American*, 86.

body; Ruth's home is penetrated and she is held hostage; and Esther's body is dominated by Buck when he hits her and holds her hostage in a bank robbery. In this way women's bodies become a site where men perform and contest their masculinities, which is a fundamental tenet of patriarchy and its enactment in hegemonic masculinity. Indeed, this reinforcement of gender difference is essential in the way men construct their self-image, a factor illustrated by the ways in which Buck's actions are validated by Ruth's submission to them, reflecting both the fragility and dominance inherent in men's gendered identities. A more specific example of this complexity occurs during the bank robbery, where Ruth uses symbols of domesticity, such as her dress and covered basket, as a cover for weaponry. In so doing she demonstrates a self-conscious play on gender and racial expectations in order to find power. However, this performance is only in support of the men, and she is then shown strapping Buck's gun-belt around his waist. This is symbolically indicative of Buck's acquisition of masculinity through the submission of the feminine to his greater power: indeed there is no practical reason in the text requiring Ruth to perform this task and it therefore exists purely as symbol for these broader forces.

It is important to conceptualize this emphasis on gender binaries as an important reflection on the historical issues surrounding the Black Power Movement, a movement that black women supported and participated in, but which also endorsed a rigorous separation between genders and was organized in often patriarchal ways.[71] As E. Francis White asserts, there lies an inherent contradiction between the construction of: 'black nationalism as an oppositional strategy that both counters racism [...] [but also] attempts to construct utopian and repressive gender relations.'[72] Certainly, Tracye Matthews agrees that the issue of gender was a primary factor in the organization and functioning of black nationalist groups such as the Black

---

71   Bettye Collier-Thomas and V.P. Franklin (eds), 'From Civil Rights to Black Power: African American Women and Nationalism', in *Sisters in the Struggle: African American Women in the Civil Rights and Black Power Movements* (New York: New York University Press, 2001), 171.

72   E. Francis White, 'Africa On My Mind: Gender, Counter Discourse and African-American Nationalism', *Journal of Women's History* 2 (1990): 73.

Panther Party. However, the movement's attitude towards gender was not monolithic or static over time but, rather, can be seen as a negotiated phenomenon influenced by complementary theories of gender roles, the nature of the women's liberation movement, and concern for the nature of black family structures, particularly those headed by black women. Therefore, Matthews illustrates the ways in which competing gender ideologies and influences sit within a movement typically classed as patriarchal to the point of misogyny. Such competing ideologies informed an often contradictory and changeable approach to gender and women's participation in black nationalist movements.[73]

This marginalization of women's interests and their use as vehicles to construct men's identities is not only demonstrated through the portrayal of black women, but also in the characterization of Esther. Esther, a white saloon prostitute, is introduced to the audience when Preacher intrudes on the white bounty hunters to create a distraction for Buck, who will kill them. Esther initially asks Preacher to leave the establishment, saying 'I've got my reputation to think about.' Preacher responds by quoting Bible passages that contradict her and then he chastises her attitude in front of the other men, humiliating her. This action creates a bond between all the men, who partake in Preacher's patronizing view of her as she stares between Preacher and the white men. This occurs despite the fact that the men essentially agree with her attitude and supporting her demand for him to leave would have saved their lives. This scene demonstrates a male bond that minimalizes racial difference in the face of gender discrepancies; in the face of such gender difference men's focus is shifted to masculine sameness in the face of the feminine other. Whilst it could be argued that male sameness is exploded by Buck and Preacher's murder of the whites Buck also uses this scene to strike Esther, further reinforcing the perception of men's dominance and capacity to derive identity through opposition to

---

73   Tracye A. Matthews, "No One Ever Asks What a Black Man's Role in the Revolution Is': Gender Politics and Leadership in the Black Panther Party, 1966–71', in *Sisters in the Struggle: African American Women in the Civil Rights and Black Power Movements*, eds Bettye Collier-Thomas and V.P. Franklin (New York: New York University Press, 2001), 230–242.

the feminine One wonders, then, about the extent to which films such as Buck and the Preacher fundamentally destabilize notions of white patriarchy, or rather call only for a reshaping of patriarchy to grant access to a more racially diverse masculine performance.[74]

Conclusion

Buck and the Preacher is a significant re-visioning of the Western genre and of representations of the historical West. Although not the first black western, or the first to present black characters as significant to the narrative structure, it does act as the culmination of a broader movement for cultural recovery amongst rights-based organizations and it also reflects the broader social disillusionment with white hegemonic power structures and masculinities. It therefore reflects the search for an alternative to exclusionary white masculinities and to an exclusionary white conceptualization of the past. The film does not simply echo the generic structures of traditional westerns and insert black characters into traditionally white roles but, rather, presents a diversity of black experiences and positions racism and the struggle of minority groups against it as essential to the broader American experience. In so doing the film problematizes conceptualizations of the West that have marginalized or ignored the voices of racial minorities and celebrated this space as integral to the formation of a hegemonic white national identity and inevitable landed conquest. By pointing to the West as racially diverse and as a site of contested meanings and identities within and between different gendered, racial and class groups, this film presents a fundamental challenge to the historical construction of hegemonic masculinity at the personal and structural levels.

74   Indeed, one could argue that it is this reshaping of patriarchy rather than a refutation of it that leads to 'remasculinization' according to Susan Jeffords. Jeffords, *The Remasculinization of America*, 37–42.

It also presents a more historically realistic West than those Westerns that focus exclusively on white stories. More than this, though, *Buck and the Preacher* poses a challenge regarding the right and capacity of traditional mainstream media structures to present alternative voices and attempts to recover these otherwise lost voices. Although the film may point to continuities between the represented past and present, this is undertaken under the broad umbrella of a discontinuity: this narrative would not and could not be told in a context other than in the post-Civil Rights era, when blacks fought for control of their stories and images. In many ways, then, this film demonstrates the breakdown of an exclusionary white masculinity and the search for alternative understandings of the past to inform a new, more inclusive version of masculinity in the present.

There are, however, significant problems with these images that curtail potential subversion. Specifically the film inverts racial hierarchies, condemning an essentialized and stereotypical Southern white racist, and relegating Native Americans to an inevitable demise at the hands of white conquest. By simply reversing racial hierarchies the film does little to engage with the racist underpinnings that institute such hierarchies and essentialize the experiences of different racial groups. Similarly the sidelining of women's experiences and diversity and the demonstration of men's domination of them in a naturalized way reinforces gender as a primary dichotomy in American society. This dichotomy allows for the construction of all masculinities unified in opposition to an unknowable 'Other'; a fundamental principle in hegemonic gender constructions and in the remasculinization of personal and national gender ideology in the 1980s as demonstrated by the Vietnam War genre and action hero films starring the likes of Sylvester Stallone and Arnold Schwarzenegger. Moreover, the use of violence is never questioned as a valid means by which to exert dominance over other groups, and such violence functions as an important means by which men construct exclusionary, hierarchical and hegemonic gendered selves. Certainly the issues noted in this film are not in themselves evidence of the ahistorical or timeless nature of an inevitable hegemonic identity. Conversely the problems associated with this representation respond to particular historical conditions during the time of production, in particular they reflect on a growing diversity in ideas regarding resistance to white structures, the use of violence as a valid means of resistance, and the difficult relationship between women, women's liberation and black rights movements. It is to suggest, however, that such limitations provide a space by which images of black resistance could both be commodified by white power structures and, also, provide a space wherein, potentially, patriarchal power is not problematized as much as some men's exclusion from it on the grounds of race is.

Conclusion

A man sits astride a horse, gazing at another two-bit settlement town and the rolling desolate hills beyond it. He is white, weather beaten and just plain tough. He and his ilk have dominated the pre-eminent American film genre. 'Who *are* those guys?' Butch Cassidy asks. Answering this question has been the central preoccupation of this volume and has necessitated an inter-disciplinary approach that engages issues of historical representation, gender and film. In examining hyper-linear history on film a distinct theoretical paradigm for understanding the ways history functions on film has been put forward. Engaging this discourse is particularly significant as historical representation in visual mediums continue to flourish and inform public and pedagogical approaches to historical knowledge. It is hoped that hyper-linear history continues to feed into this important discourse and bears fruitful understandings of cinematic representation.

Furthermore, the centrality of gender as a vehicle for transmitting hyper-linear connections between past and present is a significant indicator of the centrality of gender more generally as a historical category. In examining the 'demasculinization' of American male representation in 1950s and 1960s Westerns this work contributes to a discourse surrounding gender representation. Specifically, it contributes to a discussion regarding the ways in which masculine representation changes in American cinema over time. This provides significant insight; insight into the ways in which representations of gender reflect connections between the private and the public, the personal and the national identities; insight into the ways patterns of behaviour and enactment of power occur in American society regardless of the casualties; insight into the ways in which the gendered 'crisis points' in American history are enacted and resolved to maintain hierarchical, often oppressive, power relationships. Who is that guy?

Hyper-linear history is a paradigm through which to understand how history functions in American Western films of the 1950s and 1960s. A hyper-linear history is one that privileges both the historical ideas prevalent at the time of the filmic release and the represented past portrayed in the film. The work proposes that, rather than attempting to reconstruct the past or reflect only the historical conditions of the production context, these Western films create a fluid and mutually informing relationship between past and present, one that continually reinterprets the past and its significance in light of present concerns. Whilst this is a new paradigm when applied to the construction of history on film in historiographical terms this paradigm is not new in broader historical methodology. Historians have continually 'revised' historical knowledge and, in so doing, historians have reinterpreted the significance of the past in light of new evidence, perspectives and methods. Frederick Jackson Turner himself acknowledged this trend in Western historiography, suggesting that the interests of the present continually 'rework' understandings of the past.[1]

This work is unique in proposing that film, like other historical studies, creates a view of history that is informed by both past and present and contributes to understandings of the past and to continually updated and revised forms of historical knowledge. However, in deploying a hyper-linear history these films create a new understanding of how the past relates to, or has come to shape, present social issues. Of course film with its own conventions constructs this relationship between past and present in ways different to written history. As Robert Rosenstone has noted film is constrained, or liberated, by the conventions of genre, the visual medium, time constraints and the film-making process, which produces a work of history that conveys historical ideas in ways that are different from, though no less valid than, written histories.[2] Furthermore, re-instating the significance

---

1   Frederick Jackson Turner, 'Social Forces in American History [annual address as the president of the American Historical Association at Indianapolis, December 28, 1910]', in *The Frontier in American History*, ed. Frederick Jackson Turner (Malabar, FL: Robert E. Krieger Publishing, [1920] 1985), 330.

2   Robert Rosenstone, *Visions of the Past: The Challenge of Film to Our Idea of History* (Cambridge: Harvard University Press, 1995).

of gender as an historical category has demonstrated the ways in which gender becomes central to facilitating or carrying a hyper-linear historical relationship in Western films of this era. Gender is central to representing notions of historical change or continuity in historical film. In this examination gender in Western films of the 1950s and 1960s reveals the ways in which historical film draws on the past to illuminate the notion of male emasculation in post-Civil War and 1950s and 1960s America. The following provides both a summation of the central tenets of this argument and points to future areas of exploration opened up by it.

Three central relationships between past and present are constructed by Westerns in this period: positive continuity, negative continuity and discontinuity. These relationships impart an understanding of the past and its significance in continuing to inform present action. This understanding may, respectively, conceive of the past as a positive experience and source of future inspiration; as a negative experience yet a path to construct meaningful change is unclear; or a relationship between past and present that is ruptured to the extent that the future will no longer be meaningfully informed by the past. In constructing these relationships these films are selective in their portrayal of the past, condensing historical events, and accelerating the historical process in a way that has been labelled 'hyper-linear'. This hyper-linear process allows for connections between historical time periods. For the most part these links are exemplary, though at times films verge on illustrating a causal connection between an historical phenomenon in the past and an historical effect in the present. In this work these hyper-linear connections exist between the represented Civil War and post-Civil War period and the 1950s and 1960s America.

Whilst there are problems associated with history on film, just as there are problems associated with historical constructions across all mediums, conceiving of history in a hyper-linear way can also be extremely meaningful. A hyper-linear relationship in cinema reflects the capacity for film to explore the ways in which the past has direct relevance to the present. Hyper-linear history, at its core, impresses the importance of historical understanding in coming to a sense of one's identity at a personal and national level as depth of understanding can only be garnered through the establishment of relationships between past and present. Pedagogically this may prove a useful way to approach film as a teaching and learning tool when film is approached in the spirit of critical analysis. It is also meaningful in the sense that it is an approach that does not discard the importance of the past – or of gender – in representation.

Although these are the central relationships identified within the film sample explored here, there is certainly potential to explore the ways in which hyper-linear history constructs different relationship between past and present and different understandings of this connection based on an alternative film sample or using different forms of history on film. Moreover, it is expected that the categorization of individual films is open to contestation depending on the audiences and interpretation of the filmic elements. Such contestation is inherent in any historical study, where sources are open to reinterpretation despite thorough engagement by scholars. Ultimately the applicability of this model to historical films outside of the Western genre or to films produced outside of this national and/or temporal context, is yet to be determined and is certainly an avenue for future study. It is hoped that this research opens a new dialogue regarding the methodological and theoretical understandings of the historical film, central as film is to shaping public knowledge of the 'real' historical past.

In addition, these ideas provide a building block in further analysis of the Western film in that it avoids the either/or method that has come to dominate in the field recent. This either/or method has created a seemingly arbitrary division between gendered and historical analysis and between popular and academic understandings of historical knowledge. This is an analysis that seeks to understand the nature of historical representation in the Western distinct from conceiving of the genre in ahistorical and archetypal terms or as a reflection of societal preoccupations at the time the Western was released. Westerns display historical ideas in a more complex and suggestive fashion, and because of this it is difficult to accept that the genre can realistically be relegated to stereotype or archetype removed from the past it purports to represent. Hyper-linear history attempts to grapple with the complexity of this rendition of the past. It also reinstates the centrality of gender analysis. Unlike written history, where gendered voices can be effectively silenced or naturalized by the author, the nature of the visual medium does not allow for such treatment. Indeed, it can be argued that film has been a revolutionary medium in the portrayal of gender, and gender history, precisely because the body, its movement, adornment, construction, treatment and use in performance cannot be sidelined.

Ultimately, one of the central ways in which history is constructed in these films is through the representation of gender, and particularly through the portrayal of masculinities. In its consideration of film, history and gender can be conceived of as truly multi-disciplinary. In acknowledging this these films demonstrate the centrality of gender as a distinctly historical category whose manifestations and privileged forms change over time in accordance with shifting social conditions and values. Gender, along with race, class and age, can be seen as deeply historical and one of the primary facets of individual identity and, more broadly, a major fault line upon which power and authority are constructed in American society. Indeed, considering the importance of gender ideology in shaping national institutions, informing economic behaviours and creating shared values regarding behavioural forms despite the gulfs in other forms of experience, gender identity assumes particular significance. Ultimately these films use gender as a historical tool, with masculine gender performance coming to represent continuities and discontinuities between past and present in terms of social values, individual experiences and national ideology. Rather than conceptualizing gender as a discrete category, these Westerns see gender as a means of communicating historical ideas, which is used in conjunction with other techniques and historical cues.

The argument reinstates the historical contingency of gender and the importance of grappling with gender as a means of coming to grips with the ways in which power and power relationships are enacted in American (and Western) societies. It suggests a 'demasculinizing' prequel to Susan Jeffords' assertion that the image of the American man was 'remasculinized' in the 1980s by showing that the image of the American man, and the validity of hegemonic gender manifestations, were re-evaluated in the 1950s and 1960s.[3] These Western films hyper-linearly create a parallel between the gender crises occasioned in the post-Civil War period with the 'second

---

3   Susan Jeffords, *The Remasculinization of America: Gender and the Vietnam War* (Bloomington: Indiana University Press, 1989).

Civil War' or 'Second Reconstruction' of the Civil Rights period. These parallels meditate upon an image of the white man that was increasingly fractured along various lines of identity and forced into competition to the point that a demasculinization of that image occurred. Such an analysis is significant in assessing the ways in which privileged forms of identity undergo periods of stress and transition before they ultimately adapt to meet new social expectations and re-confirm a 'patriarchal equilibrium' that maintains men's high status collectively and maintains inter-masculine hierarchies with various impacts on men individually.[4]

The Western films of the 1950s and 1960s examined here, and potentially Western films more broadly, portray a white hegemonic masculinity under threat. This American man is both individual and, also, embodiment of existing gender ideology as it relates to the narrative of the American past and American institutional values. Whilst the relationship between past and present in these films may send a variety of messages regarding the validity of traditional hegemonic gender forms, in accordance with the relationships of positive and negative continuity and discontinuity, it is important to stress the inherent subversiveness of these examinations. This subversiveness exists in the sense that by self-consciously examining masculinity, these films illustrate that masculinity is not assured or unchanging but rather there exists multiple masculinities all vying for status, and sometimes simply for survival, in competitive relationships with each other. This takes on added significance when considering the significance of the frontiersmen as a manifestation of the foundational tenets of American ideology: conquest of available land, capacity to exercise redemptive violence unilaterally, and rugged individualism. How these films account for and reconcile this challenge to individual and nation varies – for some the redemption of the individual and nation is possible, and hegemony is reinstated as an ideal masculinity whilst for others no such redemption can be found. To the extent that men's gender performance is de-naturalized, placed in historical context and performed actively (for example, through

4   Judith M. Bennett, *History Matters: Patriarchy and the Challenge of Feminism* (Manchester: Manchester University Press, 2006), 77–81.

demonstrations of exhibitionist violence, through costume and through inter- and intra-gendered competition) these films challenge hegemonic gender values. The films ultimately reflect on a phenomenon of 'demasculinization' taking place in both historical contexts, occasioned by gendered, economic, and technological shifts. At the same time they also reflect upon the ways in which masculinities can adapt to changes and challenges to status and, therefore, the ways in which a potentially subversive representation of masculine uncertainty and change can be contained and patriarchy itself maintained.

In gendered terms, the most subversive fault line upon which masculinity is destabilized sees something amiss with hegemonic gender performance itself and its association in patriarchal institutions. In films such as *The Wild Bunch* (Sam Peckinpah, 1969) the illusion of a benevolent patriarchy has given way to a 'reality' of mercenary men, lacking morality or even group solidarity forced into patterns of violent confrontation with no apparent means of breaking the trap of violence and assuming alternative identities that may be more socially or personally beneficial. Other films demonstrate the ways in which particular modes of being masculine are out-dated and being superseded by other, alternative masculine forms. In so doing, they are intrinsically subversive to a patriarchy that grounds itself in claims of natural and unchanging permanency. Moreover, the impacts on the individual men in these films is quite distressing, trapped as they are within modes of being that are no longer socially relevant and lacking the adaptive skills (and sometimes the will) to change. This immutability leaves them destined to death, both 'real' and metaphorical. Even in films such as *The Man Who Shot Liberty Valance* (John Ford, 1962), which views the passing of previous masculine forms nostalgically, as the generation that 'gifted' civilization to a new breed of men, the cost is a chance at family, respectability and even life itself.

This volume has also examined how access to resources, particularly gun technology, and racial identity have also impacted upon the ways men have understood and performed their genders. In terms of its examinations of the intersections between capitalism and gender performance and access to resources this volume provides new insights. Money, accumulation and guns are often conceptualized in scholarly work as 'natural' elements of the genre or 'natural' symbols of hegemonic masculinity. Here, however, we have seen the distinctly historical way in which these elements have been represented. Far from seamless components of the genre or necessary narrative devices these representations change over time and are used to actively construct interplay between gender identity and historical realities. In racial terms it has been suggested that the hyper-linear history of Native Americans and black Americans in the filmic past and the Civil Rights present in many ways presents challenges to hegemonic white masculinity and the national values such masculinity embodies. At the same time that these alternative ways of being highlight the shortcomings of white patriarchal institutions some of these representations, illustrated here potentially in *Buck and the Preacher* also illuminate the ways in which a future remasculinization could occur. This occurs when such films do not necessarily repudiate patriarchy or its values but rather simply features men who refuse to be denied access to patriarchy because of their race. They reflect an appeal to the centrality of masculine sameness regardless of fractures along other lines of identities.

These Westerns also locate challenges to white masculine gender forms through threats posed by women. Typically scholars have considered women in these films as signifiers; however, this volume has sought to render such a message complex. Westerns are capable of, and do, position women in roles that convey depth of character and a capacity to engage in the public and private realms in meaningful and complex ways. Rather than feminine naivety many demonstrate the capacity for self-conscious gender performance and an exploration of gender stereotypes that positions them as distinctly historical subjects. In their complexity these characters do not blindly support patriarchy or individual men, but rather attempt to negotiate a role within this patriarchy. This role allows them to motivate, mould and commentate upon men's roles in American society. Women may participate in quite politically active ways – as temperance advocates, Quakers, or even, as Amy Kane asserts, as 'feminists'. Like Cresta Lee, other women find that their exclusion from patriarchal power opens avenues for a multiplicity of identities and movements within liminal spaces that are rarely or not available to men. Others do not resist but use existing gender ideology, calling upon their roles as wives, mothers, daughters and even at the core their status as women (particularly white women) to manipulate men's gender performances to meet their own ends.

This reflection is facilitated by a hyper-linear connection constructed by films between the past and the present. These films reflect a Western past where traditional gender roles were being tested on a number of fronts. White women in the West, some of whom had been transported away from traditional kin, friendship and community networks from which their traditional identities had derived, were forced by necessity into increasingly flexible gender performances. Whilst some women reconciled their different circumstances within traditional gender paradigms others found their experiences of Western life, the Civil War and activism within moral, racial and suffrage movements could not be so easily contained. It is particularly potent that this past is called up in films in the context of the 1950s and 1960s where an ideology of women's domesticity was trumpeted as a means to aid post-war American development at the same time that ruptures were reappearing in women's willingness to be contained within this sphere. Underneath the veil of domesticity many women were increasingly agitating for autonomy, empowerment in their sexuality, employment, education and personal relationships, which became particularly prominent in the post-McCarthy period. Women's experiences were, of course, mediated upon other fracturing lines of identity such as class and race, which had varying effects upon women's gender identity and advocacy.

This would culminate in the second wave women's liberation movement of the 1960s and 1970s, which would directly challenge the patriarchal foundation of American society and the impact of hegemonic gender performances on individual experiences. It is interesting to note that the challenge of the women's liberation movements at their height in the 1970s was met by a popular culture that was increasingly becoming 'remasculinized'. This itself is extremely significant because it demonstrates the capacity of multiple masculinities to find commonality and solidification in the face of women's challenge to power, which could completely destabilize patriarchal authority. Men may face intra-masculine competition as men vie for access to patriarchal power that may be denied to them based on their race, class, or other grounds. This competition may be painful to individual men and cause ruptures in traditional patriarchal institutions but is necessary for patriarchy to adapt to changing historical conditions and maintain the hierarchy of men's gendered identity collectively. In this context Westerns are important to witness this liminal period of gender challenge and contestation in much the same way that the 'hard body' films and Vietnam War films are central to witnessing the solidification of a remasculinized male image.

The conclusions reached here open important doorways for further research in multiple discourses. In terms of history on film it is hoped that hyper-linearity as a model will continue to be explored as a viable method for understanding the ways in which film can construct meaningful historical relationships between past and present. It would be interesting to continue this exploration within the Western film genre by charting the ways in which historical understandings of the past have changed over time. The applicability of hyper-linearity to Western films produced in different national and cultural traditions may also prove illuminating. The usefulness of hyper-linear history as a model to understand historical representations would also be well-explored by moving away from the Western genre and attempting to apply it instead to other historical film genres such as the war film, for example.

Secondly, it provides a base from which to explore additional elements of the Western film within their distinctly historical contexts. I would be particularly interested to engage with other elements of these films including, for example, the depiction of childhood, the use of religious iconography, the representation of alcohol dependence, and the representation (or lack of representation) of Latin Americans and/or Chinese migrants. The representations of male characters bearing physical scars, amputations or other forms of impairment as a result of military participation would provide interesting additional material in relation to the representations of men's war time experiences.

Finally, this volume opens doorways in relation to gender representation, particularly relevant to notion of demasculinization as a prequel to Jeffords' notions of remasculinization. It would be interesting to chart the ways in which other popular mediums relate to these notions of gender crisis and re-solidification over time. In addition, as Susan Jeffords has charted the remasculinization of the American man in the 1970s and

1980s it would be interesting to put the spotlight back onto women's gender performances in key genre vehicles in order to chart whether this same period marks a 'refeminization' of the American women; refeminization referring in this context to the reassertion of traditional gender ideology in relation to women's roles. Jeffords' work on the Vietnam War film and other work on the popularity of the Mafioso genre certainly suggest that a remasculinized male image was associated with the marginalization of women's voices and roles.[5] Certainly it is hoped that this examination of the 1950s and 1960s illustrates the capacity of Westerns to demonstrate an historical shift in women's roles that contributed to men's re-evaluation of their own gendered selves. A comprehensive study of women's roles and interactions across class and racial lines over time in Western films, rather than the conceptualization of women's roles in ahistorical and archetypal ways, awaits construction.

Ultimately the need to adapt to changing historiographical trends in the discipline is a key message in this analysis, which grapples with the nature of historical representation in the filmic medium, an area of growing importance due to the role of film in providing history education over traditional, written mediums. A hyper-linear paradigm could be a key means to explore the historical relationship between the represented past and the present of the filmic release. This model is a significant reconceptualization of the ways in which history is understood in the visual medium. It is hoped that this reconceptualization is a step towards re-opening an interdisciplinary dialogue regarding the relationship between the popular and the academic, between gender and history, and the connections between representation, film and the transmission of knowledge.

5   See, for example, Harry M. Benshoff and Sean Griffin, *America on Film: Representing Race, Class, Gender and Sexuality at the Movies* 2nd edn (Oxford: Wiley-Blackwell, 2009), 283–284.

Filmography

Aldrich, Robert. '4 for Texas.' 124 min. USA: Warner Bros. Pictures, 1963.
——. 'Apache.' 91 min. USA: United Artists, 1954.
——. 'Ulzana's Raid.' 103 min. USA: Universal Pictures, 1972.
Anderson, Paul Thomas. 'There Will Be Blood.' 158 mins. USA: Miramax, 2007.
Arnold, Jack. 'No Name on the Bullet.' 77 mins. USA: Universal, 1959.
Boetticher, Budd. 'Ride Lonesome.' 73 min. USA: Columbia, 1959.
——. 'Seven Men from Now.' 78 min. USA: Batjac Production, 1956.
——. 'A Time for Dying.' 67 min. USA: Corinth Films, 1969.
Bogart, Paul. 'Skin Game.' 102 min. USA: Warner Bros. Pictures, 1971.
Bradbury, Robert N. 'The Lawless Range.' 53 min. USA: Republic Pictures, 1935.
Brando, Marlon. 'One-Eyed Jacks.' 141 min. USA: Paramount Pictures, 1961.
Brooks, Mel. 'Blazing Saddles.' 93 min. USA: Warner Bros., 1974.
Brooks, Richard. 'The Last Hunt.' 108 min. USA: MGM, 1956.
——. 'The Professionals.' 117 min. USA: Columbia Pictures, 1966.
Butler, David. 'San Antonio.' 109 min. US.A: Warner Bros. Pictures, 1945.
——. 'Calamity Jane.' 101 min. USA: Warner Bros., 1953.
Clark, James B. 'One Foot in Hell.' 90 min. USA: Twentieth Century Fox, 1960.
Coen, Ethan, and Joel Coen. 'No Country for Old Men.' 122 min. USA: Miramax
Paramount Village, 2007.
Coppola, Francis Ford. 'Apocalypse Now.' 153 mins (202 Director's ed.). USA: United
    Artists, 1979.
Cosmatos, George. 'Rambo II.' 97 min. USA: TriStar Pictures, 1985.
——. 'Tombstone.' 130 min. USA: Buena Vista Pictures, 1993.
Costner, Kevin. 'Dances with Wolves.' 180 min. USA: Orion Pictures, 1990.
Curtiz, Michael. 'The Comancheros.' 107 min. USA: Twentieth Century-Fox Film
    Corporation, 1961.
——. 'Dodge City.' 104 mins. USA: Warner Bros, 1939.
Daves, Delmer. 'Broken Arrow.' 93 min. USA: Twentieth Century-Fox Film Cor-
    poration, 1950.
——. 'Cowboy.' 92 min. USA: Columbia, 1958.
——. 'The Hanging Tree.' 107 min. USA: Warner Bros., 1959.
de Troth, Andre. 'Day of the Outlaw.' 92 min. USA: United Artists, 1959.
DeMille, Cecil B. 'North West Mounted Police.' 126 mins. USA: Paramount Pic-
    tures, 1940.

——. 'The Plainsman.' 113 mins. USA: Paramount Pictures, 1936.

——. 'Union Pacific.' 135 mins. USA: Paramount Pictures, 1939.

Dominik, Andrew. 'The Assassination of Jesse James by the Coward Robert Ford.' 160 min. USA: Warner Bros., 2007.

Douglas, Gordon. 'The Charge of Feather River.' 95 min. USA: Warner Bros. Pictures, 1953.

Dwan, Allan. 'Cattle Queen of Montana.' 88 min. USA: RKO Radio Pictures, 1954.

——. 'Woman They Almost Lynched.' 90 min. USA: Republic Pictures, 1953.

Dymtryk, Edward. 'Broken Lance.' 96 min. USA: Twentieth Century-Fox Film Corporation, 1954.

Eastwood, Clint. 'High Plains Drifter.' 101 min. USA*: Universal Pictures, 1973.

——. 'Unforgiven.' 131 min. USA: Warner Bros., 1992.

Farrow, John. 'California.' 97 min. USA: Paramount Pictures, 1946.

——. 'Hondo.' 93 min. USA: Warner Bros. Pictures, 1953.

Fenton, Leslie. 'Whispering Smith.' 88 min. USA: Paramount Pictures, 1948.

Ford, John. 'Cheyenne Autumn.' 154 min. USA: Warner Bros., 1964.

——. 'Fort Apache.' 125 min. USA: Argosy Pictures, 1948.

——. 'How the West Was Won.' 162 min. USA: MGM, 1962.

——. 'The Man Who Shot Liberty Valance.' 118 min. USA: Paramount Pictures, 1962.

——. 'My Darling Clementine.' 91 min. USA: Twentieth Century Fox, 1946.

——. 'The Searchers.' 119 min. USA: Warner Bros., 1956.

——. 'She Wore a Yellow Ribbon.' 103 min. USA: RKO Radio Pictures Argosy Pictures, 1949.

Fuller, Samuel. 'Forty Guns.' 77 min. USA: Twentieth Century Fox, 1957.

——. 'Run of the Arrow.' 86 min. USA: Universal Pictures, 1957.

Goldman, Martin. 'The Legend of Nigger Charley.' 98 min. USA: Paramount Pictures, 1972.

Gordon, Michael. 'Texas across the River.' 101 min. USA: Universal Pictures, 1966.

Gries, Tom. 'Will Penny.' 108 min. USA: Paramount, 1967.

Hathaway, Henry. 'Nevada Smith.' 128 min. USA: Paramount Pictures, 1966.

——. 'North to Alaska.' 122 min. USA: Twentieth Century-Fox Film Corporation, 1960.

——. 'The Sons of Katie Elder.' 122 min. USA: Paramount Pictures, 1965.

——. 'True Grit.' 128 min. USA: Paramount Pictures, 1969.

Hawks, Howard. 'El Dorado.' 126 min. USA: Paramount Pictures, 1966.

——. 'Red River.' 133 min. USA: United Artists, 1948.

——. 'Rio Bravo.' 141 min. USA: Warner Bros. Pictures, 1959.

——. 'Rio Lobo.' 114 min. USA: National General Pictures CBS/Fox, 1970.

Heisler, Stuart. 'Along Came Jones.' 90 mins. USA: Cinema Artists, 1945.

Hellman, Monte. 'The Shooting.' 82 min. USA: Walter Reade Organization, 1966.

Hill, George Roy. 'Butch Cassidy and the Sundance Kid.' 110 min. USA: Twentieth Century Fox, 1969.

Huston, John. 'The Misfits.' 124 min. USA: United Artsts, 1961.

——. 'The Unforgiven.' 116 min: MGM, 1959.

Kane, Joseph. 'The Yellow Rose of Texas.' 69 min. USA: Republic Pictures, 1944.

Karlson, Phil. 'Gunman's Walk.' 97 min. USA: Columbia, 1958.

——. 'A Time for Killing.' 88 min. USA: Columbia, 1967.

Kelly, Gene. 'The Cheyenne Social Club.' 102 min. USA: National General Pictures Warner Home Video, 1970.

Kennedy, Burt. 'Support Your Local Sheriff.' 92 min. USA: United Artists, 1969.

——. 'The War Wagon.' 69 min. USA: Universal Pictures, 1967.

——. 'Welcome to Hard Times.' 103 min. USA: MGM, 1966.

King, Henry. 'The Gunfighter.' 81 min. USA: Twentieth Century Fox, 1950.

Kotcheff, Ted. 'First Blood.' 94 min. USA: Orion Pictures, 1982.

Kubrick, Stanley. 'Dr. Strangelove: Or How I Learned to Stop Worrying and Love the Bomb.' 1963.

——. 'Full Metal Jacket.' 116 min. USA/UK: Warner Bros., 1987.

Laven, Arnold. 'Geronimo.' 101 min. USA: United Artists, 1962.

Lee, Ang. 'Brokeback Mountain.' 134 min. USA: Focus Features, 2005.

Leone, Sergio. 'A Fistful of Dollars.' 99 min. Italy: United Artists, 1964(1967).

——. 'For a Few Dollars More.' 132 min. Italy: United Artists, 1965(1967).

——. 'The Good. The Bad and the Ugly.' 161 min. Italy: United Artists, 1966(1967).

Lloyd, Frank. 'Wells Fargo.' 97 mins. USA: Paramount Pictures, 1937.

MacDonald, Peter. 'Rambo III.' 101 min. USA: TriStar Pictures, 1988.

Mann, Anthony. 'Bend of the River.' 91 min. USA: Universal Pictures, 1952.

——. 'The Far Country.' 97 min. USA: Universal Pictures, 1954.

——. 'The Last Frontier.' 98 min. USA: Columbia, 1958.

——. 'The Man from Laramie.' 104 min. USA: Columbia Pictures, 1955.

——. 'Man of the West.' 100 min. USA: United Artists, 1958.

——. 'The Naked Spur.' 91 min. USA: MGM, 1953.

——. 'Winchester ,73.' 89 min. USA: Universal Pictures, 1950.

Marin, Edwin L. 'Colt .45.' 74 min. USA: Warner Bros. Pictures, 1950.

——. 'Fort Worth.' 80 min. USA: Warner, 1950.

Marshall, George. 'Advance to the Rear.' 100 min. USA: MGM, 1964.

——. 'Destry Rides Again.' 94 min. USA: Universal Pictures, 1939.

Mate, Rudolph. 'The Violent Men.' 96 min. USA: Columbia Pictures, 1955.

McLaglen, Andrew V. 'Chisum.' 111 min. USA: Warner Bros. Pictures, 1970.

Miller, David. 'Lonely Are the Brave.' 107 min. USA: Universal Pictures, 1962.

Nelson, Ralph. 'Soldier Blue.' 112 min. USA: AVCO Embassy Pictures, 1970.

Nicholson, Jack. 'Goin' South.' 105 min. USA: Paramount Pictures, 1978.

Peckinpah, Sam. 'Major Dundee.' 123 min. USA: Columbia Pictures, 1965.

——. 'Ride the High Country.' 94 min. USA: MGM, 1962.

——. 'The Wild Bunch.' 134 min. USA: Warner Bros Seven Arts, 1969.

Penn, Arthur. 'Bonnie and Clyde.' 112 min. USA: Warner Bros./Seven Arts, 1967.

——. 'The Left Handed Gun.' 102 min. USA: Warner Bros., 1958.

——. 'Little Big Man.' 139 min. USA: National General Pictures, 1970.

Poitier, Sidney. 'Buck and the Preacher.' 102 min. USA: Columbia Pictures, 1972.

Pollack, Sydney. 'The Scalphunters.' 102 min. USA: United Artists, 1968.

Post, Ted. 'Hang 'Em High.' 110 min. USA: MGM, 1968.

Ray, Nicholas. 'Johnny Guitar.' 110 min. USA: Republic Pictures Paramount Home Video, 1954.

Ritt, Martin. 'Hombre.' 111 min. USA: Twentieth Century-Fox Film Corporation, 1967.

——. 'Hud.' 112 min. USA Paramount Pictures, 1963.

Rouse, Russell. 'The Fastest Gun Alive.' 89 min. USA: MGM, 1956.

Ruggles, Wesley. 'Cimarron.' 131 mins. USA: RKO Radio Pictures Warner Home Movies, 1931.

Rydell, Mark. 'The Cowboys.' 131 min. USA: Warner Bros. Pictures, 1972.

Scott, Ridley. 'Thelma and Louise.' 129 min. USA: MGM, 1991.

Selander, Lesley. 'Tall Man Riding.' USA, 1950.

Sherman, George. 'Battle at Apache Pass.' 85 min. USA: Universal Pictures, 1952.

——. 'Big Jake.' 110 min. USA: National General Pictures Paramount Home Video, 1971.

Silverstein, Elliot. 'Cat Ballou.' 97 min. USA: Columbia Pictures, 1965.

——. 'A Man Called Horse.' 114 min. USA: National General Pictures Paramount Home Video, 1970.

Stevens, George. 'Shane.' 118 min. USA: Paramount Pictures, 1953.

Stone, Oliver. 'Platoon.' 120 min. USA: Orion Pictures, 1986.

Sturges, John. 'Gunfight at the O.K. Corral.' 122 min. USA: Paramount Pictures, 1957.

——. 'Last Train from Gun Hill.' 93 min. USA: Paramount Pictures, 1958.

——. 'The Magnificent Seven.' 128 min. USA: United Artists, 1960.

Tourneur, Jacques. 'Canyon Passage.' 92 mins. USA: Universal Pictures, 1946.

Vidor, King. 'Duel in the Sun.' 129 min. USA: Vanguard Films, 1946.

Walsh, Raoul. 'Saskatchewan.' 87 min. USA: Universal Pictures, 1954.

Wayne, John. 'The Alamo.' 167 min. USA: United Artists, 1960.

——. 'The Green Berets.' 141 min. USA: Warner Bros./Seven Arts, 1968.

Wellman, William A. 'The Ox-Bow Incident.' 75 min. USA: Twentieth Century Fox, 1943.

———. 'Yellow Sky.' 98 min. USA: Twentieth Century-Fox Film Corporation, 1948.

Yarbrough, Jean. 'The Over the Hill Gang.' 75 min. USA: Thomas/Spelling Productions, 1969.

Zinnemann, Fred. 'High Noon.' 85 min. USA: United Artists/Stanley Kramer Productions, 1952.

Bibliography

Books

Anderson, Mark Cronlund. *Cowboy Imperialism and the Hollywood Film*. New York: Peter Lang, 2007.

Appy, Christian. *Patriots: The American War Remembered from All Sides*. New York: Penguin Group, 2003.

Bellesiles, Michael A. *Arming America: The Origins of a National Gun Culture*. New York: Alfred A. Knapf, 2008.

Bennett, Judith M. *History Matters: Patriarchy and the Challenge of Feminism*. Manchester: Manchester University Press, 2006.

Benshoff, Harry M., and Sean Griffin. *America on Film: Representing Race, Class, Gender and Sexuality at the Movies*. 2nd edn. Oxford: Wiley & Blackwell, 2009.

Bernstein, Alison R. *American Indians and World War II: Toward a New Era in Indian Affairs*. Norman: University of Oklahoma Press, 1991.

Bingham, Dennis. *Acting Male: Masculinities in the Films of James Stewart, Jack Nicholson and Clint Eastwood*. New Brunswick, NJ: Rutgers University Press, 1994.

Bogle, Donald. *Toms, Coons, Mulattoes, Mammies, and Bucks: An Interpretive History of Blacks in American Films*. 3rd edn. New York: Continuum, 1996.

Brauer, Ralph with Donna Brauer. *The Horse, the Gun and the Piece of Property: Changing Images of the TV Western*. Bowling Green, OH: Bowling Green University Popular Press, 1975.

Brown, Dee. *Bury My Heart at Wounded Knee: An Indian History of the American West*. London: Arrow Books, 1971.

Buscombe, Edward. *'Injuns!' Native Americans in the Movies*. Cornwall: Reaktion Books, 2006.

Buscombe, Edward, ed. *The BFI Companion to the Western*. London: British Film Institute, 1988.

Buscombe, Edward, and Roberta E. Pearson, eds. *Back in the Saddle Again: New Essays on the Western*. London: British Film Industry, 1998.

Cameron, Ian, and Douglas Pye, eds. *The Movie Book of the Western*. London: Studio Vista, 1996.

Capps, Walter, ed. *The Vietnam Reader*. London & New York: Routledge, 1991.

Cawelti, John G. *The Six-Gun Mystique*. Bowling Green, OH: Bowling Green University Popular Press, 1971.

Cimbala, Paul A., and Randall M. Miller, eds. *The Great Task Remaining Before Us: Reconstruction as America's Continuing Civil War*. New York: Fordham University Press, 2010.

Cohan, Steven. *Masked Men: Masculinity and the Movies in the Fifties*. Bloomington & Indianapolis: Indiana University Press, 1993.

Cohan, Steven, and Ina Rae Hark, eds. *Screening the Male: Exploring Masculinities in Hollywood Cinema*. London & New York: Routledge, 1993.

Collier-Thomas, Bettye, and V.P. Franklin, eds. *Sisters in the Struggle: African American Women in the Civil Rights-Black Power Movement*. New York: New York University Press, 2001.

Collingwood, R.G. *The Idea of History*. Oxford: Oxford University Press, [1946]1961.

Connell, R.W. *Gender*. Cambridge: Polity Press, 2002.

——. *Masculinities*. 2nd edn. Sydney: Allen & Unwin, 2005.

Corkin, Stanley. *Cowboys as Cold Warriors: The Western and US History*. Philadelphia: Temple University Press, 2004.

Cripps, Thomas. *Black Film as Genre*. Indiana: Indiana University Press, 1978.

DeGroot, Gerard J. *A Noble Cause: America and the Vietnam War*. London: Pearson Education, 2000.

Dickstein, Morris. *Gates of Eden: American Culture in the Sixties*. New York: Basic Books, 1977.

Dippie, Brian W. *The Vanishing American: White Attitudes and US Indian Policy*. Middletown, CT: Wesleyan University Press, 1982.

Donaldson, Gary A. *The Second Reconstruction: A History of the Modern Civil Rights Movement*. Malabar: Krieger Publishing Company, 2000.

Durham, Philip, and Everett L. Jones. *The Negro Cowboys*. New York: Cornwall Press, 1965.

Eisenmann, Linda. *Higher Education for Women in Postwar America, 1945–1965*. Baltimore: John Hopkins University Press, 2006.

Engelhardt, Tom. *The End of Victory Culture: Cold War America and the Disillusioning of a Generation*. New York: Basic Books, 1995.

Etulain, Richard W., ed. *Does the Frontier Experience Make America Exceptional?* Boston: Bedford/St Martin's, 1999.

——. *Telling Western Stories: From Buffalo Bill to Larry McMurtry*. Albuquerque: The University of New Mexico Press, 1999.

Frayling, Christopher. *Spaghetti Westerns: Cowboys and Europeans in Karl May to Sergio Leone*. London: Routledge & Kegan Paul, 1981.

French, Philip. *Westerns: Aspects of a Movie Genre*. London: Secker and Warburg in association with the British Film Institute, 1973.

Friar, Ralph E., & Natasha A. Friar. *The Only Good Indian ... The Hollywood Gospel*. New York: Drama Book Specialists/Publishers, 1972.

Gates, Henry Louis, Jr. *Thirteen Ways of Looking at a Black Man*. New York: Random House, 1997.

Gilbert, James Birkhart. *Men in the Middle: Searching for Masculinity in the 1950s*. Chicago: University of Chicago Press, 2005.

Gilmore, David D. *Manhood in the Making: Cultural Concepts of Masculinity*. Yale: Yale University Press, 1990.

Glasrud, Bruce A., and Charles A. Braithwaite. *African Americans on the Great Plains: An Anthology*. Lincoln: Bison Books, 2009.

Goldman, William. *Adventures in the Screen Trade: A Personal View of Hollywood and Screenwriting*. London & Sydney: Macdonald & Co., 1983.

———. *Butch Cassidy and the Sundance Kid* [Screenplay]. London: Corgi Books, 1969.

Hall, Simon. *Peace and Freedom: The Civil Rights and Antiwar Movements of the 1960s*. Philadelphia: University of Pennsylvania Press, 2005.

Hitt, Jim. *The American West from Fiction (1823–1976) into Film (1909–1986)*. Jefferson, NC: McFarland & Company, 1990.

Holmlund, Chris. *Impossible Bodies: Femininity and Masculinity at the Movies*. London & New York: Routledge, 2002.

Horrocks, Roger. *Male Myths and Icons: Masculinity in Popular Culture*. London: MacMillan, 1995.

Horton, Andrew. *The Films of George Roy Hill*. New York: Columbia University Press, 1984.

Hughes, Howard. *Stagecoach to Tombstone: The Filmgoers' Guide to the Great Westerns*. London: I.B. Taurus, 2008.

Hughes-Warrington, Marnie. *History Goes to the Movies: Studying History on Film*. London & New York: Routledge, 2007.

Hurm, Gerd, and Ann Marie Fallon, eds. *Rebels without a Cause? Renegotiating the American 1950s*. Bern: Peter Lang, 2007.

Huston, John. *An Open Book*. London: Alfred A. Knopf, 1980.

Isserman, Maurice, and Michael Kazin. *America Divided: The Civil War of the 1960s*. New York & Oxford: Oxford University Press, 2000.

Jeffords, Susan. *Hard Bodies: Hollywood Masculinity in the Reagan Era*. New Brunswick, NJ: Rutgers University Press, 1994.

———. *The Remasculinization of America: Gender and the Vietnam War*. Bloomington: Indiana University Press, 1989.

Jeffrey, Julie Roy. *Frontier Women: 'Civilizing' the West? 1840–1880*. Rev. edn. New York: Hill & Lang, 1979.

Jones, Karen R., and John Wills. *The American West: Competing Visions*. Edinburgh: Edinburgh University Press, 2009.

Katz, William Loren. *The Black West*. Vol. 3, rev. and expanded. Seattle: Open Hand
　　Publishing, 1987.

Kerber, Linda K. and Jane Sherron De Hart, eds. *Women's America: Refocusing the
　　Past*. 6th edn. Oxford: Oxford University Press, 2004.

Kimmel, Michael S. *The History of Men: Essays on the History of American and British
　　Masculinities*. New York: State University of New York, 2005.

——. *Manhood in America: A Cultural History*. 2nd edn. Oxford: Oxford University
　　Press, 2006.

Kirkham, Pat, ed. *The Gendered Object*. Manchester: Manchester University Press, 1996.

Kirkham, Pat, and Janet Thumim, eds. *You Tarzan: Masculinity, Movies and Men*.
　　London: Lawrence & Wishart, 2003.

Kitses, Jim. *Horizons West: Directing the Western from John Ford to Clint Eastwood*.
　　London: British Film Institute, 2004.

Knadler, Stephen. *Remapping Citizenship and the Nation in African-American Lit-
　　erature*. Hoboken, NJ: Routledge, 2009.

Kolodny, Annette. *The Land Before Her: Fantasy and Experience of the American
　　Frontiers, 1630–1860*. Chapel Hill: University of North Carolina Press, 1984.

Leab, Daniel J. *From Sambo to Superspade: The Black Experience in Motion Pictures*.
　　London: Secker & Warburg, 1975.

LeMay, Dan. *Alan LeMay: A Biography of the Author of The Searchers*. McFarland
　　and Company, 2012.

Lenihan, John H. *Showdown: Confronting Modern America in the Western Film*.
　　Chicago: University of Illinois Press, 1980.

Lerman, Nina E., Ruth Oldenziel and Arwen P. Mohun, eds. *Gender and Technology:
　　A Reader*. Baltimore: John Hopkins University Press, 2003.

Mcmohan, Robert J, ed. *Major Problems in the History of the Vietnam War*. 2nd edn.
　　Lexington, Massachusetts: D.C. Heath & Co., 1995.

Malone, Michael P., ed. *Historians and the American West*. Lincoln: University of
　　Nebraska, 1983.

Malone, Michael P., and Richard W. Etulain. *The American West: A Twentieth Century
　　History*. Lincoln: University of Nebraska Press, 1989.

Maynard, Richard. *The American West on Film: Myth and Reality*. Hasbrouck Heights,
　　NJ: Hayden Book Company, Inc., 1974.

Meadows, Anne. *Digging up Butch and Sundance*. Lincoln: University of Nebraska
　　Press, 2003.

Mellen, Joan. *Big Bad Wolves: Masculinity in the American Film*. London: Elm Tree
　　Books, 1978.

Merrill, Dennis, and Thomas G. Paterson, eds. *Major Problems in American Foreign
　　Relations*. New York: Houghton Mifflin Company, 2006.

Mesce, Bill, Jr. *Peckinpah's Women: A Reappraisal of the Portrayal of Women in the
　　Period Westerns of Sam Peckinpah*. Lanham, MD: Scarecrow Press, 2001.

Milkman, Ruth. *Gender at Work: The Dynamics of Job Segregation by Sex during World War II*. Chicago: University of Illinois Press, 1987.

Milner, Clyde A. II, Anne Butler, and David Rich Lewis, eds. *Major Problems in the History of the American West*. 2nd edn. Major Problems in American History. Boston: Houghton Mifflin, 1997.

Mitchell, Lee Clark. *Westerns: Making the Man in Fiction and Film*. Chicago: University of Chicago Press, 1996.

Natoli, Joseph. *Hauntings: Popular Film and American Culture, 1990–1992*. New York: State University of New York, 1994.

Neu, Charles, ed. *After Vietnam: Legacies of a Lost War*. Baltimore: John Hopkins University Press, 2000.

Noble, David F. *America By Design: Science Technology and the Rise of Corporate Capitalism*. Oxford: Oxford University Press, 1977.

O'Connor, John E. *The Hollywood Indian: Stereotypes of Native Americans in Films*. Trenton, NJ: New Jersey State Museum, 1980.

Olson, James, and Randy Roberts, eds. *Where the Domino Fell: America and Vietnam, 1945–1995*. 2nd edn. New York: St Martin's Press, 1996.

Parman, Donald L. *Indians and the American West in the Twentieth Century*. Bloomington: Indiana University Press, 1994.

Pieterse, Jan Nederveen. *White on Black: Images of Africa and Blacks in Western Popular Culture*. New Haven & London: Yale University Press, 1992.

Podhoretz, Norman, ed. *Why We Were in Vietnam*. New York: Simon & Schuster, 1982.

Poitier, Sidney. *This Life*. London: Coronet Books, 1980.

Pratley, Gerald. *The Cinema of John Huston*. Cranbury, NJ: A.S. Barnes & Co., 1977.

Prince, Stephen, ed. *Sam Peckinpah's 'The Wild Bunch'*. Cambridge: Cambridge University Press, 1999.

——, ed. *Screening Violence*. New Brunswick, NJ: Rutgers University Press, 2000.

Rosenbaum, Jonathan. *Dead Man*. London: BFI Publishing, 2000.

Rosenstone, Robert. *Visions of the Past: The Challenge of Film to Our Ideas of History*. Cambridge: Harvard University Press, 1995.

Ross, Karen. *Black and White Media: Black Images in Popular Film and Television*. Cambridge: Polity Press, 1996.

Ross, Stephen J. *Hollywood Left and Right: How Movie Stars Shaped American Politics*. Oxford: Oxford University Press, 2011.

Rotundo, Anthony E. *American Manhood: Transformations in Masculinity from the Revolution to the Modern Era*. New York: Basic Books, 1987.

Russo, Vito. *The Celluloid Closet: Homosexuality in the Movies*. New York: Harper & Row, 1987.

Salisury, Harrison E., ed. *Vietnam Reconsidered: Lessons from a War*. New York: Harper & Row, 1984.

Sayre, Nora. *Running Time: Films of the Cold War*. New York: Dial Press, 1978.

Seal, Graham. *The Outlaw Legend: A Cultural Tradition in Britain, America and Australia*. Cambridge: Cambridge University Press, 1996.

Singer, Beverly R. *Wiping the War Paint Off the Lens: Native American Film and Video*. Minneapolis: University of Minnesota Press, 2001.

Slotkin, Richard. *Gunfighter Nation: The Myth of the Frontier in Twentieth Century America*. New York: Harper Perennial, 1993.

Smith, Henry Nash. *Virgin Land: The American West as Symbol and Myth*. Cambridge: Harvard University Press, 1950.

Sorlin, Pierre. *The Film in History: Restaging the Past*. Totowa, NJ: Barnes & Noble, 1980.

Taylor, Quintard. *In Search of the Racial Frontier: African Americans in the American West, 1528–1990*. New York: W.W. Norton, 1998.

Thomas, William G. *The Iron Way: Railroads, the Civil War, and the Making of Modern America*. New Haven & London: Yale University Press, 2011.

Tomes, Robert. *Apocalypse Then: American Intellectuals and the Vietnam War, 1954–1975*. New York: New York University Press, 1998.

Tompkins, Jane. *West of Everything: The Inner Life of Westerns*. New York: Oxford University Press, 1992.

Turner, Frederick Jackson. *The Frontier in American History*. Malabar, FL: Robert E. Krieger Publishing, [1920] 1976.

Walker, Janet, ed. *Westerns: Films through History*. New York: Routledge, 2001.

Warren, Robert Penn. *The Legacy of the Civil War*. Lincoln: University of Nebraska Press, [1961] 1998.

White, Richard. *Railroaded: The Transcontinentals and the Making of Modern America*. New York: W.W. Norton & Co., 2011.

Whites, LeeAnn. *The Civil War as a Crisis in Gender: Augusta, Georgia 1860–1890*. Athens: University of Georgia Press, 1995.

Woods, Randall. *Quest for Identity: America since 1945*. Cambridge: Cambridge University Press, 1995.

Woodworth-Ney, Laura. *Women in the American West*. Santa Barbara, CA: ABC-CLIO, 2008.

Wright, Will. *Six Guns and Society: A Structural Study of the Western*. Berkeley & Los Angeles: University of California Press, 1975.

Essays

Aleiss, Angela. "'The Vanishing American': Hollywood's Compromise to Indian Reform.' *Journal of American Studies* 25 (1991): 467–472.

Baritz, Loren. 'The Idea of the West.' *The American Historical Review* 66 (April, 1961): 618–640.

Barrett, Jenny. 'Bucking the Trend: Poitier on the Frontier.' *European Journal of American Culture* 30 (2011): 5–18.

Barsness, John A. 'A Question of Standard.' *Film Quarterly* 21 (Autumn, 1967): 32–37.

Bates, Robin. 'Connecting with Film History through Writing.' *Cinema Journal* 39 (2000): 83–89.

Bellesiles, Michael A. 'Exploring America's Gun Culture.' *The William and Mary Quarterly* 59 (2002): 241–268.

Benshoff, Harry M. 'Blaxploitation Horror Films: Generic Reappropriation or Reinscription?' *Cinema Journal* 39 (2000): 31–50.

Bernard, Louise. 'Black Cinema: A Celebration of Pan-African Film: Tisch School of the Arts New York University 22–30 March 1994.' *Black Camera* 9 (1994): 3–8.

Berry, Chris. 'The Chinese Side of the Mountain.' *Film Quarterly* 60 (2007): 32–37.

Bird, S. Elizabeth. 'Gendered Construction of the American Indian in Popular Media.' *Journal of Communication* 49 (2006): 61–83.

Bliss, Michael. 'Introduction: Times Maybe, Not Them – The Enduring Value of Sam Peckinpah's Films.' In *Peckinpah Today: New Essays on the Films of Sam Peckinpah*, edited by Michael Bliss, 1–5. Carbondale: Southern Illinois University, 2012.

Bobo, Jacqueline. "'The Subject is Money': Reconsidering the Black Film Audience as a Theoretical Paradigm.' *Black American Literature Forum* 25 (1991): 421–432.

Borden, Diane & Eric P. Essman. 'Manifest Landscape/Latent Ideology.' *California History* 79 (2000): 30–41.

Brown, Richard Maxwell. 'Western Violence: Structure, Values, Myth.' *The Western Historical Quarterly* 24 (1993): 4–20.

Burton, Howard A. "'High Noon': Everyman Rides Again.' *The Quarterly of Film, Radio and Television* 8 (1953): 80–86.

Carmichael, Deborah. "'Outlawed' in Oz: A *Film & History* Associate Editor Visits Australia.' *Film and History* 31 (2004): 16–17.

Charney, Leo. 'Historical Excess: Johnny Guitar's Containment.' *Cinema Journal* 29 (1990): 23–34.

Corkin, Stanley. 'Cowboys and Free Markets: Post-World War II Westerns and US Hegemony.' *Cinema Journal* 39 (2000): 66–91.

Cortese, James. 'Bourgeois Myth and Anti-Myth: The Western Hero of the Fifties.' *SubStance* 5 (1976): 122–132.

Cracroft, Richard H. 'The American West of Karl May.' *American Quarterly* 19 (Summer, 1967): 249–258.

Cronon, William. 'A Place for Stories: Nature, History, and Narrative.' *The Journal of American History* 78 (March 1992): 1347–1376.

——. 'Revisiting the Vanishing Frontier: The Legacy of Frederick Jackson Turner.' *The Western Historical Quarterly* 18 (1987): 157–176.

Cuordileone, K.A. "Politics in an Age of Anxiety': Cold War Political Culture and the Crisis in American Masculinity, 1949–1960.' *The Journal of American History* 87 (2000): 515–545.

Davis, Ronald L. 'Paradise among the Monuments: John Ford's Vision of the American West.' *Montana: The Magazine of Western History* 45 (1995): 48–63.

Diawara, Manthia. 'Black Spectatorship: Problems of Identification and Resistance.' *Screen* 29 (1988): 66–76.

Dippie, Brian W. 'Photographic Allegories and Indian Destiny.' *Montana: The Magazine of Western History* 42 (1992): 40–57.

Dowell, Pat. 'The Mythology of the Western: Hollywood Perspectives on Race and Gender in the Nineties.' *Cineaste* 21 (1995): 5 ps (html version).

Durham, Philip. 'A General Classification of 1, 531 Dime Novels.' *The Huntington Library Quarterly* 17 (May, 1954): 287–291.

——. 'The Negro Cowboy.' *American Quarterly* 7 (Autumn, 1955): 291–301.

Dykstra, Robert R. 'Quantifying the Wild West: The Problematic Statistics of Frontier Violence.' *The Western Historical Quarterly* 40 (2009): 321–347.

Dykstra, Robert R., and Harlan Hahn. 'Northern Voters and Negro Suffrage: The Case of Iowa, 1868.' *The Public Opinion Quarterly* 32 (1968): 202–215.

Faust, Drew Gilpin. 'Altars of Sacrifice: Confederate Women and the Narratives of War.' *The Journal of American History* 76 (1990): 1220–1228.

Fender, Stephen. 'The Western and the Contemporary.' *Journal of American Studies* 6 (1972): 97–108.

Fishwick, Marshall W. 'The Cowboy: America's Contribution to the World's Mythology.' *Western Folklore* 11 (April, 1952): 77–92.

Foster, Gwendolyn. 'The Women in *High Noon*: A Metanarrative of Difference.' *Film Criticism* 18/19 (1994): 72–81.

Gaberscek, Carlo, 'Zapata Westerns: The Short Life of a Sub-Genre (1966–72)', *Bilingual Review* 29 (2008): 45–58.

Gallagher, Tag. 'John Ford's Indians.' *Film Comment* 29 (1993): 68–72.

Gartner, Scott Sigmund & Gary M. Segura, 'Race, Casualties and Opinion in the Vietnam War.' *The Journal of Politics* 62 (2000): 115–146.

Gleijeses, Piero. '1898: The Opposition to the Spanish-American War.' *Journal of Latin American Studies* 35 (2003): 681–719.

Goldstein, Laurence. "Mama How Come Black Men Don't Get to Be Heroes?': Black Poets and the Movies: Invitation to a Gunfighter.' *The Iowa Review* 23 (1993): 110–131.

Graham, Don. 'The Women Of 'High Noon': A Revisionist View.' *Rocky Mountain Review of Language and Literature* 34 (1980): 243–251.

Hall, Mary Katherine. 'Now You Are a Killer of White Men: Jim Jarmusch's *Dead Man* and Traditions of Revisionism in the Western.' *Journal of Film and Video* 52 (2001): 3–14.

Hamilton, Emma, and Troy Saxby. "Draggin' the Chain': Linking Civil Rights and African American Representation in *The Defiant Ones* and *In the Heat of the Night.*' *Black Camera* 3 (2011): 75–95.

——. "Draggin' the Chain': Linking Civil Rights and African American Representation in *The Defiant Ones* and *In the Heat of the Night.*' In *Poitier Revisited: Reconsidering a Black icon in the Obama Age*, edited by Ian Gregory Strachan and Mia Mask, 73–96. New York: Bloomsbury, 2015.

Haywood, Robert C. "No Less a Man': Blacks in Cow Town Dodge City, 1876–1886.' *The Western Historical Quarterly* 19 (1988): 161–182.

Henderson, Brian. "The Searchers': An American Dilemma.' *Film Quarterly* 34 (1980–1): 9–23.

Henry, Matthew. "He Is A 'Bad Mother*$%@!#': 'Shaft' And Contemporary Black Masculinity.' *African American Review* 38 (2004): 119–126.

Hoffman, Donald. 'Whose Home on the Range? Finding Room for Native Americans, African Americans, and Latino Americans in the Revisionist Western.' *MELUS* 22 (1997): 45–59.

Horowitz, Daniel. 'Rethinking Betty Friedan and *The Feminine Mystique*: Labor Union Radicalism and Feminism in Cold War America.' *American Quarterly* 48 (1998): 1–42.

Horton, Robert. 'Mann and Stewart: Two Rode Together.' *Film Comment* 26 (1990): 40–46.

Hughey, Matthew H. 'Cinethetic Racism: White Redemption and Black Stereotypes in 'Magical Negro' Films.' *Social Problems* 56 (2009): 543–577.

Hunt, Dennis. 'Butch Cassidy and the Sundance Kid [Review].' *Film Quarterly* 23 (1969/1970): 62–63.

Iverson, Peter. 'Building toward Self-Determination: Plains and Southwestern Indians in the 1940s and 1950s.' *The Western Historical Quarterly* 16 (1985): 163–173.

Jeffords, Susan. 'Debriding Vietnam: The Resurrection of the White American Male.' *Feminist Studies* 14 (1988): 252–543.

Jensen, Joan M, and Darlis A Miller. 'The Gentle Tamers Revisited: New Approaches to the History of Women in the American West.' *The Pacific Historical Review* 49 (1980): 173–213.

Jensen, Richard. 'On Modernizing Frederick Jackson Turner: The Historiography of Regionalism.' *The Western Historical Quarterly* 11 (Jul., 1980): 307–322.

Joyce, Thomas Andrew. 'A Nation of Employees: The Rise of White-Collar Workers and the Perceived Crisis of Masculinity in the 1950s.' *The Graduate History Review* 3 (2011): 24–48.

Kimmel, Michael S. 'Masculinity as Homophobia: Fear, Shame, and Silence in the Construction of Gender Identity.' In *Theorizing Masculinities*, edited by Harry Brod and Michael Kaufman, 119–141. London: Sage Publishing, 1994.

Kitses, Jim. 'All That Brokeback Allows.' *Film Quarterly* 60 (2007): 22–27.

Klotman, Phyllis R. 'About Black Film ...' *Black American Literature Forum* 12 (1978): 123–127.

Korstad, Robert and Nelson Lichenstein. 'Opportunities Found and Lost: Labor, Radicals and the Early Civil Rights Movement.' *The Journal of American History* 75 (1988): 786–811.

Larson, T.A. 'Dolls, Vassals and Drudges – Pioneer Women in the West.' *The Western Historical Quarterly* 3 (1972): 5–16.

Lavik, Erlend. ''No Obstacle but the Means': Film History and the Postmodern Challenge.' *Rethinking History* 13 (Sept., 2009): 371–394.

Leigninger, Robert, Jr. 'The Western as Male Soap Opera: John Ford's Rio Grande.' *Journal of Men's Studies* 6 (1998): 135–135.

Lerner, Neil. ''Look at That Big Hand Move Along': Clocks, Containment and Music in *High Noon*.' *South Atlantic Quarterly* 104 (2005): 151–173.

Leyda, Julia. 'Black-Audience Westerns and the Politics of Cultural Identification in the 1930s.' *Cinema Journal* 42 (2002): 46–70.

Limerick, Patricia Nelson. 'What on Earth Is the New Western History?' *Montana: The Magazine of Western History* 40 (Summer, 1990): 61–64.

Lyne, William. 'No Accident: From Black Power to Black Box Office.' *African American Review* 34 (2000): 39–59.

McCammon, Holly J, and Karen E Campbell. 'Winning the Vote in the West: The Political Successes of the Women's Suffrage Movement, 1866–1919.' *Gender and Society* 15 (2001): 55–82.

McCammon, Holly J, Karen E Campbell, Ellen M Granberg, and Christine Mowery. 'How Movements Win: Gendered Opportunity Structures and US Women's Suffrage Movements, 1866–1919.' *American Sociological Review* 66 (2001): 49–70.

McKanna, Clare V., Jr. 'Alcohol, Handguns, and Homicide in the American West.' *The Western Historical Quarterly* 26 (1995): 455–482.

Malone, Michael P. 'The 'New Western History': An Assessment.' *Montana: The Magazine of Western History* 40 (1990): 65–67.

Marcus, Alan, and Fred Zinnemann. 'Uncovering an Auteur: Fred Zinnemann.' *Oral History* 12 (2000): 49–56.

Margolis, Harriet. 'Stereotypical Strategies: Black Film Aesthetics, Spectator Positioning, and Self-Directed Stereotypes In 'Hollywood Shuffle' And 'I'm Gonna Git You Sucka.'' *Cinema Journal* 38 (1999): 50–66.

Markoff, John. 'Margins, Centers and Democracy: The Paradigmatic History of Women's Suffrage.' *Signs* 29 (2003): 85–116.

Martin, Pete. 'Bang! Bang! Bang! Three Redskins Bit the Dust.' *The Saturday Evening Post* (3 August 1946), 26, 61–62, 66.

Metzger, Scott Alan. 'Pedagogy and the Historical Feature Film: Towards Historical Literacy.' *Film and History* 37 (2007): 67–75.

Mieder, Wolfgang. "'The Only Good Indian Is a Dead Indian': History and Meaning of a Proverbial Stereotype.' *The Journal of American Folklore* 106 (Winter, 1993): 38–60.

Miller, D.A. 'On the Universality of *Brokeback*.' *Film Quarterly* 60 (2007): 50–60.

Miller, Mark Crispin. 'In Defense of Sam Peckinpah.' *Film Quarterly* 28 (1975): 2–17.

Mirams, Gordon. 'Drop That Gun!' *The Quarterly of Film, Radio and Television* 6 (1951): 1–19.

Modleski, Tania. 'A Woman's Gotta Do ... What a Man's Gotta Do? Cross-Dressing in the Western.' *Signs* 22 (1997): 519–544.

Modleski, Tania, and Maggie Greenwald. 'Our Heroes Have Sometimes Been Cowgirls: An Interview with Maggie Greenwald.' *Film Quarterly* 49 (1995–1996): 2–11.

Moses, A. Dirk. 'The Public Relevance of Historical Studies: A Rejoinder to Hayden White.' *History and Theory* 44 (Oct., 2005): 339–347.

Moskowitz, Eva. "'It's Good to Blow Your Top': Women's Magazines and a Discourse of Discontent, 1945–1965.' *Journal of Women's History* 8 (1996): 66–98.

Mottram, Eric. "'The Persuasive Lips': Men and Guns in America, the West.' *Journal of American Studies* 10 (1976): 53–84.

Movshovitz, Howard. 'The Still Point: Women in the Westerns of John Ford.' *Frontiers: A Journal of Women's Studies* 7 (1984): 68–72.

Mulvey, Laura. 'Looking at the Past from the Present: Rethinking Feminist Film Theory.' *Signs* 30 (2004): 1286–1292.

——. 'Visual Pleasure and Narrative Cinema.' *Screen* 16 (1975): 6–18.

Neale, Steve. 'Masculinity as Spectacle: Reflections on Men in Mainstream Cinema.' In *Screening the Male: Exploring Masculinities in Hollywood Cinema*, edited by Steven Cohan and Ina Rae Hark, 9–20. London: Routledge, 1997.

Newman, Vicky. 'Cinema, Women Teachers, and the 1950s and 1960s.' *Educational Studies* 32 (2001): 416–438.

Nolletti, Arthur, Jr. 'Conversation with Fred Zinnemann.' *Film Criticism* 18/19 (1994): 7–29.

Nussbaum, Martin. 'Sociological Symbolism of the 'Adult Western'.' *Social Forces* 39 (October 1960–May 1961): 25–28.

Oshana, Maryann. 'Native American Women in Westerns: Reality and Myth.' *A Journal of Women Studies* 6 (1981): 46–50.

Osterweil, Ara. 'Ang Lee's Lonesome Cowboys.' *Film Quarterly* 60 (2007): 38–42.

Pearce, Roy Harvey. 'The Significance of the Captivity Narrative.' *American Literature* XIX (March, 1947): 1–20.

Peek, Wendy Chapman. 'The Romance of Competence: Rethinking Masculinity in the Western.' *Journal of Popular Film and Television* 30 (2003): 206–219.

Philp, Kenneth R. 'Termination: A Legacy of the Indian New Deal.' *The Western Historical Quarterly* 14 (1983): 165–180.

Price, John A. 'The Stereotyping of North American Indians in Motion Pictures.' *Ethnohistory* 20 (1973): 153–171.

Prince, Stephen. 'Historical Perspective and the Realistic Aesthetic in *High Noon*.' *Film Criticism* 18/19 (1994): 59–71.

Quinn, Eithne. "'Tryin' to Get Over': *Super Fly*, Black Politics, and Post Civil Rights Film Enterprise.' *Cinema Journal* 49 (2010): 86–105.

Reid, Mark A. 'The Black Action Film: The End of the Patiently Enduring Black Hero.' *Film History* 2 (1988): 23–36.

Rich, B. Ruby. 'Brokering *Brokeback*: Jokes, Backlashes and Other Anxieties.' *Film Quarterly* 60 (2007): 44–48.

Ridge, Martin. 'Frederick Jackson Turner, Ray Allen Billington, and American Frontier History.' *The Western Historical Quarterly* 19 (Jan., 1988): 5–20.

——. 'The Life of an Idea: The Significance of Frederick Jackson Turner's Frontier Thesis.' *Montana: The Magazine of Western History* 41 (Winter, 1991): 2–13.

——. 'Turner the Historian: A Long Shadow.' *Journal of the Early Republic* 13 (Summer, 1993): 133–144.

Riley, Glenda. 'Annie Oakley: Creating the Cowgirl.' *Montana: The Magazine of Western History* 45 (1995): 32–47.

——. 'Frederick Jackson Turner Overlooked the Ladies.' *Journal of the Early Republic* 13 (1993): 216–230.

Robbins, William G. 'In Pursuit of Historical Explanation: Capitalism as a Conceptual Took for Knowing the American West.' *The Western Historical Quarterly* 30 (1999): 277–293.

——. 'Laying Siege to Western History: The Emergence of New Paradigms.' *Reviews in American History* 19 (Sep., 1991): 313–331.

——. 'Triumphal Narratives and the Northern West.' *Montana: The Magazine of Western History* 42 (Spring, 1992): 62–68.

——. 'Western History: A Dialectic on the Modern Condition.' *The Western Historical Quarterly* 20 (Nov., 1989): 429–449.

Rondinone, Troy. "'History Repeats Itself': The Civil War and the Meaning of Labour Conflict in the Late Nineteenth Century.' *American Quarterly* 59 (2007): 397–419.

Rosenstone, Robert. 'History in Images/History in Words: Reflections on the Possibility of Really Putting History onto Film.' *American Historical Review* 93 (1988): 1173–1185.

——. 'JFK: Historical Fact/Historical Film.' *The American Historical Review* 97 (Apr., 1992): 506–511.

———. 'What's a Nice Historian Like You Doing in a Place Like This?' *Rethinking History* 13 (Mar., 2009): 17–25.

Rosenthal, Nicolas G. 'Representing Indians: Native American Actors on Hollywood's Frontier.' *The Western Historical Quarterly* 36 (2005): 328–352.

Schackel, Sandra. 'Barbara Stanwyck: Uncommon Heroine.' *California History* 72 (1993): 40–55.

Schein, Harry. 'The Olympian Cowboy.' *The American Scholar* 24 (1955): 309–320.

Shively, JoEllen. 'Cowboys and Indians: Perceptions of Western Films among American Indians and Anglos.' *American Sociological Review* 57 (1992): 725–734.

Shultz, Robert T. 'White Guys Who Prefer Not To: From Passive Resistance ('Bartelby') to Terrorist Acts (*Fight Club*).' *The Journal of Popular Culture* 44 (2011): 583–605.

Springer-Delgado, Kirsten C. 'Building a Better Soldier: Gendered Conflict from the Omniscient Cowboy to Rambo.' *Film and History* (2004/2005): 1–60.

Stantis, George M. 'Rifles and Revolvers.' In *Icons of the American West: From Cowgirls to Silicon Valley*, edited by Gordon M. Bakken, 277–292. Santa Barbara: Greenwood Reference, 2008.

Starris, Andrew. 'James Stewart.' *Film Comment* 26 (1990): 29–30.

Stoddard, Jeremy D., and Alan S. Marcus. 'The Burden of Historical Representation: Race, Freedom, and 'Educational' Hollywood Film.' *Film and History* 36 (2006): 26–35.

Swerdlow, Amy. 'Ladies' Day at the Capitol: Women Strike for Peace Versus HUAC.' *Feminist Studies* 8 (1982): 493–520.

Taillon, Paul Mitchell. 'Casey Jones, Better Watch Your Speed!: Workplace Culture, Manhood and Protective Labor Legislation on the Railroads 1880–1910s.' *Australasian Journal of American Studies* 30 (2011): 20–38.

Thompson, Frank. 'Reprinting the Legend: The Alamo on Film.' *Film and History* 36 (2006): 20–25.

Thompson, Gerald. 'Another Look at the Frontier Versus Western Historiography.' *Montana: The Magazine of Western History* 40 (1990): 68–71.

Tompkins, Jane. '"Indians": Textualism, Morality, and the Problem of History.' *Critical Inquiry* 13 (1986): 101–119.

Toplin, Robert Brent. 'Cinematic History: Where Do We Go from Here?' *The Public Historian* 25 (2003): 79–91.

Udall, Stewart L. 'The 'Wild' Old West: A Different View.' *Montana: The Magazine of Western History* 49 (1999): 64–71.

Udall, Stewart L., Robert R. Dykstra, Michael A. Bellesiles, Paula Mitchell Marks, and Gregory H. Nobles. 'How the West Go Wild: American Media and Frontier Violence a Roundtable.' *The American Historical Quarterly* 31 (Autumn, 2000): 277–295.

Van Horne, Winston A. 'The Concept of Black Power: Its Continued Relevance.' *Journal of Black Studies* 37 (2007): 365–389.

Warshow, Robert. 'Movie Chronicle: The Westerner.' In *Film Theory and Criticism: Introductory Readings*, edited by Gerald Mast, Marshall Cohen and Leo Braudy, 453–466. Oxford: Oxford University Press, 1992.

West, Elliott. 'A Longer, Grimmer but More Interesting History.' *Montana: The Magazine of Western History* 40 (1990): 72–76.

———. 'Shots in the Dark: Television and the Western Myth.' *Montana: The Magazine of Western History* 38 (1988): 72–76.

White, Francis E. 'Africa On My Mind: Gender, Counter Discourse and African-American Nationalism.' *Journal of Women's History* 2 (1990): 73–97.

White, Hayden. 'The Public Relevance of Historical Studies: A Reply to Dirk Moses.' *History and Theory* 44 (Oct., 2005): 333–338.

Whitehall, Richard. 'The Heroes Are Tired.' *Film Quarterly* 20 (1966–7): 12–24.

Wills, John. 'Pixel Cowboys and Silicon Gold Mines: Videogames in the American West.' *Pacific Historical Review* 77 (2008): 273–303.

Wilmington, Mike. 'Small-Town Guy: James Stewart Interviewed by Mike Wilmington.' *Film Comment* 26 (1990): 32–54.

Woodward, C. Vann. 'The Irony of Southern History.' *The Journal of Southern History* 19 (1953): 3–19.

Worster, Donald. 'New West, True West: Interpreting the Region's History.' *The Western Historical Quarterly* 18 (1987): 141–156.

Wright, Gavin. 'The Civil Rights Revolution as Economic History.' *The Journal of Economic History* 59 (1999): 267–289.

Index

African Americans
appearance in Westerns 41, 208–212, 238
cinema 213, 227–228, 238
Black Power Movement(s) 225, 233, 240–241
Civil Rights Movement 22, 23, 33, 37–38, 67–68, 78, 104, 108, 126, 130–131, 135, 197, 200, 209, 211, 214, 225–226, 234, 237
experiences of the American West 37–38, 209–210, 214–219
migration 33, 207, 216–218
policy concerning 22, 37–38, 214, 221, 223, 227
war, experiences in *see* military service
women, representation of 220, 223–224, 239–242
see also under stereotypes
American Civil War 16–21, 22, 24–25, 29, 39, 46, 64, 84, 108, 111–112, 132, 135–136, 140, 148–149, 155, 200, 253
American frontier, closing of *see* nostalgia
American West, mythology of 29, 62, 148, 165–166
animals 53, 59, 116, 124, 128, 167, 187, 233
assimilation 39, 102, 112, 125, 130–133, 229, 232, 239

Belafonte, Harry 212, 227, 229, 232, 234–236
Bible 84, 116, 124, 134, 222–223, 241

Blaxploitation 4, 212–213, 228–229, 233, 235
breadwinner(s) 21, 61–62, 89
Broken Arrow fn. 67, 103, 144

capitalism 19, 22, 27–28, 31, 34, 36, 44, 45, 59–64, 70, 106, 152, 160, 168, 169–170, 173, 174, 184, 186, 192–193, 195, 230, 233–234
children, representation of 109–110, 112, 121, 123, 128, 166–167, 170–171, 189, 216, 239, 254
citizenship 22, 112, 131, 210, 220–223
Civil War *see* American Civil War
Cold War 22, 61, 79, 85, 89, 141, 147, 155, 162–164, 173, 197
Comancheros, The 123
consumer culture 140–141, 152, 173
costume 53–54, 95

Eastwood, Clint 52–53, 92, fn. 192

family, representation of 20, 69, 71, 74, 89, 148, 189, 206, 220, 241
Fastest Gun Alive, The 92, 144, 163
Feminine Mystique, The see Friedan, Betty
film theory
historical authenticity 53, 110, 135, 203
hyper-reality 204
pedagogy 1, 4, 245, 247–248
Rosenstone, Robert A. 2, 155, 203–204, 246

Forty Guns 94–95
Friedan, Betty 23, 68, 79

gender theory
    binaries 21, 23, 25, 35, 72, 78, 113–114,
      183, 188, 224, 240
    crisis of masculinities 14, 19, 30, 36,
      43–46, 61, 96, 245, 254
    'cult of the body' fn. 73
    demasculinization 6–7, 14, 85–86,
      98, 100, 113, 137, 144, 173, 176, 181,
      190, 193, 207–208, 245, 250
    hard masculinity 22, 47, 51, 53–54,
      70, 113, 193, 219, 222, 254
    homosocial bond(s) 10, 26, 28,
      46–47, 60–61, 117, 190–191,
      193, 195
    homosocial competition 28, 31, 43,
      50, 191
    Kimmel, Michael 35, 43, 45, 89
    'patriarchal equilibrium' 32, fn. 33,
      93–94, 191, 228–229, 250
    patriarchy, definition of 11
    remasculinization 6–7, 10, 14,
      113–114, 144, 158, 207–208, 229,
      242–243, 249, 252–255
    'self-made man' 19, 31–32, 43
Goldman, William 204
Gunfighter, The 123, 144, 163, 171
guns
    as fetish 142, 157–158
    gunfighter fn. 36, 50, 144
    history of 147–151, 218–219
    as phallic symbol 137, 142–143
    shoot-out 30, 82, 94, 114, 128,
      142–143, 145, 166, 170, 233, 237
    see also violence

Hang 'Em High 92, fn. 212
Hepburn, Audrey 108, 118, 120
Hill, George Roy 178–179, 196, 202–203

history, techniques to convey 84–85,
    134–135, 178–179, 183, 202–204,
    216–217, 224–225
Hombre 9, 50, 179
Hud 9, 50, 179
Huston, John 109
hyper-linear history 2–4, 7–8, 10–13,
    15–16, 18, 25–26, 40–42, 44–46,
    50, 66, 68–70, 73–74, 82, 95,
    100, 102, 108, 112, 129, 132, 143,
    146–147, 155, 183, 185, 198, 203,
    206, 215, 224, 238, 245–249
    discontinuity 4, 16, 215, 226
    negative continuity 5, 16, 60, 128,
      134, 147, 160, 162–163, 166, 173,
      180, 187, 205
    positive continuity 4, 15–16, 96, 118,
      128, 133, 159, 161, 172–173, 190
hysteria, representation of 49–51

interventionism 4, 8, 40, 42, 63, 67–68,
    104, 135, 155, 162, 166, 169–174,
    175–177, 179–181, 187, 189, 196–
    199, 201–202, 205–206, 221

Johnny Guitar 72, 140

Korean War 22, 83, 89, 163

labour
    masculinities, intersection
      with 27–34, 43–44, 61–62
    organizations 29–30
    representation of 36–37, 47–50,
      57–61, 92, 192
Lancaster, Burt 108–109
landscape 55–56, 169, 184–185
law and order, representation of 48–49,
    86–87, 147, 152–153, 156–157,
    160–161, 168, 191, 196, 198,
    216, 237

Leone, Sergio 59–60
Little Big Man 9, 103

McCarthyism 78, 82–83, 253
Magnificent Seven, The 60, 176, 187–190
Man from Laramie, The 49, 123
Man Who Shot Liberty Valance, The 53, 56, 58, 140, 144, 211, 251
Manifest Destiny 14, 55, 68, 103, 117, 155, 197
Mann-Stewart Westerns 49, 53–55
marriage 68–69, 71, 82, 94, 98, 108, 111–112, 125, 189
Mexican-American War 145, 154
Mexican characters *see* Mexico
Mexico 9, 96–97, 145–146, 155, 166–173, 176, 187–188
military service 6–7, 18–19, 21–25, 36, 39, 51, 65, 89, 111, 145, 154, 175, 189, 197, 200, 209–210, 219–222, 254
miscegenation, representation of 118, 125
music 94–95, 116, 134, 224

naming 54, 59, 115, 127, 158, 188, 191, 193–195, 230–231
Native Americans
    actors 40, 118–120
    Battle of Little Big Horn 128, 135
    Iron Eyes Cody 119
    migration 39, 112, 130
    policy concerning 39–41, 125, 128, 130–135, 221
    'pro-Indian' Western cycle 39–41, 103–106, 109, 126, 140, 163
    rights movements 34, 39, 112, 130–131, 135, 238
    war, experiences in *see* military service
    see also under stereotypes
Newman, Paul 50, 177, 179, 193
nostalgia 9, 25, 29, 31, 33, 58, 139, 140, 143, 145, 147, 167, 170, 185–186

'Organization Man' 184

paternalism 128, 132, 162
Peckinpah, Sam 146, 162, 165–166, 171
Poitier, Sidney 207, 212, 215–216, 219, 227, 229–233

Rambo 7
Reconstruction 13–20, 24–25, 27–31, 33, 35, 37, 39–42, 46, 70, 72–73, 77, 102–103, 111–112, 132, 136, 148–149, 155, 200, 206–207, 210, 214, 216–217, 219–221, 225, 237, 239, 247, 250
Ride the High Country 58, 160
Rio Bravo 56, 83

Scott, Randolph 145
Searchers, The 50, 108
Second Reconstruction 17, 37–38, 41, 250
sexuality 23, 35, 45, 52, 69, 77, 80, 109, 111, 118, 122, 161, 170, 181, 183, 220, 230–232, 234, 239, 253
Shane 56, 65
Shooting, The 9, 58, 64
Social Darwinism 28–29
Spanish-American War 177, 198–202
stereotypes
    African Americans, representations of 212, 215, 220, 226–227, 230–237
    gender, representations of 21, 72, 96, 122, 158, 208, 252
    historicity of 101–102, 107–108, 126, 129, 136, 248
    Native Americans, representations of 104, 106–107, 114, 116–117, 119, 121, 238–239
    negative stereotype(s) 104, 126, 213
    proverbial stereotype(s) 132–133
    self-directed 235

white representation(s) 106, 119–120, 124–128
Stewart, James ('Jimmy') 46, 48–54, 58, 103

technology 140–141, 164–166, 183–184
automobile 140, 166, 174
bicycle 140, 183, 184–185
guns *see* guns
masculinities, intersections with 27, 142–144, 158–159
print 29
railroad 29, 75, 139–141, 166–169, 173–174, 177, 183–185, 191, 193
Turner, Frederick Jackson 11, 74, 105, 186, 208, 246
typecasting 52–53, 234, 236

'Vietnam Syndrome' 176
Vietnam War 5–8, 40–41, 102, 112–113, 147, 164, 166, 172–176, 180, 187–188, 197, 208, 210, 243, 254–255
My Lai massacre 110
violence
in the American West 30, 147–149, 160, 218–219
censorship of 161
as defensive 123–124, 126, 230–231, 244
film technique 146, 196
as gender regulator 55, 60, 84, 89–90, 98, 137, 139, 141, 153, 159–160, 166, 190, 243
as immoral 55, 67–68, 102, 117, 121, 126, 137, 143–144, 156, 158, 162, 165, 169, 172, 186–187
as nihilistic 59, 65, 85, 92, 141, 168, 196, 251
as redemptive 65, 85, 163, 195, 250–251
see also guns

Wayne, John 50, 52–53, 58, 83, 175, fn. 211
Western categories
Acid Western 9
dime novel 29, 62, 148
nihilistic Western 61, 160, 191
'professional' Western 56, 60, 176–177, 187, 189–190
psychological Western 25, 50
revisionist Western 9, 26, 58, 105
see also Native Americans, 'pro-Indian' Western cycle
'South of the Border' Western
see Western categories, 'professional' Western
television Western 8–9, 35, 63, 142, 145, 211
Zapata Western 7
'Western Civil War of Incorporation' 160
women
as autonomous 99, 122, 181–182
as 'civilizing' agents 25, 56, 71, 76, 80
education, experiences in 23, 28, 32, 68, 73, 78, 80, 183
feminism 21, 23–24, 70, 73, 80–81, 92, 182–183, 197
frontier, experiences in 21, 74–77
labour, experiences in 23, 78–79
as liminal space 72, 77, 252,
as mediator 87, 101, 112–113, 117, 120
'New Woman' 73
as property 114, 170, 224
rape 67, 121–122, 124, 181, 183
as sisterhood 98–99
war, experiences in 20–21, 23–24
World War II 21–23, 34, 52, 61, 68, 130, 162

Zinnemann, Fred 83–85, 90, 96